Poverty Amid Plenty in the New India

India has one of the fastest-growing economies on earth. Over the past three decades, socialism has been replaced by pro-business policies as the way forward. And yet, in this "new" India, grinding poverty is still a feature of everyday life. Some 450 million people subsist on less than $1.25 per day, and nearly half of India's children are malnourished. In his latest book, Atul Kohli, a seasoned scholar of Indian politics and economics, blames this discrepancy on the narrow nature of the ruling alliance in India that, in its newfound relationship with business, has prioritized economic growth over all other social and political considerations. In fact, according to Kohli, the resulting inequality has limited the impact of growth on poverty alleviation, and the exclusion of such a significant proportion of Indians from the fruits of rapid economic growth is in turn creating an array of new political problems. This thoughtful and challenging book affords an alternative vision of India's rise in the world that its democratic rulers will be forced to come to grips with in the years ahead.

Atul Kohli is the David K. E. Bruce Professor of International Affairs and a Professor of Politics at Princeton University. He has edited and authored numerous books including *The State and Poverty in India* (1987), *Democracy and Discontent: India's Growing Crisis of Governability* (1991), and *State-Directed Development: Political Power and Industrialization in the Global Periphery* (2004).

Poverty Amid Plenty in the New India

ATUL KOHLI

Princeton University

CAMBRIDGE
UNIVERSITY PRESS

CAMBRIDGE UNIVERSITY PRESS
Cambridge, New York, Melbourne, Madrid, Cape Town,
Singapore, São Paulo, Delhi, Mexico City

Cambridge University Press
32 Avenue of the Americas, New York, NY 10013-2473, USA

www.cambridge.org
Information on this title: www.cambridge.org/9780521735179

First published 2012

Printed in the United States of America

A catalog record for this publication is available from the British Library.

Library of Congress Cataloging in Publication data
Kohli, Atul.
Poverty amid plenty in the new India / Atul Kohli.
p.   cm.
Includes bibliographical references and index.
ISBN 978-0-521-51387-6 – ISBN 978-0-521-73517-9 (pbk.)
1. Poverty – India.   2. Income distribution – India.
3. India – Economic condition – 1991–.   I. Title.
HC440.P6.K64   2012
339.4'60954–dc23   2011028645

ISBN 978-0-521-51387-6 Hardback
ISBN 978-0-521-73517-9 Paperback

For
Tara

Contents

Tables and Figures

TABLES

FIGURES

Preface and Acknowledgments

Over the last three decades India's has been among the world's fastest-growing economies. And yet poverty in India has come down only slowly, leaving some 450 million Indians to subsist on less than $1.25 per day; in addition, nearly half of India's children continue to be malnourished. In the pages that follow I analyze both the political origins of this pattern of development, on the one hand, and how the resulting social context of poverty amid plenty is molding Indian politics, on the other. The argument is that, over the last three decades, the Indian state has prioritized economic growth as a goal and established a partnership with Indian business groups in order to achieve this growth. This pro-business ruling alliance has facilitated both rapid economic growth and widening economic inequality. Growing inequality along rural-urban, regional, and class lines has limited the impact of growth on poverty alleviation. A state with its primary focus on growth has also pursued a variety of social programs only half-heartedly. The exclusion of a significant proportion of Indians from the fruits of rapid economic growth is in turn creating a host of new political problems for India's democratic rulers, ranging from how to win the electoral support of the many while facilitating gains for the few, to insurrection by dissatisfied groups, to farmer suicides; the ambitions of India's political class for India to be a global player also suffer. The book suggests that inclusive growth in India is not likely either via pure market-oriented solutions or as a result of an active civil society. Although these will be ingredients of a longer-term inclusive pattern of change, state intervention will remain critical for facilitating inclusive growth in the short to medium term. Given the inadequacies of the Indian state, however, prior political and bureaucratic changes remain necessary for facilitating inclusive growth in the near future.

Books take time to write, preferably uninterrupted time. My first and foremost thanks are thus to Princeton University for its generous leave policy. Much of this book was conceptualized and written over two years of sabbatical leave. I was associated during those two years with the Center for the Advanced Study of India at the University of Pennsylvania. I would like to thank both the founder-director of the center, Francine Frankel, and the current director, Devesh Kapur, for providing congenial intellectual affiliation. I presented materials from this book at two seminars, one at Harvard University and the other at the Jawaharlal Nehru University. The comments of seminar participants helped me rethink some issues. I would like to thank Prerna Singh and Ashutosh Varshney for the opportunity to present at Harvard and to Niraja Gopal Jayal for the same at JNU.

Detailed comments on the entire manuscript from Rob Jenkins and Kanta Murali were much appreciated; these comments were helpful during revisions. I owe additional thanks to Kanta for her help double-checking all the data and for making the tables and figures in the book more reader-friendly. Among those who read parts of the manuscript, I would like to acknowledge the following for helpful comments: Amrita Basu, Supriya Roy Chowdhury, Niraja Gopal Jayal, Phillip Mader, Pratap Mehta, R. Nagaraj, Prerna Singh, and Ashutosh Varshney. The graduate students in my India course during 2010–11 (Omar Bashir, Barret Bradstreet, Siddhartha Chatterjee, Rohit De, Jason Hepps, Dinsha Mistree, Kanta Murali, and Vinay Sitapati) read the manuscript and reacted to various portions of it; these reactions made me realize where the argument was not clear and where it needed to be strengthened or modified. I very much appreciated the opportunity to share discussions with this cohort of first-rate Princeton graduate students.

I do a lot of my writing in public places. Large parts of this book were written during the hours spent over coffee at the Starbucks on Germantown Avenue in Philadelphia. I appreciated the daily chitchat there with Charlie, Nan, and Cathy. Part of the book was typed by my longtime secretary, Edna Lloyd. She retired in the middle of my writing. I miss her and owe her much gratitude for years of congenial work relations. A number of other staff members of the Woodrow Wilson School at Princeton, including Sandy Paroly, helped with other parts of the book. Lindsay Woodrick, my current secretary, helped pull the whole manuscript together. Thanks to all of them. I also need to thank my editor at Cambridge University Press, Marigold Acland, for her encouragement and support in the writing of this book.

Finally, some personal acknowledgments. My parents and my brother and his family continue to be my base in India. That the family home in Lucknow is always there is a source of great comfort. More so, longish conversations with family and family friends in Lucknow are always informative. My sister and her family in California remain a cherished part of my extended connections. I share my daily life with Marie Gottschalk and Tara Kohli; they mean the world to me. Marie has been part of all the books I have written. I am deeply grateful to her for shared love, companionship, constantly intelligent conversation, and her keen insights about society and politics. My daughter, Tara, adds immensely to my life. Her antics, including her periodic visits to my study to check on how my work was going, provided much-needed breaks from my lonely academic pursuits. I watch with fascination her growing interest in India. I dedicate this book to her, hoping that her India will be a more livable society than the one that I grew up in and that I have studied over the past few decades.

Introduction

India in the recent past has been a country of socialist and contentious politics, sluggish economic growth, and numerous poor and illiterate people. Beginning around 1980, India's political economy started moving in a new direction. Over the next three decades Indian democracy put down firmer roots, socialist rhetoric was discarded for pro-business policies, and the economy grew rapidly. Unfortunately, this "new" India remains a country of numerous poor, illiterate, and unhealthy people. Significant pockets of violence also continue to dot the political landscape. How the apex of the political economy in India, but not the bottom half, has undergone some basic changes since 1980 is the subject of this book. A central theme of the book is that the pro-business tilt of the Indian state is responsible both for the progressive dynamism at the apex and for the failure to include India's numerous excluded groups in the polity and the economy.

One has only to recall the decade of the 1970s to underline some key features of the "old" India. During that decade Indira Gandhi sought to move Nehru's socialism in a populist direction, committed the Indian state to alleviating poverty, mobilized the poor, and centralized power in her person. Opposition forces undertook their own mobilization against Indira Gandhi. Political polarization produced a series of rapid political changes in the late 1970s: the proclamation and rescinding of a national Emergency, Indira Gandhi's electoral defeat, the inability of opposition forces to provide stable government, and the return of Indira Gandhi to power. Populism and instability hurt economic growth, leading to a lackluster decade for the economy. Moreover, Indira Gandhi's rhetorical commitment to the poor was not translated into meaningful outcomes; a sluggish economy and an organizational inability to intervene on behalf of the poor remained major obstacles.

As national elections were concluded in 2009, some striking features of a new Indian political economy were evident, along with some important continuities with the old India. Following three decades of mostly steady and rapid economic growth, the elections were normal and peaceful. Competing political parties largely agreed on the basic approach to the economy: a commitment to economic growth and indigenous capitalism; a modest opening of the Indian economy to global forces; and some commitment to the poor. No major political party argued for socialism. A firmly rooted democracy, a shared commitment to growth and national capitalism, and fairly rapid economic growth are key features of India's new political economy.

This, however, is not the full picture. Three decades of economic growth have been accompanied by growing inequality. The gains for the poor have been modest, and their dissatisfaction has often spilled into a variety of political arenas. Well aware of these trends, India's premier political party, the Congress, contested the 2009 elections on a platform of "inclusive growth" and won. It remains unclear whether future economic growth will be more inclusive than that of the recent past. A rhetorical commitment to the poor and an inability to translate this commitment into real gains for the poor remain shared features of the old and the new Indian political economy. Nevertheless, even on the issue of poverty, there are some important differences between then and now. A sluggish economy and organizational deficiencies were major obstacles to helping the poor during the pre-1980 period. In the new context of a buoyant economy, public resources to help the poor are available. Some of these are indeed being devoted to improving the employment, education, and health conditions of the poor. What remains in doubt, however, is the depth of the commitment of India's pro-business leaders to the poor; some of these newer policies are mainly driven by electoral pressures. However, even if electoral pressures and normative concerns create some real pro-poor commitment at the apex, as in the past, the state's capacity to reach the poor continues to be limited; improving this capacity will remain a precondition for successful state intervention on behalf of the poor.

Admirers of the changing Indian political economy focus mainly on its apex. They variously describe contemporary India in such glowing terms as a "tiger uncaged," "emerging global power," and "India shining." These observers often attribute the underlying dynamism to a process of economic liberalization that they believe began in 1991. By contrast, many critics argue that the gains of liberalization are being exaggerated and that such costs as growing inequality, neglect of the poor and the marginalized, and the threat to national sovereignty are being underestimated. In this book I take both the gains and the costs of India's economic liberalization seriously. More important, I treat the process of economic liberalization as only part of a broader and deeper set of political and economic changes afoot in contemporary India.

By global standards, economic liberalization in India has arrived slowly, proceeded haltingly, and remains incomplete. It is difficult to attribute both significant economic gains and the lingering misery of many to these limited changes. The deeper drama in India is instead one of a basic realignment of state and class forces. Starting in the late 1970s and early 1980s, Indian leaders abandoned their anticapitalist rhetoric and, along with that, any commitment to economic redistribution or to a broad-based polity. The state instead prioritized economic growth and production. This shift had already occurred in the countryside during the second half of the 1960s, with the so-called green revolution. By the 1980s, a state and producer alliance that was aimed at boosting production became a nationwide phenomenon. Over the next three decades the Indian state and business groups, especially big business, solidified their political and economic alliance. This ruling alliance is now so well entrenched that many observers do not shy away from characterizing India as "India incorporated." It is my argument in this book that a close alliance between the state and big business is responsible both for releasing economic dynamism and for limiting the spread of the resulting gains. Management by a narrow ruling alliance in India's vibrant democracy also poses significant political challenges, especially that of accommodating the struggling, excluded masses.

The book is divided into three main chapters: political changes; the state and the economy; and regional variations. The time period covered in each section is from around 1980 to the present. In this introduction I first outline the assumptions that inform and distinguish my interpretation. I then introduce the themes that are subsequently developed in some detail in each of the main chapters of the book.

UNDERLYING ASSUMPTIONS

The book provides a distinctive interpretation of India's contemporary political economy. While the focus is on empirical analysis, even casual social observers recognize that facts seldom speak for themselves. How facts are arranged and interpreted is deeply influenced by underlying theoretical assumptions and normative commitments. Since this volume is aimed at a broad audience, I will avoid theoretical and philosophical controversies that mainly attract scholars. Instead, I will outline in brief the assumptions and commitments that I embrace and that inform the interpretation developed in this book; those uninterested in such issues can skip this brief section without much loss.

The state-society frame of reference that structures my scholarship harkens back to the classical political sociology of Marx and Weber. Several key assumptions help distinguish this scholarly tradition from other competing ones. First, not only Marx and Weber but also other classical sociologists, including Durkheim, shared the view that social reality is sui generis. From this standpoint, the study of society, including that of politics and economics, requires societal-level concepts and theories that go well beyond aggregating individual-level phenomena. These foundational assumptions of modern political sociology – especially in the writings of Durkheim – often developed in opposition to the economic individualism of other classical thinkers, such as that of Adam Smith. From the very beginning, then, the sociological tradition that I embrace took a different fork in the social science road than economics, eschewing methodological individualism, on the one hand, but insisting that markets and states are deeply embedded in societies, on the other.

Of course, Marx and Weber differed on profound issues. While Weber found much of use in Marx, he also argued persuasively that the politics and culture of a society could not be reduced to the underlying class forces, especially in the short to medium term. At the same time, both Marx and Weber appreciated the importance of economic factors in molding longer-term processes of historical change. These theoretical sensibilities, then, constitute the second important set of initial principles on which the state-society framework rests. Along with Weber, I view markets as hierarchical arenas; markets not only help generate efficiency, they also create inequalities of power and wealth and of life chances. I also share the Weberian assumption that state and society, or patterns of authority and association, are empirically interrelated but analytically autonomous. This assumption does not preclude a serious consideration of class and economic forces in the study of politics. On the contrary, for anyone studying complex societies in detail, these initial assumptions provide useful flexibility, allowing one to focus on the impact of state on society when studying some problems and to reverse the casual focus – examining, say, the class determinants of political structures and processes – when investigating other issues. This scholarly posture puts me at odds both with strict Marxism and with neoclassical economics and its offshoot, the rational choice approach to the study of politics.

Analytical predispositions often condition the normative preferences of scholars. In the past, for example, Marxists have often been sympathetic to the goals of revolution and communism, and many neoclassical economists today hold that free markets are capable of solving major societal problems. In a parallel fashion, the state-society frame of reference that I adopt shares an elective affinity with social-democratic preferences. This affinity is rooted in the core assumption that states and societies have their own partially autonomous logics of action that, in turn, mutually influence patterns of political and social change. This assumption allows one to imagine the possibility of democracy in poor societies, to argue for a vigorous role for states in promoting economic growth and welfare provision, and at the same time to worry about the growing power of capital in political and social life.

POLITICAL CHANGE

India is a deeply political society. Ever since independence, a highly interventionist state has been very much in command of the economy. Since the state structures the life chances of many, power in Indian democracy is contested vigorously, from the top to the bottom. The winners in turn use their positions and power just as vigorously, at times in the interest of the general good, but just as often for narrow, self-serving ends. The recent economic liberalization has reduced the role of the state in Indian society, but only somewhat. The state still sets the basic direction of the economy and controls enormous resources, and access to the state continues to attract the energies of numerous Indians, including those of businessmen. A full understanding of contemporary Indian political economy, then, must begin with an analysis of the economically relevant political changes in the nature of the Indian state.

I provide such an analysis of the Indian state in the first chapter of the book, developing two main themes. First, the Indian state has become a lot more pro-business over the last three decades than it had been previously. These shifting class preferences of the Indian state are deeply consequential for the choice of economic policies and for patterns of economic change in India. A second main theme concerns the political challenges thrown up by the pursuit of a narrow, pro-business ruling alliance. Ever since Indian leaders abandoned the rhetoric – if not always the practice – of populism in order to embrace economic growth as a priority and business groups as a main ally, they have struggled to come up with a formula for political legitimacy that might enable electoral support of majorities while catering to narrow interests. It may be useful to introduce both of these themes at this point.

India, of course, is a private enterprise economy, and has always been so. In this limited sense, the Indian state has never been deeply anti–private enterprise. During the Nehru years, a vague commitment to socialism – which was part and parcel of India's anticolonial nationalism – provided the ruling ideology. While much of the economy remained in private hands, public enterprise was privileged, and big business was viewed with suspicion. For political reasons Indira Gandhi in later years accentuated the anticapitalist bias of the Indian state. Ironically, when faced with new political and economic problems, she herself reordered the priorities of the Indian state during the early 1980s; she slowly but surely started emphasizing the need to improve production and sought a working alliance with big business. Thus began a new phase in India's political economy that is the focus of this book.

By the early 1980s the world was changing, with pro-market ideas and practices in ascendance. Within India too, socialism was becoming discredited as the failures of antipoverty programs and of public sector enterprises accumulated. When Rajiv Gandhi came to power, he and his technocratic team used the occasion to make a clean break with socialism, opening room for Indian capital to flourish. The loudly announced liberalization of 1991 opened the Indian economy to global forces, but only incrementally. The pace and scope of economic opening in India has been carefully orchestrated by India's nationalist rulers; the goal has been to preserve the well-being of indigenous business groups. More than that, the Indian state in recent years has become an active supporter of Indian business groups, protecting their interests here, subsidizing them there, willingly succumbing to their pressure elsewhere, and promoting public-private partnerships in a variety of arenas.

If the Indian state has taken the lead in constructing a state-business ruling alliance, Indian business groups have hardly been mere passive recipients of manna from above. The power and influence of Indian business has grown enormously in recent decades, a power that business groups have used to mold state behavior. This power is both diffuse and well organized. One obvious example of diffuse power is the growing weight of the private sector in the overall economy; for example, the share of the private sector in overall investment surpassed that of the public sector for the first time during the second half of the 1990s and has remained significant since. The role of foreign direct investment and of portfolio investment in the Indian economy has also grown. Any government that wants such investment to continue must take into account the needs and interests of private investors. A different type of example of the diffuse power of business is the growing corporate control of the media. That the modern media influence the culture and values of a society is no secret. While much of what the Indian media target are consumer tastes, political values are hardly far behind. By influencing what issues get covered and how they get covered, as well as via editorials, the privately controlled media in India today attempt to shift the political preferences of Indian society in a pro-business direction.

Beyond such diffuse power, Indian business also wields power strategically and in a well-organized fashion. Electoral finance is an example of how Indian business uses the power of money to influence India's major political parties. Part of the explanation of the economic policy convergence across political parties in India is a dependence of these parties on resources controlled by the wealthy. Corruption at all levels, including at the apex, is another example of how Indian business secures political support for economic profitability. Indian business, especially big business, is also quite well organized. A number of chambers of commerce provide expression to business interests at various levels of the Indian polity. The most significant of these at the national level is the Confederation of Indian Industry (CII). Relatively recent in origin, the CII epitomizes the growing state-business collaboration in India. The Indian government helped the CII emerge as a leading voice of business. The CII, in turn, supports government initiatives when they are pro-business and pressures the government to move in their direction when they are not.

The clearest manifestation of the growing state-business alliance in India is the changing pattern of state intervention in the economy. Over the last three decades the Indian state and business have increasingly converged on such crucial issues as the approach to labor; the pace and pattern of external opening of the economy; and, most importantly, on how to enable Indian business to improve productivity and production. These issues of political economy will be discussed in the second main section of the book. Related political changes include some symbolic changes and changes in political behavior that underline the growing legitimacy of the state-business collaboration in India. For example, a joint delegation of India's political and economic elite to the World Economic Forum at

Davos to present a case on behalf of "India incorporated" has become a regular occurrence; can anyone imagine such state-business collaboration in Nehru's or Indira Gandhi's India? As another example, India's leading economic policy makers now publicly ask Indian business groups: how can the government help? Would businessmen like a seat at the table when critical decisions are made? This too was not likely to occur in a socialist India. These examples, then, reflect slow, steady, but major changes at the apex of the Indian political economy.

Changes at the apex are precisely that, changes at the apex. India, however, is a large country with numerous poor citizens who live in a democracy, and a fairly mobilized democracy at that. The Indian state can thus never fully be a handmaiden to Indian business. More precisely, India's political leaders cannot afford to be seen as too close to or subservient to Indian capitalists. The political management of a narrow ruling alliance, then, is the second important theme running through the first part of the book. In the past, both socialism and populism have enabled the mobilization of electoral majorities. Ever since the abandonment of these mass incorporating ideologies, India's leaders have struggled to devise new ruling arrangements that will enable them to serve narrow interests without alienating the majority. The struggle to devise such new arrangements is manifest in both the electoral and institutional arenas.

Over the last three decades several legitimacy formulas have competed for success in the electoral arena, none of which has sought a real economic incorporation of India's poor. The Congress Party, for example, has tried to capitalize on a combination of the popularity of the Gandhi family and shifting economic philosophies. Because attempts to "sell" economic liberalization have resulted in only limited electoral success, the Congress has in recent years moved a little to the left, maintaining its core commitment to economic growth and Indian business, but also promising "inclusive growth." The Bharatiya Janata party (BJP) is India's other major political party. Instead of dividing the electoral pie along economic lines, the BJP has sought to define majority and minority interests along ethnic lines, championing the interests of India's Hindu majority. In many multicultural democracies ethnic nationalism has provided a convenient cloak for the pursuit of narrow class interests. This is true in the case of the BJP as well, but so far the appeals of Hindu nationalism have failed to provide a foolproof formula for electoral success. Sensing these limits, the BJP too has tried to "sell" its "competence," or to offer "services" to the poor, but with only limited success. A variety of lesser parties in India also compete for electoral success by mobilizing around such ascriptive themes as caste politics, religion and/or regional nationalism. Some of these parties simply do not have any real developmental commitments, while in other cases ascriptive themes hide a variety of economic ambitions. Even India's communist parties are now struggling to devise an electoral strategy that will permit them to attract business and investment without alienating their lower-class base.

Once elections are won, the challenge faced by India's rulers is how to pursue narrow, pro-growth, pro-business policies without losing popular support and legitimacy. The hope of India's rulers is that economic growth will be rapid enough to lift all boats and thus to maintain their political support. Short of that, a variety of institutional experiments meant to insulate decision makers from popular pressures are under way. At the national level, for example, economic policy making is increasingly in the hands of very few technocrats, many of whom do not have a popular political base. The institutional location of key decisions is also being shifted away from elected bodies to such well-insulated sites as a secretariat in the office of the prime minister or even in a revived Planning Commission. A different type of ongoing institutional experimentation is an apparent decentralization, which enables the most important economic decisions that facilitate growth to remain the prerogative of narrow national elites – who then repeatedly claim success – while shifting much of the blame for failed policies downward to states and localities. These regional and local failures include a failure to stimulate economic growth in India's poor states and a failure to implement a variety of pro-poor policies. Numerous political problems, then – demagogues in power, corruption, failing institutions, political violence – become the "responsibility" of lower-level governments, freeing the national elite to bask in the glow of "India shining."

Excluded groups, of course, do not simply accept elite efforts to institutionalize illusions of inclusion. They express their dissatisfaction in both the electoral and nonelectoral arenas. Caste politics, especially movements of backward and lower castes, are one frequent manifestation of protest politics in the electoral arena. Some of the regional nationalist movements are also efforts to mobilize the dissatisfaction of those with regional identities into the electoral arena. While protest along class lines is not frequent in India, communist parties have achieved electoral success in a few of India's regions. Conflicts around identities and interests are often fought in India in nonelectoral arenas as well.

Examples include: organized labor goes on strike; informal workers struggle to get organized; farmers come in truckloads to the national capital to demand subsidies and higher agricultural prices; feminist movements protest dowry deaths and a variety of other injustices against women; NGOs organize marginalized groups to protest their further marginalization by planned "development" projects; regions with grievances demand greater control over their own political fate; conflicting caste groups take up arms, to fight both each other and the police; ruling parties fail to mobilize civil servants and the police as Hindus kill Moslems; and the truly marginalized – say, the tribals – join revolutionary groups that now hold sway over a significant number of districts in central India. And when all else fails, the destitute simply kill themselves, a phenomenon that has become common enough in the Indian countryside to acquire a name: "farmer suicides."

STATE AND ECONOMY

Over the last three decades India's economy has grown briskly, at a rate of nearly 6 percent per year. Since this acceleration of growth marks a real departure from the sluggish economy of the past, many Indians rightly take pride in the new "rising" India. Rapid growth indeed opens up possibilities for attacking deeply embedded socioeconomic problems of India. Unfortunately, rapid growth has been accompanied by growing economic inequality along a variety of dimensions, and India's numerous poor have not shared proportionately in the economic gains. In the second section of the book I analyze the political and policy determinants of these economic trends, focusing especially on the impact of the state-business alliance on patterns of growth and distribution.

Among the notable characteristics of India's rapid economic growth is the fact that it is driven mainly by national resources and is concentrated in the service sector, especially in communication and business services. The changing patterns of state intervention in the economy have molded these outcomes. The Indian economy, especially its industrial sector, grew at a fairly sluggish rate during the 1970s, even more slowly than during the earlier post-independence period. Concluding that India's left-leaning socialist model of development was responsible for this sluggishness, both Indira Gandhi and Rajiv Gandhi abandoned socialism during the 1980s for a more pro-growth, pro-business model of development.

The details of these policy shifts – both the causes and consequences – will be analyzed in due course. To introduce the main issues, starting in the early 1980s, Indira Gandhi's government initiated a series of pro-business policy reforms. First, the government withdrew some important constraints on big business expansion and encouraged private enterprise to enter areas hitherto reserved for the public sector. Second, the government encouraged the expansion of the private sector by providing both tax relief to big business and a policy framework for the development of private equity markets. Third, labor activism was discouraged. And fourth, new investment in public sector enterprises was discouraged. More generally, Indira Gandhi started courting Indian big business, declaring that populism and socialism were now on the back burner and that the government's new priorities were improvements in productivity and production.

Rajiv Gandhi intensified the Indian government's pro-growth, pro-business, and antilabor stance. At the ideological level, he made a clean break with the socialist past. Among policy changes, state control over activities of private Indian firms such as entry into production, production decisions, and expansion in size were eased further. Indian business groups were also provided significant concessions on corporate and personal taxes. Enhanced credit and lower taxes on the middle class were aimed at boosting demand. Fully committed to growth, the government also hoped to boost the pace of public investment, especially in infrastructure. Unfortunately, enhanced public investment combined with tax concessions led to extensive borrowing, which in turn paved the way for the financial crisis of 1991. Rajiv Gandhi also sought to open India's economy to global forces but was stymied by a variety of domestic pressures, especially pressures from threatened Indian business groups.

These pro-growth, pro-business policy changes during the 1980s reflected in part the changing priorities and views of India's political elite, and in part the growing political significance of India's business class. The important consequences included the emergence of an activist, growth-oriented Indian state, on the one hand, and the growing role of the private sector in the Indian economy, on the other. These trends, in turn, led to both higher rates of investment and improvements in the efficiency of investment, contributing to more rapid economic growth. While the major beneficiaries were established big business firms, the relative ease of entry and growth also enabled new players like the politically well-connected Reliance group to emerge as giants, competing with the likes of Tatas and Birlas.

The financial crisis of 1991 provided the occasion for a second round of important changes in India's economic policy regime. This time the focus was on India's global economic links. The changes in the domestic industrial policy regime deepened along the pro-business lines initiated during the 1980s: further easing of controls on the private sector, allowing business to enter new areas of production and to grow; tax concessions; and a freer hand for producers to deal with organized labor as they saw fit. The more noticeable and even dramatic changes were in India's external economic relations, including trade, foreign investment, and financial relations. For example, the currency was devalued, tariffs were lowered, the foreign investment regime was liberalized, and some restrictions on external financial transactions were eased. While these changes were indeed significant by India's past standards, when viewed in a comparative perspective – especially in comparison to, say, Latin America – India's opening to the world remains relatively modest. The truly significant change in India over the last three decades has been the shift away from socialism and an adoption of a growth-first model of development, involving the warm embrace of state and business groups.

I will analyze the causes and consequences of the post-1991 policy changes in Chapter 2. Among the main themes I will develop is the fact that India's ruling elite had been waiting for the right occasion to introduce significant economic policy changes. While the financial crisis of 1991 provided such an occasion, deeper changes in both the global and the national political economy were the real catalysts. Notable among the global changes were the disintegration of India's main ally, the Soviet Union; the impending membership of India in the WTO; and the growing availability of portfolio investment in the world capital markets. Within India the obstacles to external liberalization had also eased during the 1980s, especially with the emergence of an outwardly oriented faction among India's capitalist class.

As to consequences, compared to the 1980s, India's economic growth has improved during the post-1991 period – especially in recent years – but not dramatically. The role of the private sector in the Indian economy has grown steadily. This has led to higher rates of savings and investment in the economy. The role of foreign investment in the Indian economy has also grown. By contrast, the shrinking share of public investment has become a drag on overall economic performance. This is not only because of such growth bottlenecks as India's poor infrastructure, but also because India's poorer states and the large agricultural sector are not growing as rapidly as they could with the support of public investment.

If the pro-business tilt of the Indian state has helped the Indian economy grow more rapidly, the distributional impact of this shift has been largely adverse, especially during the post-1991 period. Of course, more rapid growth is bound to help the poor somewhat. On the whole, however, the state-capital alliance for growth in India is leading to widening inequality along a variety of dimensions: city versus countryside; across regions; and along class lines. Not only does rapid economic growth not benefit as many of the poor as it could if inequality were stable, but the balance of class power within India is shifting decisively toward business and other property-owning classes. Political and policy determinants of distributive trends, then, are the other set of issues analyzed in the second section of the book.

The history of post-independence India is replete with promises of redistribution and repeated failure to implement such policies. The underlying reasons include the class-based nature of state power and the organizational inability of the state to confront entrenched interests, especially at the lower levels. As the Indian state became more and more committed to economic growth during the 1980s, earlier redistributive commitments, like land redistribution and tenancy reform, lost luster as policy options. While these policies had never succeeded much, starting in the 1980s even their desirability became questionable. Also, very few new efforts emerged during the 1980s to improve primary education or the health of India's poor. The state's focus was instead mainly on growth promotion. However, the redistributive picture during the 1980s was not totally bleak. Since public investment was maintained at a high level, publicly supported growth in agriculture put a brake on the growing rural-urban divide, and continuing public investment kept India's poor states from falling further behind in their relative rate of economic growth. Moderate levels of inequality ensured that some of the fruits of rapid economic growth reached India's poor.

By contrast, economic growth during the post-1991 period has been accompanied by growing inequality. India's poor have not benefitted greatly from this growth, creating a situation of want amid plenty. Some of the growing inequality is inevitable in the sense that the fruits of growth accrue disproportionately to those who own capital and take risks, and to those who possess scarce talents. However, redistributive problems in India are exacerbated by a variety of sins of omission and commission on the part of the Indian state. In the most recent phase of India's development, the Indian state has basically catered to the winners in the new economy, without intervening much on the behalf of those left behind. The occasional corruption scandal that erupts in public underlines the fact that not all of the pro-business tilt is aboveboard. It is this activist role of the state – some driven simply by a commitment to growth and some by emerging crony capitalism – that has further contributed to growing inequality. The Indian state thus continues to support Indian capital in various ways so as to enable it to grow. A plethora of public-private partnerships are also beginning to absorb public initiative and resources. By contrast, with declining public investment, India's agrarian sector and poorer states are falling behind. Since new private capital has not rushed into these areas, inequality in India continues to grow, and the country's poor do not benefit as much from growth as they might under a modified policy regime.

The buoyant economy of recent years has generated new public revenue in the hands of the Indian state. Given democratic pressures, some of this revenue is now being committed to helping the poor. This is reflected in enhanced investment in primary education and public health, on the one hand, and in the creation of new employment opportunities via public work programs, on the other. Since this new investment is not accompanied by new organizational initiatives, however, the capacity of the state to truly reach the needy remains limited. Still, these are important new initiatives; their success will become clear only over the next decade or so. Meanwhile, what is clear is that the Indian state's approach to helping India's poor has undergone a basic change. In socialist India, the hope was to alter substantial inequality by redistributing assets; much of this failed and has by now been abandoned. The new approach is more consistent with the principles of an evolving capitalist political economy: instead of attacking substantial inequality, the Indian state now hopes to promote equality of opportunity.

REGIONAL VARIATIONS

India's subnational diversity finds expression in its federal structure. Political and economic changes in Indian states continue to diverge along several dimensions, including economic growth, distribution, poverty alleviation, and quality of governance. In this volume I do not provide anything close to a full analysis of regional diversity across India. What I provide instead, in the third section of the book, are snapshots of a few of India's important states that shed light on some typical variations across Indian states. The main analytical theme that continues in this section is that varying patterns of politics and authority across Indian states, especially the underlying state and class/caste relations, are a key determinant of regional developmental dynamics.

Three political tendencies compete for ascendancy in India's states: *neo-patrimonial, social-democratic,* and *developmental.* While most Indian states exhibit all of these tendencies, some states during some periods have emerged more clearly as neo-patrimonial or social-democratic or developmental, with discernible developmental consequences. For example, where neo-patrimonial tendencies are ascendant, state-level governments simply lack public purpose. Instead of using state authority and resources to pursue the public good, ruling elites in these settings use their power for personal and sectional gains. Bihar and Uttar Pradesh typify these *neo-patrimonial* states of India. Politics in these and a few other states of India – where neopatrimonialism has been ascendant during recent periods – tends to be under-institutionalized and instead characterized by some shared traits: the political arena is dominated by a single leader surrounded by loyal minions; modal political relationships are vertical, of a patron-client type; bureaucracy is politicized; symbolic appeals are used regularly to build diffuse political support; the zero-sum quality of politics makes those excluded from power feel totally excluded; and instead of carrying out any systematic public policy, leaders channel public resources for personalistic and narrow gains.

Understanding the causes and consequences of such neo-patrimonial tendencies in some of India's states is a complex research problem. I shed some light on these issues by focusing on one of India's major states, Uttar Pradesh. Among the key proximate causes of neo-patrimonial politics as modal politics in U.P. is the pervasiveness of ascriptive politics, especially the politics of caste. In the past – say, during the 1950s and 1960s – the Congress Party exercised its hegemony in U.P. mainly by depending on Brahmins. While state politics during this early phase was not totally devoid of public purpose, the gains were monopolized by the upper castes, fueling cynicism. The eventual challenge to Brahmanical domination took the form, not of class politics, but of a challenge by the middle castes. As ascriptive politics is want to do, the political upsurge of the middle castes lacked any coherent ideology or organization; it quickly became a politics of symbolic gains (e.g., with a focus on "reservations") and of personalism and corruption. The most recent political challenge by the lowest castes in the form of rule by the Bahujan Samaj Party has only accentuated these tendencies toward symbolic gains, personalism, and corruption. As to consequences, a focus on ascriptive politics has detracted attention in U.P. from issues that might serve the interests of the state as a whole, such as economic growth; the decline in public investment from the central government and apparent decentralization have only accentuated these problems. A focus on symbolic gains as a strategy for mobilizing fellow caste members also continues to detract attention from any systematic redistribution. The net result is that in states like U.P. both growth and distributive gains have been meager.

Indian states in which governmental authority is used more constructively can be conveniently thought of as states in which politics of either the left or the right dominate. Given democracy, these ideological tendencies can of course shift. Nevertheless, it is fair to characterize certain states of India such as Kerala and West Bengal during recent periods as India's left-leaning states, where *social-democratic* tendencies have been ascendant. Politics in these states is typically characterized by mobilized lower classes and castes, on the one hand, and by the presence of a well-organized left-of-center political party that systematically incorporates this mobilized support into a social-democratic power bloc, on the other hand. The presence of this power bloc, in turn, has added public purpose to the politics of India's left-leaning states. I will later use the example of West Bengal to demonstrate how politics of this type emerged and how it has been used to pursue certain constructive ends, such as tenancy reforms.

While the redistributive successes in West Bengal are distinctly mixed – and the ruling forces of the left have lost power as the book goes to press – the case does suggest the proposition that redistributive success is most likely when effective governmental power rests on a broad political base; in such cases, rulers can minimize the hold of upper castes and classes on the regional state, successfully organize the middle and lower strata into an effective power bloc, and then use this power to channel resources to the poor. This proposition finds further support when we juxtapose India's southern states against the neo-patrimonial states of India's "Hindi heartland." In spite of middling growth rates, poverty has come down relatively rapidly in all of India's southern states. This is in part a result of the fact that the social base of political power in these states has been relatively broad; the narrow domination of Brahmins was effectively challenged quite early in the twentieth century, and subsequently the middle and lower strata have provided active support to the ruling parties. The social base of state power in the southern states is thus distinct from that in Hindi-heartland states, where Brahmanical domination was challenged only more recently. The other factor that has contributed to the success of pro-poor politics in the South is the relative superiority of the bureaucracy. A broader social base of power and more effective state machinery has led to better education and health provision in the South; the subsidized public distribution system has also been better managed. Higher rates of literacy in the region have in turn further contributed to ongoing political scrutiny, setting some limits on neo-patrimonial excesses. In the more radical southern state of Kerala, land redistribution, higher wages for the landless, and gender equality have also been achieved.

Finally, following economic liberalization and the related shift of initiative from the center to the states, a few of India's states have actively and effectively promoted business and industry. These are India's more right-leaning states, approximating *developmental states* of sorts, in which the government has worked closely with business groups to promote economic growth. I will later use the example of Gujarat to demonstrate the developmental tendency in some of India's states. In addition to Gujarat, where the state government has mainly sought to promote manufacturing, leaders in other states such as Karnataka and Andhra Pradesh have actively supported service industries, and in Punjab and Haryana, agriculture and agriculture-related industries.

Gujarat has long been one of India's more industrialized states, and the state government has long exhibited pro-business proclivities. Some of this was challenged during the 1970s, when Indira Gandhi's populist upsurge led to the ouster of the commercially inclined Patels from Gujarat's ruling circles. That, however, did not last long. As the upper strata of Gujarat reasserted their political weight, the political challenge faced by ruling elites became that of catering to these narrow interests while mobilizing electoral majorities. Gujarat in recent decades has created a "tradition" of sorts of fomenting deliberate riots against one set of victims or another so as to capture state power for narrow elites. The most recent manifestation of these trends is Narendra Modi, who has created an efficient, pro-business government with the help of the well-established business class of Gujarat and a relatively well-organized BJP that has mobilized a pro-Hindu majority against Muslims.

To sum up, in this book I analyze the political economy of contemporary India from a number of vantage points. In the first part of the book I analyze the changing nature of the Indian state itself, focusing especially on its evolution away from socialism and toward becoming an active partner of Indian capitalism. How this pro-business state intervenes to promote growth and distribution is the main issue analyzed in the second part of the book. I suggest that the pro-business proclivities of the Indian state have helped release economic dynamism, but have not strengthened the impulse to intervene effectively on behalf of India's poor.

The same themes are then analyzed across Indian states to demonstrate how neo-patrimonial, social-democratic, and developmental tendencies remain aspects of the Indian polity. I will conclude then by situating the Indian case in a broader, comparative context and by focusing on the key challenge faced by India's democratic rulers, the challenge of inclusive growth.

I

Political Change

Illusions of Inclusion

India is governed as a vibrant democracy. While the quality of government provided by India's democracy remains uneven, the survival and institutionalization of democracy in a large, poor, multiethnic society is India's singular achievement. In this chapter I provide some background materials that help shed light on how and why democracy has put down roots in India. The focus of this chapter, however, is on the changing character of India's contemporary democracy. In the discussion that follows, two themes are emphasized. First, the Indian state over the last few decades has become more and more pro-business. I analyze both the causes and consequences of this important shift. And second, the political management of a narrow ruling alliance creates numerous electoral and institutional challenges, especially the challenge of how to deal with the excluded masses. I analyze the political strategies pursued by both the rulers and the ruled.

I. BACKGROUND

By the time the British left India in the mid twentieth century, key elements of what would eventually become a sovereign, democratic Indian state were already in place. Summarizing a complex history, one might suggest that the British left behind such moderately well-functioning state institutions as a civil service, an army, and a judiciary. Indian nationalists, in turn, knit together diverse elements of India's political society and adopted a parliamentary democracy with full adult suffrage. Thus, avowedly working against each other, the colonial rulers of India and

19

Indian nationalists together laid the foundations of the modern democratic Indian state.[1]

The British ruled India for nearly two centuries, first via the East
India Company and then from 1857 on, more directly, via the British
crown. The British developed an administrative system in India to ensure
the taxation that financed colonial rule, a judiciary to ensure private
property and contracts, and an army both to impose rule and to project
power in other regions of the empire. Unlike other British colonies, such
as those in Africa, India played a fairly central role in Britain's global
empire. Favorable trade balances with India helped pay Britain's imperial
expenses, and the British Indian army helped Britain expand and police
its empire. There is no doubt that the British rule in India was despotic,
racist, and exploitative. And yet it is the case that the British, for their own
purposes, created and left behind in India a well-functioning, professional
civil service, an apolitical army, and a British-style judiciary. Indian rulers
inherited and eventually built on these institutions, adding a degree of
stability to sovereign India.

Under the leadership of the likes of Gandhi and Nehru, Indian nationalists mobilized successfully against British colonial rule. The motives
of those who led and those who joined India's nationalist movement
were, of course, mixed: patriotism, dislike of the British, self-interest.
Leaving aside communist revolutions such as China's, India's nationalist movement was one of the most significant anticolonial mass movements in the developing world. Three characteristics of this movement
turned out to be especially consequential for India's long-term political
development. First, the nationalists created "unity in diversity": India's
diverse ethnic, class, and caste groups joined the anticolonial movement, finding an institutional expression in the Indian National Congress,
which later evolved into India's premiere ruling party, the Congress.
Second, the Congress not only provided a big tent for incorporating
a variety of identities and interests, but also did so while committed
to democracy, both for India and also, to a degree, within the nationalist movement. And third, when confronted with the severe inequality and tensions of India's rigid hierarchical society, Gandhi and other
Indian nationalists always chose the path of gradual change over decisive

[1] For a somewhat more detailed version of my own interpretation of the colonial impact
on Indian politics, see Kohli (2004), Chapter 6. For two important formulations by
historians that are more or less consistent with my views, see Chandra et al. (1998) and
Sarkar (1989).

challenges. While the commitment of the nationalists to inclusion, democracy, and gradualism augured well for creating a stable and open polity, it also implied a slow – nay, very slow – pace of change for India's vast poor majority.

Nehru was India's nearly unchallenged ruler for some fifteen years following independence.[2] These years were the crucible of modern India: state power was consolidated; democracy put down roots; and the foundations of a state-guided, industrializing economy were laid. Unfortunately, these achievements were not without costs. In spite of a rhetorical commitment to socialism, India's poor did not benefit much from this pattern of development. This too was a long-term pattern in the making. As in other countries, India's leaders faced difficult trade-offs in their policy decisions. The pattern of choices reflected the fact that India's leaders at this early stage prioritized political goals over economic ones, and within economic choices – which we will discuss in the next chapter – the commitment to redistribution was more rhetorical than real.

India's nationalist movement enjoyed widespread support, and, as a result, leaders of the movement such as Nehru and others were considered deeply legitimate within India. Early in the life of the republic, the leaders put this political capital to good use by adopting a constitution that continues to provide the framework for governing India. Reflecting the elements of a shared consensus within India's political class, the constitution committed India to a British-style parliamentary democracy with full adult suffrage. The act of adopting full adult suffrage was quite radical; it is explicable if one keeps in mind that the nationalist struggle was fought in the name of all Indians, rich and poor, literate and illiterate, men and women. On other key elements of the constitution there was less consensus, but those defeated in one issue area often felt they had won in other areas, avoiding debilitating conflict. For example, the right of private property had to be weighed against the rights of tenants and landless workers in the countryside to own land via land reforms; the "left" forces generally lost this battle as private property became a fundamental right. Conversely, there was significant disagreement about how interventionist in the economy the Indian state would be; the "right" lost this battle, with "socialism" becoming enshrined in the constitution as a guiding principle of the Indian political economy.

---

[2] For good studies of politics in India during the Nehru era, see Kothari (1970), Weiner (1967), and Chandra et al. (1999). For a good biography of Nehru, see Gopal (1984).

Decolonization brought with it serious challenges of governance.[3] The creation of Pakistan led to violence and bloodshed, massive migration of refugees, and a war with Pakistan. Nearly two-fifths of British India had been ruled by semisovereign Indian princes; creation of a modern state now necessitated political consolidation. Disparate nationalists like Nehru and Patel agreed that the armed force they had inherited from the British needed to be not only maintained but strengthened in order to deal with such challenges. Faced with nation-building challenges, then, a key colonial institution came to occupy the heart of the sovereign Indian state. The same was also the case of a second key institution, the Indian Civil Service (ICS), but here there was less agreement at the top. The ICS had, of course, been the central institution by means of which the British in India had extracted taxes and maintained law and order. The nationalists had often viewed the ICS as part of the exploitative colonial framework. The left-leaning leaders of the Congress, including Nehru, wanted to transform the ICS into an institution that would promote development. By contrast, Patel and others on the right argued that India could not be governed without the ICS and won. Indian nationalists changed the name of the ICS to the Indian Administrative Services (IAS) and chose to maintain and build on this colonial creation. Here, then, is a good example of how the political goals of good governance in India often trumped more transformative goals, such as that of creating a developmental state.

In the political sphere, following independence, Indian nationalists had to quickly devise strategies for winning elections. While the Congress already had some experience with elections in British India, and as nationalist leaders enjoyed broad popularity, full adult suffrage raised new challenges. With the British gone and, with them, the anticolonial nationalist unity, the challenge now was to secure the electoral support of India's numerous poor and illiterate citizens. Citizens more in name than in substance, most of India's poor and illiterate during the early life of the republic remained entrenched at the bottom, bound by patron-client ties dominated by the property-owning upper-caste members of India's village society. Given its weak organizational capacity to penetrate villages, the Congress Party built its political support on the backs of the village "big men," generally the landed members of the higher castes. Congress rulers were in a position to channel public resources to these big men,

---

[3] A recent historical study that covers these and most other important political developments in post-independence India in great detail is Guha (2007).

who in turn mobilized all those who depended on them to support the Congress. Thus were built long chains of patronage that stretched from New Delhi to India's vast rural periphery. Lingering nationalist legitimacy and machine politics enabled the Congress to repeatedly win elections, with two important consequences. First, elections and democracy became increasingly routine. Second, this routinization came at what was by now becoming a familiar cost: the interests of the powerful in society were becoming deeply embedded within India's core political institution, the Congress Party, further diluting its rhetorical commitment to socialism.[4]

As the Indian state consolidated power and Nehru's hold over the Congress Party became firm, Nehru felt more and more comfortable in confronting the challenges posed by Indian federalism. British India already had elements of federalism built into its ruling structure. Regional groupings were also important within India's nationalist movement. Though the Indian constitution created India as a federal polity, the principles and boundaries of regional entities were not fully defined, and indeed are still evolving today. India is, of course, a multilingual, multiethnic society. Though organizing Indian federalism along linguistic lines – a Tamil state for these who spoke Tamil, a Punjab state for those who spoke Punjabi – was a natural option, Nehru and others resisted such a design in the aftermath of the bloody partition between India and Pakistan, lest a linguistic reorganization encourage secessionist tendencies. During the 1950s, however, numerous linguistic groups mobilized, demanding their own states within the Indian federal structure. After much back-and-forth, Nehru and other Congress elite in New Delhi agreed in 1958 on power-sharing arrangements, leading to a linguistic organization of Indian federalism.[5] In retrospect, it is clear that this major concession by Nehru from a position of strength – by then the Indian state had consolidated central power, and Nehru was firmly in command – did much to accommodate India's ethnic diversity. At the same time, however, it is important to underline the trade-off: from here on, New Delhi would have to depend on state capitals – which were often less progressive in terms of social commitment and less competent – to pursue a whole range of development policies, including land reforms, education, and the management of the police and thus of law, order, and corruption.

India lost a war with China in 1962, and Nehru died in 1964. These developments created a sense of crisis in India. Just below the level of

---

[4] This theme is well developed in Frankel (1978).
[5] For a good study of this episode, see Dasgupta (1970).

popular mood, however, key institutions of the Indian polity had by now acquired a firm shape. The army – even a defeated army – and the civil service were well-organized, professional bodies that helped stabilize governance. While the Congress Party was hegemonic, it was a big-tent party, incorporating diverse interests and identities. A federal structure was in place. And most important, democracy had put down firm roots; elections were by now the main vehicle for acquiring and legitimating power. None of this is to minimize the serious political problems that India still faced: the economy remained sluggish, especially India's agricultural economy, causing food shortages, inflation, and political dissatisfaction; identity-based demands were far from settled; and, most important, a vast majority of India's poor and illiterate citizens remained economically and politically marginalized. Nevertheless, the framework of a stable democratic polity was now in place.

Following Nehru's death, the struggle to replace him was settled peacefully by the "syndicate" – a group of powerful second-tier leaders of the Congress Party – who chose a mild-mannered man named Shastri for the leadership position. Unfortunately, Shastri himself died shortly thereafter. Looking for a leader whom they could control but who would also be popular in elections, the syndicate now chose Nehru's daughter, Indira Gandhi, to head the Congress Party and to become India's new prime minister. Thus began in the mid-1960s a new era in Indian politics that was dominated by Indira Gandhi and that ended only with her assassination in 1984.[6] Important political changes during the Indira Gandhi period included the declining popularity of the old Congress Party; the emergence of a variety of new political demands from below; the adoption of a populist posture by Indira Gandhi and the related creation of a new type of top-down, personalistic Congress Party; and growing political conflict, leading to the temporary suspension of democratic rights, followed by a return to democracy in 1980 and a slow but steady shift away from mobilization and populism and toward a more pro-business approach to the national political economy. In what follows I will discuss some of these background changes only in a highly abridged form, setting the stage for a more detailed discussion of the post-1980 period in the rest of the chapter.

By the mid-1960s the twin pillars of Congress's hegemony over Indian politics – nationalist legitimacy and machine politics – were, if not quite

---

[6] Good studies of the Indira Gandhi period include Frankel (2005), Guha (2007), Rudolph and Rudolph (1987), and Carras (1979). Also see Jayakar (1992).

crumbling, certainly weakened. The simple passage of time was bringing forward a post-nationalist generation of leaders and followers. The spread of democracy and commerce, in turn, had begun to undermine the relations of patron-client domination upon which Congress's electoral machine rested. Numerous poor and illiterate citizens were thus becoming freshly available for political mobilization. New political parties flourished in this changing political context. The Congress Party nearly lost the national election in 1967. In the aftermath, Indira Gandhi sought to rebuild Congress's electoral fortunes by shifting it further to the left. As she adopted the slogan *garibi hatao* (alleviate poverty) to reflect Congress's modified political position, the Congress "old guard" resisted. At this point Indira Gandhi split the old Congress Party, created a new Congress Party in her own image, and became immensely popular among India's numerous poor.

During the 1970s, Indira Gandhi was India's most important political leader, though hardly an unchallenged one. Indian politics during this decade became quite contentious, with Indian leaders attaching a high premium on winning and maintaining power. As discussed earlier, political and developmental goals competed even during the Nehru period, with political priorities often trumping developmental ones. By now, however, not only was politics very much in command (e.g., economic policies served political needs), but the substance of politics itself had shifted – more populist and anticapitalist than during the Nehru period, on the one hand, and more personalistic and top-down, on the other. Indira Gandhi's soaring popularity, especially among the poor and the marginalized, enabled her to concentrate vast powers in her own person. The roots of this power, however, were shallow: the new Congress Party lacked any coherent ideology or organization, and Indira Gandhi's diverse followers were held together by little more than her leadership appeal and vague populist promises. Instead of moving toward a well-organized social democracy, for which many had hoped, India's political system became centralized, personalistic, and powerless, at least in terms of implementing developmental goals.

The top-down polity that Indira Gandhi created and that was held together by her persona and by populism led to important political consequences. From the standpoint of supporters of Indira Gandhi, she reenergized a failing Congress Party, saving India from debilitating political fragmentation, and empowered India's poor majority. While such claims are not without merit, they are far from the full story. Indira Gandhi's populist policies hurt India's economic growth, and, in the absence of a well-organized support structure, her radical flourishes remained that, radical flourishes, providing no significant gains for India's poor; I will return to these issues in the next chapter. With power concentrated in her person, she started appointing second- and third-tier political officials whose power rested more on loyalty to her and less on an independent political base. The resulting organizational weakness of the Congress Party has continued to plague the party to the present day. And finally, the more Indira Gandhi concentrated power in her own person, the more opposition forces mobilized and organized against her. By the mid-1970s, then, the pro- and anti-Indira forces had become so polarized that Indira Gandhi proclaimed a national emergency, suspending democratic rights for some two years.

Indira Gandhi thus brought Indian democracy to the brink. For reasons that remain murky, she fortunately rescinded the Emergency after two years and called for new elections. While she lost these elections to a motley anti-Indira coalition, the reason she called for elections was probably the fact that democracy in India had already put down roots and that legitimacy in this system required winning elections. The anti-Indira coalition, in the form of the Janata Party, which won the election in 1977, held together for barely two years; competing ambitions and the lack of a programmatic consensus thus made the very first effort by non-Congress forces to govern India a failure. The Indira Gandhi who returned to power in 1980 was smug about the inability of the opposition to govern, on the one hand, but also chastened and changed by the traumatic political events of the second half of the 1970s, on the other.

The Emergency period, then, turned out to be yet another turning point of sorts in Indian politics. First, with democratic rights and processes in suspension, both the mobilization and countermobilization of political forces that had preceded the emergency came to a sudden halt. Even after the Emergency was rescinded, levels of mobilization in India seldom reached the feverish pitch of the pre-Emergency period. A variety of leaders, including communist leaders, seemed to recognize how much everyone had to lose with the suspension of democracy, moderating extremist politics, especially on the left. And second, working closely with her relatively conservative son, Sanjay Gandhi, Indira Gandhi during the Emergency started moderating her own leftward political and economic tilt. Thus began, especially during the post-1980 period, a new phase in Indian politics, characterized by a slow but steady abandonment of socialism for a more pro-business political economy.

II. PRO-BUSINESS TILT

The Indian state has never been deeply anti-business. Prior to independence, Gandhi worked closely with leading businessmen like Birla, and Nehru forged working relationships with Indian industrialists like Tata in planning India's future economic direction. Nevertheless, the Congress Party committed itself to socialism, creating a multiclass social base and privileging the role of the public sector in India's economic development. Indira Gandhi during the late 1960s and early 1970s accentuated these left-leaning tendencies, creating further distance and suspicion between the Indian state and Indian capitalists. Indira Gandhi soon realized, however, that her anticapitalist stance was counterproductive: in what was mainly a private enterprise economy, it not only hurt private investment and economic growth but also, and equally important for her, politically alienated businessmen who could readily switch their financial and political support to other leaders and parties. These costs were especially salient in light of the fact that her poor supporters were not well organized, and she had only minimal success in implementing pro-poor policies. Indira Gandhi thus initiated a long-term political realignment in India, a realignment that has now created a ruling alliance between the Indian state and capital.

I analyze both the causes and the consequences of this important political shift away from socialism and toward a pro-business political economy in India. Among the causes, I first focus on how and why India's political elite initiated a pro-business shift. This is followed by an analysis of the growing power of business groups within India, a power that very much molds state behavior today. As one might anticipate, the consequences of the growing state-business alliance are both political and economic. A key political challenge created by a narrow ruling alliance is how to win the support of and deal with the excluded masses. This is discussed later in this chapter. I return to the issue of the economic consequences of the state-business alliance – an acceleration of economic growth accompanied by widening inequality – in the next chapter.

State-Initiated Changes

While there is no doubt that Indira Gandhi herself initiated the pro-business tilt of the Indian state, when exactly this happened and why remains somewhat unclear. Since complex and important changes often occur in fits and starts, this lack of clarity is not surprising. During the late 1960s and early 1970s, Indira Gandhi pushed Indian politics to the left, certainly at the level of rhetoric. If judged by the actual policies she pursued, however, the record is quite mixed. As examples, she adopted an important set of agricultural policies in the mid-1960s – to be discussed in the next chapter – that led to a close alliance between the state and landowning producers, resulting in the so-called green revolution. As the Emergency approached, Indira Gandhi crushed a strike of railway workers. While this was in part politically motivated – the leader of the strike, George Fernandez, was very much part of the growing opposition to Indira Gandhi – it was also welcomed by Indian businessmen, whose economic activities had already been hurt by the railway strike. Moreover, as the pressure on Indira Gandhi to resign was growing prior to her imposition of the Emergency, a delegation of prominent Indian businessmen – led by K. K. Birla – urged her to stay in power. What all these events help underline is that Indira Gandhi's early record was a combination of left-leaning rhetoric, various failed antipoverty policies, and some quite "pragmatic" policies that were appreciated by the producer classes.

During the Emergency, politics and policy in India turned more conservative. This is true in the most obvious sense that mobilized popular forces were either put in prison or forced to get off the streets. As the public sphere shrunk, a sense of discipline in society emerged, leading to bureaucrats actually showing up for work on schedule and the trains running on time. Members of the urban middle class welcomed these changes. While businessmen and industrialists were also pleased, what they truly appreciated was a sharp decline in labor militancy. A sense of efficiency and discipline was boosted by Indira Gandhi's growing reliance on her son Sanjay Gandhi, who, in turn, argued openly against Indian communists and for clearing the slums and imposing family planning on poor Indians. Indira Gandhi sought to maintain her socialist credentials by announcing a variety of pro-poor policies, but most of these were not well implemented.

It is hard to know what would have happened if the Emergency had continued or, more plausibly, if Indira Gandhi had won the elections in 1977. What happened instead, of course, was that Indira Gandhi called for elections and lost. The brief Janata interregnum that followed revealed several emerging political trends. First, Indian politics had become a lot more contentious. With the decline of the nationalist legitimacy and the emergence of a variety of new political forces, Congress's hegemony had been challenged. Second, the opposition forces in the form of the Janata Party were unable to work together as a cohesive political force. Competing factions represented a variety of social interests and identities, and without a cohering ideology or organization, leadership ambitions tore apart the possibility of institutionalizing an alternative to the Congress Party. And third, and somewhat ironically, in spite of the growing contentiousness and the inability of the anti-Congress opposition to coalesce, the sense that democracy was the only way to go was strengthened in India. This was in part because of a factor already noted, namely, that a variety of antidemocratic forces, such as the revolutionary communists, recommitted to democracy after realizing how much they had to lose when democratic spaces were eliminated, but also in part because Indira Gandhi's electoral loss was widely interpreted as a popular vote against authoritarianism.

When the brief Janata government collapsed, new elections were called, and Indira Gandhi returned to power with a resounding majority. Even with this majority, however, Indira Gandhi was by now much less of a socialist, and India by now had become a difficult country to govern. In retrospect, it seems that Indira Gandhi's embrace of *garibi hatao* during the 1960s was mainly motivated by electoral considerations; the leftward tilt enabled her to gain support among India's poor majority, freed her of the old Congress guard, and helped her reverse Congress's declining hegemony, albeit on a new basis. Indira Gandhi lacked the political instruments – a well-organized party and/or a lower-level bureaucracy that would respond to central directives – needed to implement her antipoverty policies, and she certainly did not try very hard to push against entrenched interests. On the contrary, when difficult choices had to be made, she often made concessions to propertied classes, reserving the worst of her wrath for her political opponents. As noted earlier, during the Emergency she had already started distancing herself from her earlier commitment to the politics of *garibi hatao*. Instead, maintaining law and order and improving production had become the themes of governance during that authoritarian interlude. After returning to power in 1980, maintaining electoral popularity, providing orderly government, and promoting economic growth continued to be her key priorities.

That Indira Gandhi wanted to maintain her electoral popularity and stay in power hardly requires an explanation. All politicians want to do that. More than many others, however, Indira Gandhi was a deeply political politician. She viewed most policy decisions through the prism of their potential impact on her hold on power. She also displayed signs of paranoia, readily suspecting independent politicians of being challengers. This put a great premium on loyalty and sycophancy among the leaders of the second tier. And finally, with the accidental death of her son Sanjay

in 1980, she became quite despondent and lonely. This made her even
more wary of undertaking heroic social mobilization. The governance
agenda had by now shrunk to holding it all together, on the one hand,
and turning to the capitalists with the hope that they would produce
more, on the other.

While the Janta Party was unable to forge a coherent alternative
to Indira Gandhi, their disintegration did not mean that opposition to
Congress rule itself disappeared. On the contrary, what happened instead
was that a variety of fragmented opposition movements started emerging during the early 1980s. Unable or unwilling to accommodate these
"million rebellions" politically, Indira Gandhi readily adopted a law-and-
order approach to what were political problems. For example, a major
strike by textile workers in and around Bombay was crushed in the early
1980s, breaking the back of an important segment of unionized workers. Peasants demanding land took to revolutionary tactics in states like
Andhra Pradesh and were met by state repression. Identity politics again
came to the fore in several regions, leading to the emergence of regional
nationalist governments in such regions as the Punjab, Kashmir, and
Andhra Pradesh. Ordinary political struggles in some cases, such as that
involving the Sikhs in the Punjab, got so out of hand – at least in part
because of Indira Gandhi's political manipulation and refusal to make
timely concessions – that a decade-long battle between Sikh militants and
the national government ensued, eventually culminating in the assassination of Indira Gandhi by one of her Sikh bodyguards. Leaders of middle
and lower castes gained power with the support of Indira Gandhi in
states such as Gujarat, leading to clashes with the entrenched dominant
castes. And finally, as an offshoot of the Janta Party, the old Jana Sangh –
a Hindu religious party – was born anew as the Bharatiya Janta Party
(BJP) in the early 1980s. While in due course this party would go on to
become India's major opposition party, during this period it was associated with encouraging Hindu-Moslem violence in parts of north central
India, including the state of Uttar Pradesh.[7]

While Indira Gandhi dealt with one brush fire after another, the main
focus of her economic policy became the promotion of economic growth.
Slowly but surely, this led to a growing alliance between the state and
big business. Just after coming to power in January 1980, for example,

---

[7] I have analyzed India's growing crisis of governability during the 1970s and 1980s in
some detail in Kohli (1990). Also see a collection of essays, especially those by James
Manor, Paul Brass, and Henry Hart, in Kohli (1988).

Indira Gandhi let it be known that improving production was now her top priority. In meeting after meeting with private industrialists, she clarified that what the government was most concerned about was production.[8] A host of new policies aimed at boosting production – discussed in the next chapter – were adopted. Observers of the Indian political scene noticed the changes. India's leading daily, *The Times of India*, thus editorialized on February 22, 1981: "A change of considerable significance is taking place in India. . . . the emphasis has shifted from distributive justice to growth."

India's leading business organization at the time, the Federation of Indian Chambers of Commerce and Industry (FICCI), had produced its own analysis of factors inhibiting economic growth in India. These included constraints on and lack of governmental support for business; labor activism; the inefficiency of the public sector; and the decline in public investment, especially in infrastructure.[9] Indira Gandhi's government increasingly accepted this analysis. In spite of her socialist credentials, her antilabor stance was there for anyone to notice; she had crushed the railway strike in 1974; labor militancy had declined sharply during the Emergency; and she stood by in the early 1980s as the massive textile workers strike was defeated. The new pro-growth rhetoric and policies also assured businessmen that a new economic order was emerging. Most reassuring to businessmen were the advisors Indira Gandhi now surrounded herself with; gone were the left-leaning "Kashmiri Brahmins" of the pre-Emergency period, now replaced by individuals well known for their pro-business sympathies.

The underlying changes that triggered the pro-business political shift were both of the slow-moving type – changes that accumulated slowly but surely, not always noticed in daily newspaper reports – and of the more noticeable variety. Among the slow changes was the accumulating evidence that India's economic growth throughout the 1970s had been fairly dismal; accelerating production was thus very much on the political agenda. The context within which higher rates of growth were to be achieved included the important fact that the significance of capitalism in the Indian economy, both in the countryside and in the cities, had grown steadily.[10] The more this happened, the more anachronistic

[8] See, for example, the lead editorial ("All for Production") in *Economic and Political Weekly*, August 30, 1980.
[9] See "FICCI's Blueprint," *Economic and Political Weekly*, January 26, 1980, p. 135.
[10] See Nayar (1989), pp. 330–50.

became claims of the state controlling the "commanding heights of the economy," especially in the face of a poorly performing public sector. A growing reliance on the private sector for growth was thus increasingly probable.

Among the short-term changes, it was clear to Indira Gandhi by 1980 that the politics of *garibi hatao* had run out of steam; antipoverty policies like land reform had proven difficult to implement; ineffective socialism had hurt economic growth; and, by contrast, putting the weight of the state behind private producers had helped agricultural production, leading to the green revolution in the 1960s.[11] The economic lessons were hard to ignore. Politically too, Indira Gandhi and her advisors calculated that a realignment with big capital might not be too costly, in part because the poor were already loyal to her, but also because state support of business might lead to higher growth and thus to lower inflation, an outcome that India's largely poor electorate would appreciate.

The global context of India's political economy was also changing in significant ways. Free market ideas were ascendant around the world. While Indira Gandhi was quite suspicious of arm twisting by the West, she was also a clever politician who recognized political necessity. Sharp increases in the price of imported oil had made India quite vulnerable to foreign exchange shortages in the early 1980s. As is common under such circumstances, India borrowed from the International Monetary Fund (IMF) and in exchange agreed to undertake some policy reforms.[12] Since such reforms generally boost the private sector at the expense of state intervention in the economy, these external pressures also contributed to the emerging pro-business shift within India.

In sum, when Indira Gandhi was assassinated in 1984, a variety of class, caste, and regional movements were already demanding more from the central government, and she had already initiated a major political and economic shift, away from socialism and toward a state and business alliance. This was the context in which her son Rajiv Gandhi succeeded her as India's prime minister. From all appearances, Rajiv was a reluctant politician. Born to India's first political family, trained as a pilot, married to an Italian woman, he was mostly a family man of few outstanding talents, but with a gracious bearing and sense of confidence that comes from a life of privilege. Indira Gandhi inducted him into politics after

---

[11] See Kohli (2004), pp. 270–77.
[12] For details see Sengupta (2001), Chapter 2.

the accidental death of her more politically inclined younger son, Sanjay Gandhi. Thereafter, Rajiv's political prominence grew rapidly. This was not because he had any special political acumen. Instead, it reflected the nature of the Indian political system, in which authority by now was both concentrated and personalistic. Unlike the situation following Nehru's death, when Indira Gandhi was selected by the syndicate to be Congress's leader, there were no second-tier leaders with independent political standing, certainly not in the Congress Party. Instead, Indira Gandhi dominated a party that was very much molded in her image, with the second-tier leaders quite dependent on her for their positions. These loyal minions needed Indira's son to step into her shoes, win elections with inherited legitimacy and popularity, and thus ensure their own power and positions.

Indira Gandhi's assassination created widespread sympathy in India for the Gandhi family, along with a fear of political destabilization. These sentiments benefited Rajiv Gandhi, who was elected the new leader of India with massive popular support. Unfortunately, Rajiv's popularity also did not have institutional roots; as the national mood shifted, Rajiv's popularity and power proved to be shallow, contributing to a variety of political failures, including the loss of elections in 1989.[13] We will never know whether Rajiv Gandhi on his own could have rebuilt his political base or not. He too, unfortunately, was assassinated in 1991 by a suicide bomber sympathetic to the Tamil Tigers of Sri Lanka.

Once in power, Rajiv Gandhi sought to make a clean break with the past, at least in terms of ideology and style of politics. As someone without a political past, he was not encumbered by prior political commitments. Unlike his mother, he had no need to defend his "socialist" credentials. Of course, Indira Gandhi's commitment to socialism was deeply strained by the end of her political career. Rajiv dropped any and all pretense of socialism and committed himself instead to a more "liberal" beginning in India.[14] He created a technocratic image – he and his coterie were often dubbed in the media the "computer boys" – expressed disdain for the old Congress culture of corruption and inefficiency, and sought to "liberalize" India's economy. Of course, all this was easily expressed in rhetoric and in symbolic politics but harder to put into practice.

---

[13] This argument is developed in some detail in Kohli (1990).

[14] During his very first budget speech, for example, the word "socialism" was not even mentioned once. Of course, when faced with declining popularity later in his tenure, Rajiv again embraced "socialism." By then, however, the image of a break with the past had stuck.

Rajiv Gandhi inherited numerous political problems from his mother, especially the growing militancy in the Punjab. Rajiv sought to use his considerable popularity to accommodate the demands of the Sikh regional nationalists. Unfortunately, as already noted, his popularity proved to be shallow and short-lived. As his party lost elections in one region after another, indicating his declining capacity to attract the popular vote, Rajiv's capacity to accommodate demands also declined. A return to a law-and-order approach to political problems then underlined once again the incapacity of leaders in India to translate their popularity into meaningful outcomes.

The one policy area in which Rajiv's governance strategy seemed to make headway was a growing alliance with Indian business. This too, however, was less a function of Rajiv's planned strategy and more a function of the growing power of Indian business groups. As a matter of fact, motivated by the need to make the Indian economy more efficient, Rajiv Gandhi wanted to open it up to foreign goods and investment. The economic dimensions of such a shift are discussed in the next chapter. What needs to be pointed out here is that Rajiv's efforts to "liberalize" India's economy ran up against numerous political obstacles, especially opposition from threatened indigenous Indian business groups.[15] In the end, Rajiv Gandhi gave up his efforts to open up the Indian economy; Indian business groups won this round of the battle. What this battle underlined was the growing power of Indian business during the 1980s. A business sector that had been unable to thwart Indira Gandhi's flirtation with socialism during the 1960s and 1970s had by now become significant enough politically to limit any hurried opening of the Indian economy. By accepting these constraints, Rajiv Gandhi signaled a working partnership with Indian business groups.

During the 1980s Indira and Rajiv Gandhi thus cemented a political alliance between the Indian state and India's indigenous business groups. Looking for economic growth, Indira Gandhi first started courting business groups. Business groups, in turn, took advantage of the new political opening and boosted profits and production. As the role of the private sector in the economy grew, so did the power of private actors. Rajiv Gandhi experienced this growing power of business groups. He continued his mother's focus on prioritizing economic growth, but thought that the best way to do so was to open India's economy to the world. Unable to push through these liberalizing reforms, he accommodated the demands

[15] See Kohli (1989).

of Indian big business, especially the demands to dilute internal regulations and for protection from external competition. As the state and business alliance firmed via trial and error, and socialism was discarded, a key political challenge facing India's rulers became how to win the electoral support of India's poor. This background helps to make sense of the growing importance of caste and religion in Indian politics during the late 1980s and 1990s.

Rajiv Gandhi lost the elections in 1989 and was assassinated while campaigning in 1991. Having abandoned socialism, the Congress Party and Rajiv Gandhi increasingly had trouble attracting popular support during this period. As Rajiv's popularity declined rapidly during the second half of the 1980s, one notable political development was the rising popularity of the BJP. The BJP mobilized on a platform of Hindu nationalism and rekindled latent Hindu-Muslim tensions.[16] The issue of building a temple where a mosque stood in the city of Ayodhya attracted national attention, catapulting the BJP into political prominence. Both the rapid decline in Rajiv's popularity and the equally rapid ascendance of the BJP underlined the fact that Indian politics had lost its institutional moorings; nothing coherent had replaced the old Congress Party, and in the resulting vacuum, rapid mood swings could alter the political fortunes of competing elites. That symbolic politics could be used to shift the national electoral mood was also noticeable in the efforts of V. P. Singh – India's prime minister for a brief period following the defeat of Rajiv Gandhi – to mobilize India's middle castes by offering them "reservations" in public institutions, that is, quotas for public jobs and for admission to publically controlled educational institutions, similar to those offered earlier to India's underprivileged scheduled castes.

Except for the communists, it is notable that by the late 1980s none of India's major political parties – the Congress, the BJP, and the Janata – were parties of the left. The Congress had moved away from socialism; the BJP was explicitly a party on the political right; and the Janata was composed of many former Congress leaders who could not agree on a common platform. For a country that had enshrined the rights of the poor in its constitution, this was a remarkable political shift. It was as if everyone in India had pretty well concluded that there was no alternative for India's development but to facilitate economic growth, and that there was no other way to promote growth but to support private business

---

[16] See, for example, Jaffrelot (1996).

groups. This unspoken emerging consensus among members of India's political class provided a powerful base of support for the growth of a state-business alliance.

As a sign of the changing power relations within India, the greatest threat to big business in India during the 1990s and beyond has come, not from the left, but from global competition. A Congress government in 1991 attempted once again to open India's economy to external forces, this time with more success.[17] Much has been made, both within India and abroad, of India's "economic liberalization" in 1991; some observers even divide the history of independent India into pre- and post-1991.[18] While some of the liberalizing changes were real and important, it is easy to exaggerate their importance. There is no doubt – and there is no need to deny – that India's economy started opening up more and more during the post-1991 period. By global standards, however, India remains an economy that is mainly driven by Indian producers producing for the Indian market.[19] I will discuss these economic issues in more detail in due course. What needs to be underlined here is that the liberalizing reforms of 1991 represented elements of both change and continuity: important changes in terms of India's external relations, especially economic relations, but also considerable continuity when it came to protecting the interests of indigenous Indian business groups, which have continued to flourish in the aftermath. The immediate questions for political analysis, then, are what had changed by 1991 that enabled a weak Congress government within India to initiate India's economic opening, and what forces moderated this liberalizing thrust.

India experienced a financial "crisis" in 1991, and this crisis provided the occasion for India's economic opening. But the real factors that were pushing India's decision makers toward external opening were deeper. These included changes both in India's external environment and in the domestic political context, especially the fact that Indian business split politically during the 1980s, with a significant, technologically modern faction willing to experiment with a more open economy.

Foremost among the significant external changes was the decline and disintegration of the Soviet Union. This change was profoundly consequential for India. First, the Soviet Union was an important trading

---

[17] See, for example, Jenkins (1999) and Corbridge and Harriss (2000).
[18] Not surprisingly, many economists consider 1991 to be a critical dividing line. See, for example, Panagariya (2008).
[19] See Nayar (2001).

partner (India–Soviet Union trade was close to $6 billion towards the end of the 1980s) that, in exchange for a variety of goods, provided India with oil, armaments, and defense materials. Much of this exchange did not involve the use of hard currency. With a sharp decline in exports to Russia, the issue of maintaining and upgrading defense forces became intimately related to the availability of hard foreign exchange. Improving export earnings and maximizing other sources of foreign exchange thus became issues of national security. While never publicized as such, these issues created a new sense of urgency for liberalization. Closely related to this, the disintegration of the Soviet Union also meant the loss of a military and political ally, creating pressure to shore up relations with the United States. As most leaders of developing countries understand, improved political relations with the United States, in turn, often involve closer economic relations, especially the opening of one's economy to American goods and capital.

A second important global change that developed over the 1980s was the growing availability of investable resources – in foreign exchange, to boot – in the form of portfolio investment. While a Faustian bargain – mainly because of their volatile nature – they appeared attractive to foreign exchange–starved Indian decision makers. Even to Indian businessmen, portfolio investment appeared less threatening – it is in some ways more akin to selling one's shares in public, over which one has some control – than competitive products produced via direct foreign investment, not to mention acquisitions and mergers.

And finally, it was clear to Indian decision makers the that WTO was going to happen (it actually came into being in 1994), and that India would be a signatory to the WTO agreement. Given the WTO's requirements, it was also clear that import quotas would have to go, and that tariffs would have to come down within some defined period. These external considerations were also important reasons why India had to liberalize in the early 1990s.[20]

While India's "world" thus indeed changed over the 1980s, some very important changes within India also must be taken into account to explain the economic opening of 1991. Most important, the resistance of some of Indian business groups to external opening softened, though within limits.[21] While it is something of an oversimplification, one could say

---

[20] For such an argument, see Sengupta (2004).
[21] The changing political role of Indian business is well analyzed in Kochanek (1996a) and Kochanek (1996b).

that during the 1980s Indian capital was basically split in its political preferences. On one side were the more modern, technologically sophisticated industries that depended on imports for technology and were often export-oriented. They favored a more open, competitive economy. And on the other side were the older business houses that had matured during the import substitution regime. They were considerably more wary of external opening. As will become clear later, the actual political process surrounding economic liberalization was more complex than this characterization might suggest. Nevertheless, with some significant business names and organizations willing to support the opening of the economy, India's pro-liberalization policy makers were emboldened. In sum, then, changing global conditions and splits within the ranks of Indian capital provided the new structural conditions within which the technocratic elite pushed through some significant policy changes in the early 1990s.

Beyond the structural changes, the political process of economic liberalization was also revealing of the underlying power dynamics. As the balance-of-payments situation deteriorated throughout 1990, the issue of India approaching the IMF for a "structural adjustment" type of loan was at the forefront; India accepted such a loan in 1990, with a caretaker government in charge. Then in April 1991, just a couple of months before the "big bang" announcement of new liberal economic policies, India's leading chamber of commerce, the CII, floated a "theme paper" arguing for radical shifts in Indian economic policy toward a more open and competitive economy.[22] When the Congress government, with Manmohan Singh as finance minister, actually announced the policy shift, the main forces supporting such a shift included the narrow political leadership, the technocratic policy elite, a segment of Indian capital, and some external actors, expressing their preferences mainly in the form of the policy conditionality set by the IMF.

In spite of India's being a fairly mobilized democracy, it was then the case that major economic policy changes arrived with only a narrow base of support. If further evidence were needed to support this claim, notice, for example, that critical reforms in industrial policy in 1991 were made as executive decisions. Anticipating nationalist opposition to global opening, the government used legal technicalities – they included the policy changes in a "statement" rather than in a "resolution" – to avoid any discussion or a vote in the parliament. Similarly, the efforts to reduce fiscal deficits over the next few years encountered opposition. Once again,

[22] See Kochanek (1996b), p. 538.

as yet another example, the government reduced some fertilizer subsidies and increased petroleum prices (in September 1992) only after the parliament had gone into recess. Such examples could be readily multiplied. The simple point, however, is that liberalizing reforms were pushed forward by a narrow coalition, and that an element of "stealth," aimed at circumventing nationalist and popular opposition, clearly characterized the politics of economic liberalization.[23]

The "big bang" rhetoric of a dramatic policy shift aside, India's economic policies changed only incrementally during the 1990s, responding not only to objective changes but also to the evolving views of key policy makers and to a variety of political pressures. Early reforms included internal deregulation of industry, attempts to tame the deficit, and slow but steady external opening. The industrial policy reforms included further elimination of licensing requirements on the private sector, relaxation of restrictions on when big firms might be considered illegal monopolies, tax concessions to business, and some efforts to defang India's well-entrenched and activist labor movement. India's private sector rightly interpreted these policy changes as highly favorable to them. The stock market boom that followed was probably not unrelated to what was interpreted as a sharply pro-business policy shift.

In line with the IMF's "structural adjustment" prescriptions, a second important element of early reforms included efforts to cut the budget deficit. Since it was difficult to increase revenues – especially in light of tax concessions to the corporate sector – the burden of these efforts fell on reducing expenditures. After some early success during the first three years or so, these soon ran into numerous problems. For example, cutbacks in subsidies were resisted by such politically consequential groups as farmers and exporters; further cuts in social expenditures were likely to cost electoral support; and the decline in public investment was widely being associated with the continuing industrial recession. Even big capital started arguing for greater public investment in such areas as infrastructure. Concerned about economic growth, then, the Indian government by 1994 chose not to accept further IMF loans. The leaders started arguing that further budget cuts were neither possible nor desirable. The decline in current expenditures came to a halt. The reduction in budget deficits that was actually achieved unfortunately came at the expense of social spending and public investment.[24]

---

[23] See Jenkins (1999) for a focus on the element of "stealth" in policy making.
[24] See Kumar (2000).

The attempt to integrate the Indian economy with the global economy was, of course, the third major component of the reform initiative.
The political process of India's global opening turned out to be quite
contentious, and in the end a variety of pressures, especially business
lobbying, limited the speed and scope of such an opening. For example,
within two or three years of the "big bang" opening, as the balance of
payment crisis eased, a variety of Indian business houses came together –
in a group the press dubbed the "Bombay Club" – to oppose India's
external opening.[25] They argued that rapid liberalization would destroy
India's indigenous industry, especially its capital goods industry; according to them, tariffs should be brought down very slowly, and the inflow
of foreign investment should be limited. Citing Korea as their model,
they asked for more government help and for a more selective integration
with the global economy. The nationalist element in this business protest
found a strong echo in the *swadeshi* (economic nationalist) politics of
India's main opposition party at the time, the BJP. A variety of more
diffuse issues – such as intellectual property rights and the rapid opening
of trade in commodities and services – also fed the nationalist wrath of
India's political class. The BJP mobilized these sentiments effectively in
the mid-1990s, putting the ruling Congress government on the defensive.
The early momentum of reforms thus got bogged down in the usual complexities of India's democratic politics. The results included a steady but
relatively slow-paced integration of the Indian economy with the global
economy, a trend that has largely continued to the present day.

Of the major policy reforms initiated in 1991, then, internal deregulation has proceeded the furthest; global opening has been real but slow
and modest; and the attempts to trim current public expenditure have
not made much headway. Two other areas of reform – the privatization
of public enterprises and labor reforms – were also discussed at the early
stages and have been discussed periodically since. Anticipating serious
political opposition, however, various governments have mostly left these
policy reform areas alone. A pattern thus emerges. Internal deregulation
and the modest global opening were either demanded by Indian business
groups, especially by big business, or were new policies that a significant
faction of Indian business could live with. The unwillingness or inability to privatize public enterprises and/or to tame India's organized labor
underline the fragmented nature of state power in democratic India. The
politics of continuing budget deficits is in part a result of similar democratic pressures, but it also highlights the commitment of Indian policy

[25] Kochanek (1996a), pp. 168–70.

makers to economic growth and their related willingness to use public expenditures to facilitate this outcome. In spite of much pro- and antireform rhetoric about India going neoliberal, therefore, both the political process and the process of policy reform reflect a much more complex pattern of state intervention in the economy: while some liberalization is real, the Indian state remains activist, willing to support and work closely with Indian business, while at the same time, state actors remain hemmed in by a variety of democratic political pressures.

In the new millennium the BJP and the Congress were in danger of becoming indistinguishable, at least as far as their core approach to Indian capitalism was concerned. Of course, the BJP remained a party of Hindu nationalism, and the Congress remained committed to secularism. Their economic approaches, however, were quite similar: both were committed to a partial opening of the Indian economy, but both also championed the interests of indigenous capitalists. The BJP fluctuated between emphasizing its capacity to govern, on the one hand, and its Hindu nationalist credentials, on the other. When in power, BJP leaders generally emphasized their performance; when out of power, they just as often depended more on their affiliated storm troopers – the Rashtriya Sevak Sangh (the RSS) and/or the Bajrang Dal – to mobilize ethnic resentments for political gain.[26] By contrast, under the influence of Sonia Gandhi, Rajiv's Italian-born widow, the Congress Party recommitted itself to a milder version of *garibi hatao*. While fully committed to economic growth and Indian capitalism, Congress leaders now also sought to create more equal opportunity for India's poor by focusing on education and health and to help India's rural poor directly via public works programs. Resources generated via higher rates of economic growth made these programs a real possibility, but the poor quality of local administration made their implementation difficult. Still, the mild political shift to the left, along with some old-fashioned populist move, such as the canceling of loans taken out by farmers from public sector banks, situated the Congress Party favorably to make a modest political comeback in 2009.

The Rising Power of Business

The focus of the discussion so far has been on how state elites in India have shifted India's political economy away from its socialist leanings

---

[26] See Basu (2001).

and toward a more pro-business orientation. While a variety of contex-
tual variables have been discussed, the focus of the analysis has been
top-down, that is, on the changing role of the state in society. One important societal change that now needs to be analyzed in some detail is the
growing power of business groups within India. While state elites, for
their own reasons, created a pro-business opening in India in the early
1980s, business groups took advantage of this and have continued to
grow in significance. While business groups in India are not quite "hegemonic" in the Marxist sense of that word, India is by now very much a
capitalist political economy in which Indian capital exercises enormous
indirect and direct power.

The power that business groups exercise in a political economy operates in different spheres and at various levels. At the most indirect level,
the more important the role of private business groups in the economy,
the more the decision makers need to take account of business preferences
in their decisions. This is because the performance of the economy is an
important determinant of the legitimacy of any set of rulers. At a more
direct level, it matters whether business groups are well organized or not,
and whether they speak in one or multiple voices. The deliberate impact
of business groups on politics, in turn, can vary anywhere from quite
diffuse and decentralized – say, in molding a society's political values – to
much more concentrated and strategic – say, in seeking to influence policy choices. The disproportionate control over economic resources also
enables businessmen to "buy" politicians and to influence the positions
of political parties and the conduct of elections, not to mention the possibility of holding political office themselves. In India over the last couple
of decades, the power of business has grown in most of these spheres.

The Indian economy is now clearly dominated by private capital, especially by businesses located in cities, both big and small. Some simple data
helps demonstrate this and related points. For the purposes of analyzing
the political impact of business, it first makes sense to decompose India's
gross domestic product (GDP) into segments that originate in the public
sector, the agricultural sector, and the nonagricultural private sector. This
is because the public sector can be readily influenced by the ruling elite;
the agricultural sector – though mostly in private hands – tends to generate diffuse political preferences; and the nonagricultural private sector,
especially big business, tends to be both concentrated and organized and
thus well positioned to be politically quite influential. The evolving shares
of these three sectors within India's GDP are charted in Figure 1.1. The
pre-1980 story the chart tells is a familiar one: the role of the public sector

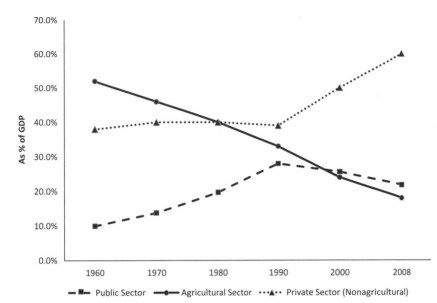

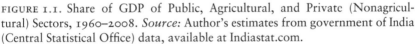

FIGURE I.I. Share of GDP of Public, Agricultural, and Private (Nonagricultural) Sectors, 1960–2008. *Source:* Author's estimates from government of India (Central Statistical Office) data, available at Indiastat.com.

in the economy grew; the share of agriculture declined, mainly because of its relatively slow growth; and urban private capital maintained its relative share. Since about 1980, and especially since 1990, the change has been quite dramatic: while the shares of both the agricultural and the publicly controlled economy in the overall economy have continued to decline, that of nonagricultural private capital has risen sharply. While not evident in the chart, the role of organized private capital in the gross domestic product has also risen sharply, from some 12 percent in 1980 to nearly 20 percent in 2004–5.[27] Stated somewhat differently, nearly 60 percent of production in India now originates in the activities of city dwellers, a social segment that the Europeans of an earlier era characterized as the bourgeoisie; the Indian political economy has become very much a bourgeois political economy.

If Figure I.I tells a story about economic output, Figure I.2 gives us a sense of who invests in the economy and thus tells a slightly different political story. Rates of capital formation in India have risen steadily, especially in recent years, helping explain India's rapid economic growth.

[27] See Majumdar (2008), Table 2, p. 20.

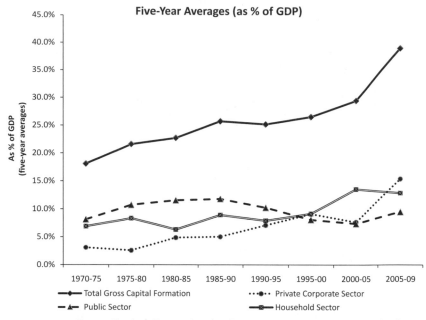

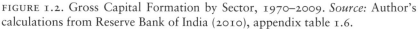

FIGURE 1.2. Gross Capital Formation by Sector, 1970–2009. *Source:* Author's calculations from Reserve Bank of India (2010), appendix table 1.6.

For a political analysis, it is important to focus on the changing composition of who is saving and investing. Following the pro-business political shift initiated by Indira and Rajiv Gandhi during the 1980s, the rates of capital formation in the private corporate sector have risen steadily. The private corporate sector surpassed the public sector as an agent of investment and growth sometime during the 1990s. The contribution of the private corporate sector to overall capital formation has increased sharply in recent years. This reflects the favorable conditions for the private corporate sector created by the Indian state. The growing role of the private sector, in turn, enhances the power of the corporate sector because any government in India desiring economic growth must establish favorable conditions for the corporate sector to create profits, reinvest, and boost production.

More telling evidence of the growing role of private capital in India is provided in Figure 1.3. The data in this figure charts the share of private capital (what in India's official statistical parlance is called "paid-up capital of nongovernmental companies") in the total capital of all companies. It is clear that up until 1980, the share of public sector capital grew and that of private capital declined. During the 1980s, private and

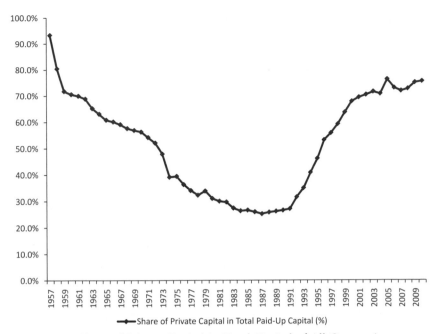

FIGURE 1.3. Share of Private Capital in Total Capital of All Companies, 1957–2010. *Source:* I borrowed the idea of presenting the data in this manner from Pedersen (2000). I updated Pedersen's data from government of India, Ministry of Corporate Affairs (Companies at Work in India, 1957 to 2007), available at Indiastat.com.

public capital maintained their shares, suggesting that economic growth during this period was fueled by both private and public capital. Since 1990, what is noteworthy is the steadily growing share of private capital. About three-quarters of all the capital invested in India's companies is now private capital.

Many observers celebrate the "uncaging" of India's entrepreneurial talent. There is no denying that many new small and medium-sized industries, often technologically sophisticated and organized as modern companies, have emerged over the last three decades, especially in the service sector. It is nevertheless the case that industrial leaders in India at present are often the same groups that were leaders in the past. While groups like Reliance are relative newcomers, Tatas, Birlas, Bajaj, Larsen and Toubro and a host of other leaders are of distant origin. This continuity underlines the point that India's economic giants not only remain well entrenched – with all their well-established political connections – but have also grown handsomely in the era of "liberalization."[28] There is also very little evidence to suggest that the level of concentration among India's private business groups has declined;[29] if anything, evidence on capital stock and sales suggests that concentration has increased. Moreover, the growth of the organized private sector has not been accompanied by a proportional gain in employment, and the share of wages in the total wealth generated in the organized private sector has declined. The concentration of big business, in turn, readily translates into disproportionate political power via a variety of mechanisms to be discussed later.

The role of foreign investment in India has also increased since 1991, though not dramatically. Direct foreign investment in India has averaged some $3 billion per annum over the last two decades; it was as high as some $35 billion in 2009, though it declined quite sharply – by as much as a third, to some $24 billion – in 2010, possibly because of a variety of corruption scandals. While these amounts are far from insignificant in influencing the structure and performance of the Indian economy, they are small when compared to foreign investment inflows into China during the same period (nearly $100 billion in 2010).[30] Portfolio investment has also grown rapidly in India, making additional funds available for investment via the stock market, but also adding volatility.

It should be clear from this discussion that the Indian economy is now dominated by the activities of private capital, both big and small, both domestic and foreign. Within this changing economy, indigenous big business houses continue to be the most significant. India's political leaders created the conditions that allowed this development to unfold but, over the last two decades, the political leaders in turn have had to learn how to operate in this dramatically altered economic context. To repeat, the most important lesson for India's politicians has been that, if they want to promote economic growth, they cannot afford to go against the interests of private capital. The private sector is now the main motor of capital accumulation. The state now needs to ensure the conditions for the smooth functioning of the private sector. This still leaves numerous important economic choices open – for example, national versus foreign capital, big versus medium-sized and small business, and/or how inclusive economic growth should or could be. Nevertheless, the changing

---

[28] Ibid.

[29] See Alfaro and Chari (2009).

[30] As a qualification, it should be added that the figures for China can be misleading insofar as a significant component of "foreign investment" in China originates from the Chinese diaspora based in Hong Kong, Macao, and Taiwan.

economic context has created broad limits within which political leaders, parties, and bureaucrats committed to economic growth need to operate: socialism is out; pro-business policies are to be preferred; and modest social democracy, with an emphasis on modest, is probably the outer limit at the left edge of the political spectrum.

So far I have documented the growing role of the private sector in the Indian economy and asserted that this changing class context molds Indian politics. This assertion now needs to be both explained and qualified. As already noted, business classes influence politics in India via both indirect and direct mechanisms; these first need to be clarified. The indirect impact on politics of a changing economic context emerges as political leaders learn the new limits of their choices. This learning, in turn, generally occurs over time, through a process of trial and error. Some examples will help clarify the underlying mechanisms. Indira Gandhi turned to socialism to ensure her political position but learned that such a stance hurt economic growth, especially as the private sector emerged as the main source of economic growth, leading to modified political preferences. Rajiv Gandhi sought to open India's economy too fast, and India's business groups set vocal limits on that possibility. When Manmohan Singh finally opened India's economy in 1991, he received kudos the world over, especially in the pro-business press, which dubbed him the global "finance minister of the year." All of these political economy "moments" generated negative and positive incentives that constituted future lessons for politicians.

A most dramatic moment of learning of this kind followed the national elections of 2004. As soon as it became clear that the Congress Party would form only a minority government, India's stock market crashed, fearing that Congress would need the support of the communists in order to govern. Sonia Gandhi immediately announced that key economic decisions would remain under the control of such pro-business leaders as Manmohan Singh, P. Chidambaram, and Montek Singh Ahluwalia. Capital markets calmed down. This was a very Latin American moment for India, in the sense that capital flight is an ever-present fear in countries like Brazil that, in turn, sets policy constraints in the dependent economies of Latin America. For India, this was a new development, underlining for all and sundry that capital in India is also quite capable of voting with its feet, and that these votes matter more than popular verdicts.

As to qualifications, the claim that business groups can set direct limits on Indian politics, merely by their dominant role in the economy, ought to be understood more as an emerging tendency than as a hard-and- fast rule. There will always be leaders who do not accept these constraints. For example, some leaders might hold that high rates of economic growth ought not to be the only priority. Their ideology and support networks may lead them instead to a position that a somewhat lower rate of economic growth might be preferable if it enables modest redistribution of the fruits of growth. At times, India's communist parties have seemed to have some such option in mind, though they too in recent years have courted capital in order to facilitate growth. Moreover, if the fruits of growth are not shared, dissatisfied citizens may create a political reality that encourages leaders willing to work against emerging "market" constraints; the fact that populist budgetary expenditures tend to increase prior to elections is an example of such a counterpressure. And finally, below the national level, class constraints on political behavior in India operate quite unevenly; these constraints are most significant in regions with strong private sector–led growth but are less important in the less dynamic regions, where politicians readily rule via personal and populist appeals.

Beyond indirect power, business groups in India also seek to influence politics via numerous more direct and deliberate actions. It helps to categorize these direct actions as either more or less coordinated. For example, numerous business houses and businessmen in India seek to mold political values, alter the preferences of political parties, and curry favor with politicians. While these actions may often be uncoordinated, the fact is that they move in a similar pro-business direction, and given the fact that these efforts are often backed by considerable economic resources, their cumulative impact tends to be both systematic and significant. By contrast, business houses are also quite well organized into a number of important chambers of commerce. These chambers seek to mold Indian politics in a pro-business direction via a much more coordinated set of actions.

Over the last two or three decades business groups have felt increasingly confident of their position in India. With this self-confidence, they have started using their economic resources to mold India's political values. Before elaborating on this point, however, an important caveat is in order: this discussion is tentative, because: (a) it is difficult to ascertain changing values; (b) it is even more difficult to delineate how and why values are changing; and (c) all this is especially problematic when the trends under discussion are of fairly recent origin and have not been well researched. Nevertheless, a few comments are in order, especially because of the importance of the subject.

One important instrument that business groups have used to influence political values in India is the media. As is well known, the Indian media are vibrant.[31] Over the years corporate control of the Indian media has grown, especially in television. Most newspapers in India have always been controlled privately, but there is evidence to suggest that simultaneous ownership of print and television has also grown over time. While some political parties own newspapers, and government control of radio and a few television channels continues, given that most parties and the national government have in recent years moved in a pro-business direction, they do not really provide a ready check on the growing business influence over the media.

If this much is clear, it is more difficult to establish the impact of such growing business control of the media on political values. First, access to media in India is distributed highly unequally; for example, nearly 60 percent of Indian families do not own a television, and, given high rates of illiteracy, access to newspapers is also quite skewed. And second, apart from the media, political values in any setting are molded by a variety of forces: family and religious values, the activities of political parties, socialization in schools, and life experience.

What we do know is that the attitudes of Indians as a whole have in recent years not moved in a pro-business direction. If any clear trend is evident in changing attitudes, it is mostly in the opposite direction. For example, the World Values Survey provides a reliable source of information on changing national values.[32] Between 1989 and 2007, they have periodically sampled the views of Indians toward business. On the question of whether private or government ownership of industry is to be preferred, support for private ownership doubled between 1989 and 2007 (from 11.2 to 23.2 percent) but tripled for government ownership (from 11.4 to 33.1 percent). The answers to another question on a government versus a private role in selecting the management of industry moved in the same direction. How does one interpret such survey results? If the results are to be trusted, it ought to be clear to even a casual observer that these views are at odds with the growing pro-business views entertained by India's elites. One possible interpretation of this public opinion data, then, is that the skewed economic benefits of India's model of development have a counterpart in public opinion: a significant proportion of the

---

[31] Some of the factual information about Indian media is taken from Anand et al. (2006)
[32] I am indebted to my Princeton colleague Amaney Jamal for directing me to the data from the World Values Survey.

population is still not sympathetic to Indian business. These are probably the groups that have not always benefited from pro-business policies, do not have access to the media, and as a result of both life experience and relative lack of exposure to the media, do not partake in the growing pro-business views entertained by elite Indians.

This interpretation is actually supported by the data when one disaggregates the responses to the World Values Survey questions just cited by class and education. For example, in response to the question of whether public or private ownership of industry/business is to be preferred, support for private ownership among India's upper classes jumped from some 20 percent in the mid-1900s to 31 percent by 2007. By contrast, support for public ownership among India's lower classes over the same time period jumped from some 24 percent to 40 percent. When respondents are categorized by level of education, a similar pattern is evident: support for private ownership among the well educated jumped from some 13 to 26 percent, and for public ownership among the less educated from 13 to 38 percent. While all such survey data ought to be interpreted with care and caution, it is a better guide to changing attitudes than the mere impressions of observers. What the data suggest is that support for business among India's well-educated, upper-income groups has increased, but not so among the poor and the illiterate.

What role the corporate-controlled media have played in these evolving attitudes is difficult to establish. What we do know are the following facts: corporate control of the media has increased; the Indian media reach better-educated, better-off Indians more readily than poor, illiterate Indians, especially those who live in the villages; and support for business groups has increased among the literate and the better-off. The values propagated in the media often tend to be pro-business. While this is obviously true of the business press – for example, such magazines as *Business Today*, and *Business and Economy*, *Business Digest* (published by one of India's leading chambers of commerce), the Indian edition of *Forbes*, and newspapers like the *Economic Times* – it is also true of such mainstream magazines of middle-class India as *India Today*. Take, for example, that magazine's recent special issue published to commemorate thirty-four years of publication (December 28, 2009). One important story ("A Question of Conscience," pp. 24–7) in this issue reviews the social sector policies of the new Congress government, stressing the wastefulness of such government programs because of corruption and poor management. When discussing India's communist party rule in West Bengal in the same issue, the magazine has no hesitation in mixing it's anticommunist editorial views with apparent news stories (for example, see p. 106 and pp. 35–8). By contrast, the magazine puts a lot more stock in such poverty-alleviating schemes as those run by Indian Corporations in partnership with NGOs to provide vocational, "market-driven skills" (pp. 40–3). While examples are only that, examples, readers of this and other similar media in India will readily recognize that they are anything but anomalous.

A tentative proposition may then be advanced: growing support for private business among India's upper- and middle-class groups results in part from the fact that they have benefited the most during the recent pro-business era, and in part because the modern media help them interpret their upward mobility in terms of a pro-business mind-set. Elements of the latter probably include media propagation of negative attitudes toward government intervention, labor unions and left-leaning politicians and intellectuals on the one hand, and, on the other hand, a more positive image of the private sector, markets, technocracy, businessmen as self-made heroes, and of pragmatic, "nonideological" politicians and thinkers.

The impact of business on political values in India is likely to grow in the future, both via growing control of the media and possibly as a result of such new trends as the growth of private educational institutions. That not everyone will embrace the efforts of business groups to create hegemony and that some, or maybe even many, may challenge these deliberate efforts are possibilities that cannot be discounted. In any case, all that lies in the future. Another significant political arena in which the influence of business groups and of money is already well established is that of electoral politics. Among the well-known aspects of Indian politics are the facts that elections in India are costly affairs, that political parties depend on moneyed groups to finance elections, and that moneyed groups, in turn, expect politicians to return favors. However, hard evidence on the murky give-and-take that links politicians, political parties, and business groups is difficult to come by, especially because most such transactions involve black money and violation of one existing law or another. A few comments based on what we do know will provide a sense of the growing role of what in India is described as "money power" in politics.[33]

The rich in all democracies seek disproportionate political influence. What makes the Indian case somewhat unique – and "somewhat" needs to be underlined, because these practices are widespread in other parts of

---

[33] I am drawing here on Sridharan (2006). Also see Kapur and Vaishnav (2011).

the world as well – is how much of the Indian money-politics exchange takes place "under the table," almost normalizing corruption. This results in part from archaic laws governing financial contributions to political parties in India, but it also reflects habits of behavior that continue even as the laws are changing. There are other compulsions too, on both those who give money and those who receive it, to keep these transactions as opaque as possible. For example, businessmen worry about the views of their shareholders and do not want to be seen as too close to any single party; politicians, in turn, want to keep up the appearance of not being in anyone's debt. Most important, though, is a deeper issue: democracy is supposed to be a system in which all citizens are legally and politically equal, irrespective of their socioeconomic status. When the rich seek disproportionate political influence in a democracy, the practice reeks of violating the core norms of the system, and so is best kept "under the table."

While the Congress Party in India began as a party funded mainly by small contributions, all that is far back in the past. Well before independence, Mahatma Gandhi had forged connections with a variety of moneyed interests who contributed to the Congress, and the Congress, in turn, argued their case – for example, demanding tariff protections – to the British. Following independence, the Congress was nearly hegemonic in India during the Nehru years. In spite of Nehru's commitment to a state-regulated economy, private business groups supported the Congress, both in order to ensure that Nehru's socialism remained limited and, more important, in order to establish individual political connections that helped loosen the grip of a variety of state regulations on the private sector. As Indira Gandhi centralized power, she also centralized the task of mobilizing finances for the Congress Party at the top. By now the political context had also changed: competing political parties were trying to raise funds. In order to bolster her socialist commitments, Indira Gandhi created new laws to limit contributions to parties, and her socialist commitment threatened to alienate business groups from the Congress. The corrupt practices linking money and politics intensified in this changed context.

Growing political competition accentuated the need of politicians for money to finance elections. Growing state regulation of the economy, in turn, created a need on the part of businessmen to lubricate the wheels of the state. These mutual needs, then, provided the framework within which the role of money in politics grew, and much of this took the form of corruption. As Indira Gandhi alienated some businessmen, she also established personal links with others. These connections brought India Gandhi money for her political activities and, in turn, helped certain businessmen enormously via governmental favors. A new type of corrupt practice also emerged during this period: foreign firms entered the fray. As India sought arms and other goods from foreign firms, agents of some firms contributed huge sums to political coffers in order to secure contracts. At times the sums involved were so substantial that they dwarfed the contributions of Indian businessmen.

Rajiv Gandhi lost elections during the late 1980s under the shadow of one such corruption scandal, namely, the "Bofors scandal," so named after the Swedish arms manufacturer Bofors. Recall that by this time the Indian political economy had already turned quite pro-business, with many state regulations on private activities diluted. Had these regulations been the main source of corrupt links between businessmen and politicians, their dilution should have led to a decline in such practices. Unfortunately, there is no readily available evidence to suggest such a trend. On the contrary, India from the late 1980s onward entered an era of governmental instability, leading to frequent elections; as election expenses multiplied, so did financial contributions from the private sector to political parties. From the standpoint of business interests, their incomes had grown throughout the 1980s; they now had more to part with. Moreover, the nature of business contributions was beginning to change. Instead of focusing mainly on establishing personal contacts within the state apparatus – at both the national and regional levels – businessmen were increasingly contributing to a variety of political parties, hoping to solidify the emerging pro-business trend across the political class.

During the 1990s, India's leading chamber of commerce, the CII, openly sought to systematize the money-politics link in Indian politics. A commission created by the chamber recommended both limits on contributions and a tax-deductible status for all such contributions.[34] The government accepted some of these recommendations. While the results have been meager – more on this later – the CII-government cooperation on this issue underlined the fact that state-capital relations in India were coming of age. The proposition that capital will exercise disproportionate political power via its financial contributions – a proposition that is nearly a truism in most advanced democracies – was now being realized in India as well.

---

[34] Confederation of Indian Industries, Task Force on Financing of Democracy and Elections, 1993, cited in Sridharan (2006).

There is no evidence to suggest that the role of money in Indian politics has either declined or become more transparent. While concrete evidence is skimpy, the trends are moving mostly in the opposite direction. Elections have become more and more expensive. Accounts in the popular press suggest that the amout of money needed to contest seats at both the state and national levels has grown steadily. This not only puts pressure on parties to collect more and more funds, but also privileges those who are independently wealthy in the electoral process. From the point of view of businessmen, one may wonder why they continue to fund political parties in the new "liberal" era. The answer is fairly simple. Even in truly liberal economies – such as the United States – businessmen continually finance politicians and parties because, liberal principles aside, there is almost no end to the number of favors modern liberal states continue to offer businessmen. All this is even more true in India, where the state remains a powerful economic actor, very much in a position to help or hurt the business prospects of private firms.

Both the Congress Party and the BJP depend heavily on Indian capital for financial support. The Congress Party depends mainly on big capital, especially from the more modern, emerging global firms that favor gradual opening of the Indian economy. The BJP, by contrast, still depends heavily on traders and small businessmen, the party's traditional base. Since acquiring national stature during the 1990s, the more economically nationalist BJP has also attracted the support of big capital, especially from older business houses that have felt threatened by India's global opening. A variety of regional parties, in turn, collect money, not so much on the basis of broad principles or policy preferences, but by offering more direct favors to businessmen. Government control over land is especially significant in creating corrupt links between politicians and businessmen. The only major political party that remains an exception to this trend is India's main communist party, the CPM. From all the evidence available, it appears that the CPM still continues to depend on small contributions to finance its activities, possibly giving it some latitude against corporate power.[35]

The growing importance of money in elections privileges the wealthy in the political system. Those with independent wealth are better situated to contest elections. As important, once in power, officeholders seek to amass more personal wealth, not only for consumption or for passing on to their progeny, but also to contest yet another round of elections.

---

[35] The information in this paragraph is drawn from Sridharan (2006).

Some evidence of the growing direct participation in elections of the wealthy is provided by a nonprofit organization in India, National Election Watch. According to their data, 300 millionaires (*crorepatis*) became members of the Indian parliament following the national elections in 2009. In a house of some 550 parliamentarians, this is a distinct majority. The number of millionaire parliamentarians had nearly doubled since the fourteenth Lok Sabha, which was elected in 2004, when their number stood at 154. Nearly half (137) of the elected millionaire parliamentarians in 2009 belonged to the Congress Party, the party of "inclusive growth," and 58 to the BJP; even the Bahujan Samaj Party (BSP), the party of the India's underprivileged untouchables, sent thirteen millionaires to the Lok Sabha.[36] While the policy preferences of elected officials are hard to extrapolate from their social backgrounds, what seems clear is that moneyed interests are not only buying influence from the outside, but are now directly embedded in the heart of India's political system.

In addition to molding political values and the electoral process, business interests also seek to influence government policies directly, especially economic policies. I will return later to the role of organized chambers of commerce in this process; that influence is aimed mainly at the framing of broad policy commitments. As often, or maybe more often, businessmen are interested in policies that may directly influence their respective industries, or even individual firms. In the recent past, business lobbying for such particularistic policies took the form of "briefcase politics," so called because of the widespread belief that business representatives passed briefcases full of cash to politicians and/or bureaucrats who were in a position to modify the policies in question.[37] The policies may concern one or more of a variety of issues such as tax concessions, limiting imports, permission to expand production, limiting competition, land use, infrastructure support at public expense, or simply jumping through various regulatory hoops more easily.

In more recent years, as the "license-permit" regime has been diluted, the character of particularistic business lobbying has also changed. While this is a relatively new trend and remains underresearched, business lobbying in India is becoming more "professional"; it is beginning to adopt the "American style" of lobbying.[38] In addition to major business houses

---

[36] This information is taken from the Times News Network story, "300 Crorepati MPs in new Lok Sabha," posted on the home page of the National Election Watch.

[37] See, for example, Kochanek (1987).

[38] See, for example, "India's New Lobbyists Use American Methods," *International Herald Tribune*, May 18, 2006.

maintaining lobbyists in Delhi and in state capitals, lobbying firms are
also emerging. These new-style lobbyists make their clients' case to government representatives via well-researched power-point presentations
and by placing newspaper stories in the business-friendly press, while still
ensuring that at least baskets of fruits and nuts – if not briefcases – are
delivered to the homes of policy makers. With the government embracing a pro-business attitude, such lobbyists are often knocking on open
doors. And yet there is no evidence to suggest that corrupt practices are
declining. Foreign firms are now using lobbyists in a big way, aimed at
both securing government favors and creating a favorable image. India's
indigenous industrialists, in turn – especially anyone who has anything to
do with land use (which is nearly everyone) – remain deeply enmeshed in
efforts to maintain favorable business-government ties.

A recent example of new forms of corruption during the liberal era
is the well-publicized G2 scandal of late 2010, so named by the media
because it involved second generation (2G) frequency-spectrum licenses
that the government sells to private investors in the telecommunication
industry. The heart of the scandal was that officials in the national government sold the licenses to favored businessmen at basement rates, costing
the national exchequer an estimated $40 billion, a sum nearly six times
what the Indian government spends on education. The scandal came to
light as relevant information involving leading politicians, journalists,
lobbyists, and businessmen was taped and leaked.[39] Leaving the seamy
and sordid details aside, the scandal helps underline some important analytical issues already discussed. The brave new era of liberal economics
does not appear any freer of corruption than the bad old era of state
intervention; on the contrary, the scale of the G2 scandal dwarfs much of
the "briefcase politics" of the socialist years, which now appear downright quaint. The freeing of a variety of industries for competition in the
private sector has been accompanied by the creation of new rules and
regulations. These regulatory instruments are now the object of manipulation by India's private sector and its agents, a variety of lobbyists who
are busy establishing cozy links with India's willing politicians, including
leaders at the highest levels.[40]

---

[39] The scandal was widely covered in the Indian media. For useful analysis of relevant issues,
see articles by Surajit Mazumdar and Ajay Singh in the news magazine *Governance Now*,
January 1–15, 2011.

[40] As the book goes to publication, the Anna Hazare movement against corruption is
spreading in India. While it is too late for me to analyze the movement, its emergence
and spread is consistent with the emphasis here on growing corruption in the liberal era.

So far in my discussion of the rising power of business, I have analyzed two sets of issues: first, the growing indirect power of business that results from the growing significance of the private sector in the economy; and second, a variety of decentralized, direct strategies used by business houses to further their interests by influencing political values, the electoral process, and government decisions and policy choices. What finally need to be discussed are the more organized activities of business groups to pursue their interests via a number of chambers of commerce.

India has three main national-level chambers of commerce and numerous more at the regional and local levels. My focus for now is on the national chambers: CII and FICCI, both mentioned earlier, and the Associated Chambers of Commerce (ASSOCHAM).[41] In the recent past – say, prior to the 1980s – FICCI represented India's more traditional big business houses, many of which had started out as the family-owned businesses of India's trading castes, and most of which had matured during the era of state-controlled economy. While business groups represented within the ASSOCHAM were also beneficiaries of the state-controlled economy, most of them had roots in firms established by the British or by collaboration between British and Indian capital. Prior to 1980, FICCI and ASSOCHAM were often distinguished culturally, with the former representing *dhoti wallahs* (dhoti being the traditional loin cloth worn by Indian men) and *tie wallahs*. During this period, the CII existed as a smaller, more specialized chamber, mainly for engineering industries.

During the 1980s, India's two main national chambers of commerce – FICCI and ASSOCHAM – were reorganized. They increasingly became mirror images of each other (with differing regional bases), and they also slowly lost ground to the newly constituted CII in terms of political influence. The CII increasingly came to represent India's more modern industries – especially engineering firms, often located in the south of India – that were more interested in exports. The CII was also run professionally and developed such close ties with the Indian bureaucracy that it came to be dubbed a "junior partner" of the government – so much so that the government's budgets on occasion during the 1990s came to be called "Tarun Das" budgets, a reference to Tarun Das, the director of CII. Over the next decade, these patterns nearly became institutionalized;

---

[41] I am drawing here on Kochanek (1996a) and Kochanek (1996b). Also see Damodaran (2008). In addition to these three chambers, the software association NASSCOM is also growing in influence; for reasons of space, I do not discuss this chamber in the following account.

for example, in the new millennium, India's economic policy makers were openly discussing the need for "public-private partnership" in industry and inviting the private sector, especially the CII, to be part of decision making.

CII's membership has grown fairly rapidly, from some 2,800 firms in 1993 to 8,238 in 2009.[42] A majority of the members are medium-sized or large firms located in such areas as Tamil Nadu, Maharashtra, and New Delhi. With offices spread throughout the country, the CII's core purposes include "influencing government policy" via maintaining close contacts with government officials, undertaking and disseminating research, and "interacting closely with Members of Parliament" so as to keep "economic legislation" flowing. The CII also increasingly collaborates with public officials in the area of defense so to promote the interests of private defense industries. While the term "military-industrial complex" remains a disparaging one even in the United States, the CII does not shy away from posting on its web page glossy pictures of India's top economic and defense officials, including commanders in uniforms, interacting with industry officials.

The major national-level chambers of commerce in India represent somewhat differing factions of Indian capital and thus do not always express unified policy preferences. The CII is the most modern and the most influential, often favoring global integration, at least in rhetoric. The FICCI has often favored a "go slow" policy on external opening but had agreed with CII and ASSOCHAM on a variety of other issues such as labor policy, reducing regulation, and maintaining public support for the private sector. Even the differences between CII and FICCI on the issue of the global opening of the Indian economy can be exaggerated; for example, when the "Bombay Club" during the 1990s argued for limiting foreign investment in India, its members included leading firms that belonged to both FICCI and CII. Overall, then, there now exists a consensus of sorts in India for moderate global opening, an opening that might maximize the interests of indigenous Indian capital. India's national chambers of commerce have done much to push this policy consensus.

To sum up the discussion of the pro-business tilt in India, this trend began in the late 1970s, slowly but surely supplanting the socialist commitment of India's leaders. By now, the trend has matured into a defining feature of the Indian political economy. It was initiated by the Indian

---

[42] The information in this paragraph is based on materials readily available on the CII's web pages.

state elites as they came to realize not only their inability to implement pro-poor policies, but also their dependence on property-owning groups for economic growth. A commitment to growth via the private sector, in turn, has strengthened the position of business groups in Indian politics. The influence that business groups exercise operates via both indirect and direct mechanisms. A robust private sector now sets the parameters within which policy decisions need to be taken. In addition, individual actions by business groups in such areas as media control, financing of elections and parties, and lobbying for specific government favors cumulatively add a systematic pro-business bias to contemporary Indian politics.

III. MANAGING A NARROW RULING ALLIANCE

The state and business ruling alliance in India is deeply consequential for India's broader political economy. I will return to the growth and distributional impact of this narrowing apex in the next chapter. The focus in this section is more on political issues: given a narrow ruling alliance, how do the political elite manage the excluded groups in a poor, mobilized democracy? The suggestion I present here is that quite a few emerging political trends in India during the post-1980 period can be interpreted as efforts to deal with the excluded masses in an elitist political economy.

In the electoral arena in India, the search is on to discover legitimacy formulas that will ensure electoral victories. Such mass-incorporating ideologies of the past as anticolonial nationalism, socialism, and populism have either lost their potency or been discarded by most political parties as party leaders prioritize economic growth and seek accommodation with Indian capital. Instead, the emergence of demagogues as leaders, the focus on caste politics, the rise of Hindu nationalism, the efforts to capitalize on the legitimacy of political dynasties, and some continuing populism can all be interpreted as efforts to appeal to the poor masses without threatening the emerging class hierarchy. I will also argue that a number of important institutional trends – a growing convergence on economic issues across political parties; the location of key economic decisions in a technocratic apex; and the "decentralization" of much else – also reflect efforts to insulate governance from mass pressures. Of course, all such efforts do not fully succeed; some of the excluded masses are devising their own strategies to cope with exclusion. The most visible of these is the growing significance of violent politics among marginalized groups.

The Electoral Arena

In spite of the fact that India's ruling alliance has become quite narrow, rulers in India must periodically win elections, elections that are mostly fair and competitive. When both power and wealth are controlled by a few, and when any fundamental redistribution of these valued goods is not on the agenda, winning periodic and fair elections poses a challenge: what can politicians offer the poor and the near-poor in return for their electoral support? This is the challenge of creating successful illusions of inclusion in the electoral arena while practicing exclusion in the real political economy. How are Indian politicians dealing with this challenge?

During the period following independence, Congress was the only game in town; electoral majorities were facilitated by some combination of anticolonial nationalism, the appeal of founding leaders like Nehru, patronage chains that channeled growing public resources to the locally powerful, and structures of patron-client domination that cemented the relations of local elites with the poor and the dispossessed in the countryside. With the decline of anticolonial nationalism and the dilution of patron-client ties, Indira Gandhi recreated the old Congress into a new Congress, with appeals to *garibi hatao*. All this has already been discussed. I have also noted that by the time Indira Gandhi returned to power in 1980, most of these older legitimacy formulas for winning elections had been exhausted. Thus began the competition for new formulas during the post-1980 period, several of which deserve attention.

The Congress Party has for the most part continued to depend on the Nehru-Gandhi family as its key source of legitimacy and popularity. This phenomenon has to be understood in terms of what the German sociologist Max Weber described as traditional legitimacy, that is, a type of legitimacy whereby citizens give the right to rule to rulers simply because they are the ones who have always ruled. Royal dynasties used to benefit from this type of habitual acquiescence, as did other famous political families in more modern settings as the Kennedys in the United States. As India's first political family, Indira Gandhi; her son Rajiv Gandhi; then his widow, Sonia Gandhi; and now her son Rahul Gandhi all seem to benefit from being descendants of Nehru, well situated to claim the right to rule simply on the basis of lineage. Of course, this is not enough; modern parties also need to offer concrete programs for governance.

In addition to relying on family charisma, the Congress Party has over the years either benefited from political circumstances or created policy programs that continue to be modified.[43] For example, Indira Gandhi in 1980 benefited greatly from the incapacity to govern of the Janta Party; she then offered herself and the Congress Party as the only viable source of governmental stability. Rajiv Gandhi, in turn, benefited handsomely from the sympathy generated by his mother's assassination. When he lost power, it was due in part to corruption scandals but also because his technocratic leadership had created a sense of indifference towards the common man. With Narasimha Rao as the leader of Congress Party in the early 1990s, there was a momentary sense that the Congress Party might well manage without a Gandhi at the helm. That, however, was short lived. It took Sonia Gandhi to help revive Congress's sagging electoral fortunes against a resurgent BJP.[44] As "economic liberalization" did not sell well in the electoral arena, Congress over the last decade has again embraced a platform of "inclusive growth." The inherited legitimacy of the Gandhi family, agents of liberalization and economic growth, and modest efforts to be inclusive are then the main elements of the legitimacy formula that Congress hopes will help it maintain the status of India's premiere political party.

As a national party, Congress during the 1950s and the 1960s attracted support from all social strata, but especially from the upper castes and classes, on the one hand, and from lower classes and castes who depended on these elites, on the other. With a commitment to "inclusive growth," the Congress is again trying to reestablish this fragile electoral coalition of the top and the bottom. A variety of middle groups were never all that well incorporated into the Congress Party. Urban traders and small businessmen were attracted to the old Jana Sangh, which later evolved into the BJP. The middle groups in the countryside, in turn, mostly family farmers from intermediate castes, slowly but surely threw their political lot in with a variety of opposition parties that championed the interests of "backward castes." The focus of most such parties was regional rather than national, and the pace of their development across Indian states has been uneven – relatively early in southern states such as Tamil Nadu, for example, and more recent in such Hindi-heartland states as Bihar and Uttar Pradesh.

---

[43] A useful source of information on the changing character of the Congress Party is Guha (2007).

[44] For a discussion of the Congress Party under Rao and Sonia Gandhi, see Manor (2011).

The legitimacy formulas generated by these parties of the middle castes have focused mainly on ascriptive and symbolic politics. Some of these parties have married their middle-caste politics with themes of regional nationalism; others have not. What they all have in common is an anti-Brahmanical commitment that is combined with a positive commitment to social justice for the middle castes. Instead of pursuing social justice via any coherent development plan, however, these parties have argued for "reservations" for "backward castes" in public institutions. Since such a strategy can benefit only a handful of well-placed members of middle castes, middle-caste parties have often had trouble consolidating support. With regional foci, these parties also have trouble forging a national coalition. The recurring failure of a "national front" or a "third front" to emerge in Indian politics is a manifestation of this failure.[45] Nevertheless, these parties keep themes of regional nationalism and of caste politics alive in India's electoral arena; the latter has now even seeped down to the lowest castes, giving rise to such parties as the Bahujan Samaj Party.[46] Moreover, these parties continue to attract significant political support in one region or another, forcing the two main national parties, the Congress and the BJP, to seek their support when forming a national government.

India's other major national party is of course the BJP.[47] As an offshoot of the old Jana Sangh, the core character of the BJP continues to evolve: when in power, it attempts to portray itself as a mature conservative party that champions Hindu nationalism; when out of power, however, it often adopts a more militant, antiminority stance, aimed at mobilizing electoral majorities.[48] Ever since the Congress Party abandoned socialism during the 1980s and embraced Indian capitalists as its main ally, it has floundered in the electoral arena, modifying its legitimacy formula this way and that. Into the resulting vacuum have stepped a variety of political forces, especially the BJP. Sensing the vacuum, the BJP came to prominence during the second half of the 1980s, when it mobilized around an issue bound to appeal to some Hindus, namely, the need to construct a temple where a mosque had stood. It is important to recall the circumstances in which this development took place. The BJP supported a non-Congress minority national government that came to power in

[45] See, for example, Ruparelia (2011).

[46] A good study of the Bahujan Samaj Party is Chandra (2004). I also discuss this issue further in Chapter 3 of this volume.

[47] Studies of the BJP include Jaffrelot (1996), Hansen and Jaffrelot (1998), Hansen (1999), and Basu (2001).

[48] For such an argument, see Basu (2001).

1989, following the defeat of Rajiv Gandhi and the Congress Party. Led by V. P. Singh, this minority government underlined important changes in Indian politics: Congress's hegemonic status had been challenged fundamentally, and nothing coherent had replaced it, with the left, the right, and the middle all jockeying for position. As V. P. Singh tried to create a permanent power bloc of the middle castes – an effort that failed – the BJP decided to unite India's Hindus by mobilizing against India's key minority group, the Muslims. The cause of a Ram temple in the city of Ayodhya provided the occasion for mobilizing Hindus, especially in western and north central India, where a sizable number of Muslims live and where the memory of Muslim rule over Hindus, if not alive, can certainly be revived.

The BJP and its affiliates, the Rashtriya Sevak Sangh (RSS) and the Bajarang Dal, caught the imagination of a substantial segment of India's majority religious community, the Hindus. While national moods are hard to capture, even with the help of public opinion polls, it is important to recall that, in the aftermath of the assassination of both Indira and Rajiv Gandhi, a sense of crisis gripped India. There was a growing sense that India was being left behind, mired in its internal fissures and fragmentation, while other countries in East Asia flourished with rapid growth and those in West Asia prospered with oil wealth. The benefits accruing to India's Muslims from Middle Eastern oil wealth only added to a sense of Hindu anxiety. An important television series depicting the Hindu epic *Ramayana* played for nearly a year during 1987 and 1988, rekindling the imaginations of many with memories of a great, but lost, Hindu past. The BJP was both a product of this mood and helped crystallize it further. The BJP argued that India was a great Hindu civilization that had been despoiled by centuries of Muslim rule, that India's current progress required a muscular internal unity of Hindus instead of a pandering to Muslims by the pseudo-secularists of the Congress Party, and that the greatness of a Hindu India could be recaptured only under the leadership of a well-organized and austere BJP.

After a decade of mobilization around this ideology of *Hindutva*, the BJP finally captured power – albeit in a minority government that it dominated – in 1998. The BJP's leader, Atal Bihari Bajpai, completed a full term as India's prime minister. After numerous short-lived governments under the leadership of non-Congress parties, this period of BJP rule created a sense in India that parties other than the Congress were capable of offering stable government. Constrained by the needs of governance, and by its coalitional partners, the BJP avoided pursuing some of its most provocative programs, such as the forced building of a Ram temple. A major exception to what was mostly a stable national government was the killing of nearly 2,000 Muslims in the state of Gujarat in 2002, a set of issues to which I will return in Chapter 3. While the BJP lost elections in 2004 to a Congress-led coalition, it is notable that in that election it ran, not on a platform of its charged *Hindutva* ideology, but more on its accomplishments, captured by the slogan "India Shining." While in power, the BJP put India on the nuclear map, mostly continued India's economic liberalization policies (though moderated somewhat in the direction of economic nationalism), inspired great fear among India's Muslims, and deeply alienated the left and secular elements among India's political class. Since losing elections for the second time in 2009, the BJP is now under new leadership, once again under the sway of its more doctrinaire arm, the RSS.

This brief review of political forces competing in India's electoral arena during the post-1980 period suggests two generalizations. First, governmental stability born of a dominant single-party rule is now gone; every national government in India since Rajiv Gandhi's has been a minority government. This may change in the future, but for now this is the new normal. And second, following Indira Gandhi's abandonment of socialism, no major party has competed for national prominence on a platform of class politics that might politicize the economic cleavages dividing India's haves and have-nots. The competing legitimacy formulas have focused instead on dynastic politics, caste-based "reservations," and religious nationalism. Save for India's main communist party – which remains mainly a regional force in certain states such as West Bengal and Kerala, and which I will discuss further in Chapter 3 – all of India's major political parties are more or less committed to supporting Indian capitalism as part of their core economic strategy. In light of political fragmentation on all other dimensions, this near consensus on matters of class and economy is explicable only against the background described earlier, namely, the growing power of business groups in India that now places broad class constraints on Indian politics.

The Institutional Arena

If, via a prolonged process of trial and error, India's major political parties are perfecting the art of creating illusions of inclusion in the electoral arena, a parallel but more deliberate effort to insulate critical decisions from popular pressures is also under way in institutional arenas. This is because, even when parties perfect the art of sidestepping economic and distributive issues, they still need to make some promises to the excluded in order to gain their support. All of India's major political parties thus continue to remain committed in some vague way to the conditions of the "common man." What else could they do in a democracy in which almost half the population is poor or near-poor? In order to ensure that these vague commitments to the common man do not generate antibusiness policies, a variety of institutional mechanisms that filter out mass demands are needed in the new pro-business politics of India. In this context, advanced industrial democracies provide a model. Notice, for example, the recent case of Barack Obama in the United States, who ran on an inclusive platform of "change," but very soon needed to rescue, subsidize, and protect Wall Street interests; these narrow pro-business decisions were, in turn, taken by a handful of hand-picked technocratic elite, who were mostly protected from popular pressures and who worked closely with business groups. While institutions in India remain a lot more fragile than those in the United States, a parallel process of devising mechanisms to protect pro-business decision making from mass pressure is also under way in India.

One important emerging tendency in the body politic, then, is to separate economic decisions from politics by concentrating the former in the hands of pro-business technocrats. While complex economic decisions in India, as elsewhere, have always been the domain of specialists, notice that during earlier periods major economic choices did reflect the mass will, even if quite imperfectly. For example, Nehru's import substitution policy regime was rooted in his anticolonial nationalism, a set of ideas that were responsible for the mass support enjoyed by the Congress Party. Similarly, Indira Gandhi's socialism emerged from her mobilization strategy around *garibi hatao*. During the post-1980 era, by contrast, the connection between politics – promises made to the masses to secure their electoral support – and economics – key economic policy decisions that set the framework for who gets what, when, and how – has been weakened. This may strengthen "economic rationality," as defined by the ruling elite, but it does so by weakening a key principle of democracy, namely, that policies ought to reflect popular preferences.

The institutional mechanism that facilitates this divergence between politics and economics is the emergence of a "two-track polity," an electoral track and an economic governance track. Mass participation is encouraged – nay, deliberately mobilized – in the electoral arena, but efforts are then made to insulate key decisions from mass pressure. For example, the political parties and the parliament are obvious institutional locales where mass preferences and policy decisions may be synchronized.

Political parties, however, increasingly play very little role in economic policy making. For example, prior to coming to power in the 1990s, just around the time when the mobilization for the Ram temple was peaking, the BJP did not have a single important economic advisor among its executive group at the apex.[49] While the BJP now has more institutional capacity to deliberate economic matters, as Congress has always had, the fact is that, when in power, leaders of both parties quickly delegate economic decisions to a technocratic elite. Notice, for example, that Sonia Gandhi's key economic decision makers include technocrats like Manmohan Singh and Montek Ahluwalia, who have little or no independent political base. Even the parliament plays hardly any significant role in modifying economic decisions taken by the technocrats. While this has always been so in India, in the past the parliament at least debated key economic choices, giving newspapers a chance to publicize them and thus adding an element of public discussion to economic choices. As discussed earlier, key decisions to "liberalize" India's economy, by contrast, have been made by a narrow group of technocratic leaders, away from parliamentary and public scrutiny. While the institutional location of key economic decision making may shift – at times in the office of the prime minister, at other times in a revived Planning Commission, and at yet other times in one ministry or another – those who make these decisions share certain characteristics: invariably they are pro-business technocrats who are appointed by political leaders and who work closely with business leaders.

A different type of institutional development that is helping solidify the state-business ruling alliance at the apex is apparent decentralization. As a federal polity, there has always been a tendency in India for national leaders to take credit for achievements – for example, successful industrial growth during the Nehru period – while shifting the blame for failures to state-level governments – for example, the failure to implement land redistribution policies during the same period. This tendency has been accentuated in recent decades, especially during the post-1991 period. As the role of the public sector in the economy has diminished, the capacity to initiate a variety of economic policies has shifted from the national to state-level governments. State governments increasingly play an active role in attracting new investment and, where possible, providing support to business groups to make these investments efficient.

---

[49] Based on the author's interview with Atal Bihari Bajpai.

Some of this decentralization is, of course, good for economic growth. I will return to that issue in due course. However, it is also the case that these policy shifts have privileged the better-off and better-governed states in comparison to India's relatively "backward" states, leading to growing interstate inequality. If the central government were directly in control of the policies that have produced these inequalities, the impact on the legitimacy of national rulers could be serious. As it is, the blame can be readily shifted to state-level elites; so, if an Uttar Pradesh fails to attract private investment, the fault lies with poor governance in that state and not with the national decision makers. The suggestion here is not that such an allegation is necessarily incorrect. What I am instead drawing attention to is the changing nature of the credit-and-blame political game in India and thus to the changing nature of legitimacy. In the past, the national government felt responsible for the less well-off states of India. The legitimacy formula now emphasizes a Darwinian, survival-of-the-fittest ethos. A paternalistic, egalitarian set of attitudes is thus being replaced with a set of beliefs that sanctions a winner-take-all system.

Further decentralization of resources and initiative to local governments is also helping shift the credit-and-blame game in the Indian political economy. During the 1990s, elections to *panchayats* – village-level governments – were made mandatory in India. Many decentralization enthusiasts hailed this as a positive development. However, those who know rural India clearly understand that power inequalities in the countryside are sharp and that public resources in these settings are readily appropriated by the powerful for private use. Only few regions of India offer exceptions to these trends. It is possible that, with repeated local elections, some of these corrupt inequalities will be mitigated. For now, however, the ineffectiveness of local governments as agents of governance and development is well understood.[50]

In spite of this knowledge, the national government increasingly wants to rely on these ineffective local governments for implementation of such programs as education, health, and public works employment-generating schemes. Instead of putting any great effort into improving the quality of local government, the national government seems content merely to channel resources to them. Why? The rationale is mainly political. By allocating some resources, the national government can claim that it is trying to include the excluded. When reports of misuse of resources at the local level appear – as they frequently do – the discussion quickly shifts to

[50] Recent studies include Ghosh and Kumar (2003) and Kumar (2006).

local government failure, to a need to cut back on misused resources, and to looking for market-type solutions rather than public sector initiatives. While there is probably no conspiracy at work, it is the case that national decision makers seem to adopt some policies that they know will fail, pursuing them for political benefit while shifting the blame for failure to others in the body politic.

A variety of political institutions in India, then – political parties, parliament, center-state-local government relations and elections, to name some of the more important ones – are beginning to adjust to the emerging power of big capital in India. Much of the process of institutional adaptation is taking the form of trial and error; there is no grand design at work. And yet a design is emerging – changes that help the powerful find a solid footing, while others are tried and discarded. For example, the national center continues to champion economic growth and pursues "rational" policies that encourage and benefit business groups, on the one hand, while a Mayawati or some other similar leader deals with the excluded masses via demagoguery and symbolic caste politics, on the other. The national center and Mayawatis of India, then, need each other in order for the new political economy to function. Similarly, failed local governments enable the national center simultaneously to claim a commitment to the poor as they put some resources into pro-poor programs, and to claim fiscal prudence in not allocating too many resources to the poor, lest they be wasted by inept local officials. Of course, just because the ruling elite are trying to manage the excluded via a variety of political strategies does not mean that they will necessarily succeed. Beyond quiet suffering, which is widespread among India's poor, the excluded also use various modes of activism to deal with their exclusion.

The Politics of the Excluded

India is a noisy democracy. Many groups periodically press more or less organized demands upon the state for one valued good or another.[51] All this is par for the course in India and has been for some time. India is also a rigid and hierarchical society in which the well-off upper castes have controlled a disproportionate share of society's valued goods. This too is par for the course in India, with many of the oppressed and the excluded accepting their fate as given. It was Mahatama Gandhi and other Indian nationalists who initiated the mobilization of India's poor

---

[51] This theme is well developed in Rudolph and Rudolph (1987). Also see Kohli (1990).

and the outcastes, hoping that democracy would create a less exclusionary society and state. As the excluded became politicized, Indira Gandhi hastened the inclusionary trend by promising the alleviation of poverty as Congress's central political goal. During the post-1980 period, however, this inclusionary rhetoric decelerated. With the Congress and other political parties in India embracing India's business groups as their main ally, the question for analysis is, how have India's excluded groups reacted? In what follows, I discuss several electoral and nonelectoral political trends that represent the political activism of the excluded as they face a new, narrowing ruling alliance at the apex.

One of the more significant expressions of the politics of the excluded in the post-1980 electoral arena is the growing significance of caste politics, especially in north central India. As discussed earlier, with socialism and class idiom taking a back seat, mobilization of caste identities has provided one political outlet for the excluded groups. These identity appeals in recent years have been especially significant in the Hindi-heartland states of India – such as U.P. and Bihar – where Brahmanical domination began to be challenged only during the 1960s and 1970s.[52] The numerically significant backward castes – many of them with small family-owned farms – were keen to challenge Brahmanical domination, both because of indignities they had suffered at the hand of Brahmins and because of lack of opportunities for their children to make a living independent of the family-owned land.

The appeals of such backward-caste leaders as Laloo Prasad Yadav in Bihar and Mulayam Singh Yadav in U.P. were potent to these backward-caste groups because they emphasized issues of dignity and of caste-based "reservations." The backward-caste parties successfully displaced the Congress as state-level parties in such states as U.P. and Bihar during the 1990s, both winning state-level elections and sending a significant number of backward-caste parliamentarians to the Lok Sabha. As already noted, these parties were unable to consolidate their support. The underlying reasons are not hard to fathom. The politics of dignity goes only so far; once some of the symbolic battles have been won, parties must come up with systematic policies that benefit their supporters. The backward-caste parties had very few such policies to offer. Their main concrete proposal – "reservations" for members of backward castes in public institutions – would benefit no more than a few offspring of backward-caste elites. With patronage as the modal form of their politics, these parties also gained

[52] See, for example, Frankel and Rao (1990). Also see Weiner (2001) and Jaffrelot (2003).

a reputation for being especially corrupt. As a result, many backward-caste members have by now lost faith in these parties as vehicles for attacking their problems of economic marginalization; these backward-caste members continue to search for new leaders.

Over the last decade or so, caste politics has permeated even lower in the caste hierarchy, now including the *dalits* or the untouchable castes, the lowest castes in the Hindu social order. In U.P., for example, the rise of the Bahujan Samaj Party (BSP) under the leadership of Mayawati is a testament to this most recent trend in the politics of the excluded. Championing the politics of dignity for *dalits*, Mayawati's electoral success is manifest in the fact that she now heads an elected government in India's largest state. Mayawati thus signifies both how the excluded groups in India yearn for political expression and the limits of such expressions faced with the avoidance of class politics. Because the untouchables constitute only a fraction of the population – less than a fifth – Mayawati has forged an opportunistic electoral alliance with the Brahmins. This is explicable only in terms of the fact that there is no social-democratic logic to a party that claims to represent the most downtrodden groups; had such logic been at work, an alliance with backward-caste parties would have made policy sense, since such an alliance may lead to broad based socioeconomic policies. Instead – and all this will be discussed in more detail in Chapter 3 – Mayawati offers dignity to the members of India's lowest castes in U.P., co-opts the elites, practices symbolic politics, and rules via personal charisma, demagoguery, corruption on a massive scale, and patronage networks.

In regions of India where middle and lower castes were mobilized well before the pro-business national shift of 1980, some combination of regional nationalism and populism continues to provide a political outlet for excluded groups. For example, non-Brahmin parties have now ruled the state of Tamilnadu for several decades. For mobilization and ruling strategies, these parties have combined charismatic leaders and themes of cultural nationalism with a variety of populist programs, such as free noonday meals at schools, debt forgiveness to farmers, and a well-run public food distribution system. In Andhra Pradesh, too, an explicit commitment by state leaders to champion "economic liberalization" has been combined with themes of Telugu nationalism and the cult of leadership in order to incorporate the excluded groups.

In only two or three Indian states have excluded groups been incorporated into the body politic via class themes. In West Bengal and Kerala, for example, communist parties have successfully put together coalitions of the lower-middle and lower classes. Since these parties govern their respective states within the constraints of a federal system, their policies tend to be, at best, mildly social-democratic. We will discuss these and other state-level issues in more detail in Chapter 3. What needs to be noted here is that state-led communist parties face a fundamental trade-off: if they emphasize only the interests of the poor and the near-poor, they are likely to alienate private investors, hurting economic growth; by contrast, the more they appease private investors, the more likely they are to alienate their core supporters.

The cumulative impact of the successes of a variety of caste, class, and regional nationalist parties at the state level, of course, is to under-cut the political support of the two main national parties, Congress and the BJP. This is what lies behind the recurring phenomenon, since Rajiv Gandhi's assassination, of minority national governments. When excluded groups realize, however, that their support of one party or another does not really produce the outcomes that they were promised or hoped for, what emerges is a trend toward anti-incumbency. We thus notice that an Indian parliamentarian has no better than an even chance of being reelected – a figure much more unfavorable to an incumbent in India than in other established democracies – and that the odds of being reelected at the state level are even worse.[53] This trend is understand-able if one keeps in mind the electoral volatility created by the ongoing search of the excluded groups for leadership that will truly serve their interests.

The political activism of the excluded groups in India is of course not limited to the electoral arena. Conflicts around identities and inter-ests are often fought in India in nonelectoral arenas as well. Examples include the activism of organized labor; the efforts of informal workers to become organized; farmers demanding subsidies and higher agricul-tural prices; feminist movements protesting dowry deaths and a variety of other injustices against women; NGOs organizing marginalized groups to protest their further marginalization by planned development projects; regions with grievances demanding greater control over their own politi-cal fate; conflicting caste groups taking up arms, to fight both each other and the police; ruling parties failing to mobilize civil servants and the police as Hindus kill Moslems; and the truly marginalized – say, the tribals – joining revolutionary groups that now hold sway over signifi-cant number of districts in central India. As noted earlier, some of this

53 One study of the impact of incumbency in India is Uppal (2007).

political activism is nearly normal in India. It would be absurd to suggest that most of it results from the narrowing state-business alliance at
India's apex; its roots are instead complex and often local. In a short
book like this one, I cannot analyze these "million rebellions" of India
in any detail.[54] I will touch only on a few that are relatively significant
and those whose trajectory is being influenced by the narrowing apex in
India.

The roots of the regional secessionist movements in the Punjab and
Kashmir are, of course, complex. It is the case, however, that the militancy
in these regions was exacerbated by the electoral calculations of national
leaders, calculations that reflected the abandonment of socialism by the
Congress Party during the post-1980 period. Take, for example, the case
of Sikh militancy in the Punjab during the 1980s.[55] The deeper reasons
behind the demands for Khalistan, or for a sovereign state for the Khalsa
(Sikhs), included the following: the demographic fact that the Sikhs and
Hindus are more or less equally divided within the Punjab and the related
fact that the Congress party has always been in fierce political competition
with the Sikh political party, the Akali Dal, for political control of the
Punjab; the growing incomes and related sense of political efficacy among
the Sikhs as a result of the green revolution; the centralizing antics of
Indira Gandhi, to which the Akalis reacted; and the fact that the Sikh
leaders could use their temple networks to mobilize the laity to counter
the power of New Delhi.

During the 1980s, timely concessions from Indira or Rajiv Gandhi
would have strengthened the hand of moderate Sikh leaders, marginaliz-
ing the extremists. Unfortunately, both Indira and Rajiv felt electorally
pressed. This was especially evident in the case of Rajiv Gandhi, who
began his tenure in office ready to accommodate moderate Sikh demands.
Having embraced economic liberalization, however, and having abandoned socialism, Rajiv was politically vulnerable, constantly worried
about ethnic factors in electoral calculations. Unwilling to appear soft
on minorities, Rajiv backtracked on his concessions to Sikhs halfway
into his term, delaying the resolution of the conflict.

The roots of Moslem militancy in Kashmir are also complex, dating
back to the less-than-legitimate process by which Kashmir became part

---

[54] On Hindu-Moslem conflicts, see Varshney (2003) and Wilkinson (2004); on labor, see
Candland (2007) and Teitelbaum (2008); on informal labor, see Agarwala (2008); on
NGOs, see Katzenstein et al. (2001); and on feminist politics, see Basu (2010).

[55] My own interpretation of this conflict appears in Kohli (1997). An important study of
the Sikh crisis in the Punjab is Brass in Kohli (1988).

of India when the British left. During the 1960s and 1970s, New Delhi established a working relationship with Kashmir's nearly feudal leaders by channeling resources to them and giving them considerable autonomy in managing internal patronage links. All this changed in the early 1980s.[56] The trigger was the post-socialist Indira Gandhi, flirting with ethnic politics as a strategy of electoral mobilization, and unwilling to accommodate independent Moslem leaders in Kashmir lest she be viewed as soft on minorities by majority voters. She created the conditions for the dismissal of an elected chief minister of Kashmir, Farooq Abdullah, in 1984. Most analysts of the Kashmir conflict in India agree that his dismissal was a critical turning point. Dismissal of an elected leader by fiat eliminated any major democratic outlet for those Kashmiri Muslims who felt marginalized and excluded in India and who sought greater autonomy from Delhi. Many of the disillusioned were, in turn, attracted to more militant movements. They received training and support from neighboring Pakistan and contributed to one of India's most drawn-out ethnic conflicts.

A different but related example of how pro-business politics might influence the activism of excluded groups is the killing of some 2,000 Muslims by Hindu mobs in Gujarat in 2002 in the so-called Godhra incident. The details of this tragic and violent episode are readily available elsewhere.[57] What is important to underline here is the role of the BJP in this gruesome incident. Recall the argument made earlier that the BJP is best understood as a party that seeks to minimize appeals to class and caste division by emphasizing the unity of all Hindus. Nothing facilitates the unity of Hindus better in India than mobilizing anti-Muslim sentiments. Gujarat is also one of India's most advanced capitalist states, with rapid economic growth but a variety of social and economic cleavages, including growing economic inequality. The Congress Party in Gujarat had created a winning electoral coalition during the 1970s by excluding the state's dominant groups while bringing together middle castes, lower castes, and Muslims around Indira Gandhi's socialist platform. The BJP displaced the Congress only by creating unity among Gujarat's religiously oriented Hindus. As the ruling party in Gujarat at the time of the killing of Muslims, it can be proposed that the BJP was probably on the lookout for occasions to strengthen its core support among Hindus. Nowhere in India is Hindu unity more needed in order for the BJP to maintain power

[56] See Kohli (1997), Varshney (1991), and Widmalm (2006).
[57] See Engineer (2003).

than in a state like Gujarat, with rapid economic growth, a powerful business community, and huge numbers of poor and marginalized groups. It was the need of the BJP to mobilize and maintain Hindu support in face of growing economic stratification, then, that led it to neutralize the state apparatus as its storm troopers mobilized Hindu mobs – often unemployed youth – to kill Moslems, further benefiting the BJP in subsequent state elections.

A very different type of nonelectoral politics of the excluded is manifest in the growing significance of violent revolutionary politics in India, the return of the Naxalites. While its historical landscape is dotted with rebellions, and even with armed rebellions, India, unlike China, has always stood as a case in which the poor and the exploited have not joined revolutionary movements. Among the more persuasive factors invoked by scholars to explain the absence of a revolution in India are the role of caste and village society in creating a decentralized pattern of exploitation and oppression, ethnic and regional fragmentation that makes it difficult for local rebellions to accumulate into a larger revolution, and the role of a powerful state – first under colonialism and then in sovereign India – in successfully repressing revolutionary upsurges.[58] The most significant exception to this acquiescent trend in recent India was the revolutionary Naxalite movement of the 1960s, which drew inspiration from the Chinese revolution, argued for a violent overthrow of India's "bourgeois-landlord state," and enjoyed pockets of strong support in states such as West Bengal and Andhra Pradesh. Consistent with the reasons invoked to explain the absence of revolutionary movements in India, it is notable that the Naxalite movement drew its support from those who lived on the margins of India's caste order, namely, the tribal population; that it operated in remote regions difficult for the state to penetrate; and that it remained regionally fragmented. While the Naxalites were eventually brutally crushed by the Indian state, their offspring, a new generation of Naxalites who share many of their earlier traits, have again emerged at the political forefront.

The strength of the new Naxalites in India has risen steadily over the last two decades. Even after the old Naxalites were crushed, pockets of revolutionary activity survived. During the 1980s, for example, urban revolutionary elite helped organize marginalized rural groups in Bihar into

[58] See, for example, Moore (1966).

a *Lal Sena* – the Red army – that fought caste indignities and exploitation by landlords, including the use of young lower-caste women for sexual pleasure. Revolutionary activity in the Telengana area of Andhra Pradesh and the Naxalbari area of West Bengal has never fully died. During the last decade or two, Naxalites have also started organizing tribal populations in remote regions of Maharashtra, Orissa, Chhattisgarh, and Jharkhand. While the roots of discontent are often local, a common theme that unites the movement is resistance to encroachment on land hitherto held as common property.

Rapid economic growth in India has increased the demand for land and for land-based products such as timber. Corrupt public officials (forest officials, local *patwaris*) often help private interests (a variety of contractors) secure access to public lands. Pressed tribal groups, who depend on these commons for their livelihood, have started joining armed revolutionary groups as a means to resist such encroachments.[59] The typical process of revolutionary politics thus involves revolutionary groups building some support among pressed tribals, creating "revolutionary justice" by eliminating local big men and corrupt officials, building further support, and establishing "liberated zones," which the state finds difficult to penetrate. It is estimated that some 10,000 to 20,000 armed fighters now help control some 200 districts in central India, an area twice the size of Kerala. No wonder India's prime minister, Manmohan Singh, in a widely reported speech on September 15, declared in 2009 that "left-wing extremism poses perhaps the gravest internal security threat our country faces."

While there is no likelihood, not even a remote likelihood, that India's Naxalites can overthrow India's government, their presence underlines the desperation of all those whose lives not only do not benefit from rapid economic growth but are actually threatened by it. The significance of Naxalites is also growing. A variety of revolutionary groups came together in 2004 to form the Communist Party of India (Maoists), an umbrella organization of sorts that gives some coherence to local and disparate activities. Five years later, the Indian state banned the CPI-Maoists, categorizing them as a terrorist organization. The national government has now launched "operation green hunt," an "antiterrorist" operation, supported by some 100,000 federal paramilitary officers, to eliminate the Naxalites. By treating a political problem rooted in exclusion from

[59] For one recent analysis of the role of tribals in the Naxalite movement, see Guha (2007).

progress as a law-and-order problem, the Indian state has again exposed its continuing inability to deliver on the promise of inclusive growth.

Finally, a tragic manifestation of exclusion and destitution is not so much rebellion, but suicide. Over the last two decades or so farmer suicides have become common phenomena in India. While neither the exact number of suicides nor good studies documenting their causes are readily available, the main outlines of the tragedy are well known.[60] Since the late 1990s, some 15,000 to 20,000 farmers have taken their own lives in India every year. These suicides have been concentrated in the low rainfall and low irrigation areas of states such as Karnataka, Andhra Pradesh, Maharashtra, and parts of Kerala and Punjab, hardly India's poorest states. Suicides have also been concentrated among cash crop farmers who were highly indebted and who took out loans from moneylenders. A common pattern has been that farmers take out large loans, make investment in irrigation hoping for large returns on their investments in such water-intensive cash crops as Bt cotton and spices, but are then deeply disappointed when the returns fall far short, either because of the fluctuating price of commodities or because of a secular decline in the prices of such liberalized commodities as cotton, leading to suicides. The deeper causes of the suicides, then, include a broader neglect of agriculture by the Indian state, especially investment in irrigation; I will return to this issue in the next chapter. Suffice to note here that numerous small farmers are no political match for the concentrated pro-business power of the Indian state. As the state focuses its resources and energies on facilitating the growth of industries and services in the cities, India's farmers are one more excluded group that remains on the margins of the high-growth economy, at times with tragic consequences.

IV. CONCLUSION

In this chapter I have analyzed some of the more important political developments in India over the last three decades. The two interrelated themes that I have discussed in some detail are the growing power of business in India, on the one hand, and the problems of incorporating the excluded groups created by this narrowing state-business alliance, on

---

[60] I am especially drawing here on Vaidyanathan (2006). Also see the special issue of the *Economic and Political Weekly* (April 22, 2006) edited by K. C. Suri for a state-by-state analysis of the subject.

the other. This focus on who wields power and who is left out emerges from this study's concern with the winners and losers in the new Indian political economy. Since an emphasis on some issues can emerge only if other issues are neglected, it is worth noting that my focus on issues of distribution of power comes at the expense of neglecting matters that might influence the life chances of all Indians, rich and poor, such as the quality of political institutions. In a chapter on political change, it might have been fair to expect a fuller discussion of institutional decline in India. This neglect is not total, however, as political parties have indeed been discussed, albeit in brief. Also, my earlier studies have focused precisely on these issues. And finally, I will visit some related issues in Chapter 3 on Indian states, where the issue of the poor quality of institutions is most pressing.

A focus on the growing power of business and on the problems of managing a narrow ruling alliance helps put in sharp relief some of the more important patterns of political change in contemporary India. Over the last three decades, a multiclass state that used mass incorporating ideologies to legitimize power has been transformed into a much narrower ruling alliance between the state and big business. This process of change was initiated by state elites as they prioritized economic growth and came to depend more and more on the private sector to produce this growth. As the process unfolded, the economic and political role of business in India grew. The more the private sector emerges as the main motor of capital accumulation and growth, the more India's political elite must create policies favorable to the private sector. And in case these indirect constraints are not sufficient, business groups in India now exercise growing direct influence on politics via the media, by financing elections, by lobbying for favorable policies, and via well-organized chambers of commerce that help propagate a pro-business political economy.

A narrow ruling alliance between state and business is responsible for both relatively rapid growth and growing inequality in India. We will analyze these issues in the next chapter. From a political standpoint, a narrow ruling alliance in a democracy creates the problem of how to accommodate excluded groups. I have suggested that a number of important political developments in India can be interpreted precisely as efforts to manage the excluded. In the electoral arena, for example, we notice major parties attempting to create illusions of inclusion, that is, creating electoral platforms that will mobilize the support of the poor without threatening the narrow ruling alliance. There are also efforts under way to insulate critical economic decisions from mass pressure by simultaneously creating a "rational" and "technocratic" apex and decentralizing the task of accommodating the noise in the body politic to lower levels of governments. Unfortunately for the rulers, such exclusionary strategies do not always succeed. Among the most recent challenges to institutionalized exclusion is the emergence of revolutionary politics, a challenge that the state hopes to meet with a law-and-order response.

2

State and Economy

Want Amid Plenty

Over the last three decades India's economy has grown at an impressive average rate of more than 6 percent per annum. While this growth rate trails well behind China's rate of more than 10 percent per annum, it compares favorably with the Latin American average of some 3 percent over the same period and puts India in the same high-growth league as South Korea, Malaysia, and Vietnam. It is also the case, however, that inequality in India has widened over this period, especially since 1990. While poverty has declined, a variety of human development indicators remain abysmal. In this chapter I analyze these broad economic patterns, focusing on their political and policy determinants and emphasizing the impact of the state-business alliance on patterns of growth and distribution. My argument is that the state-business alliance has led to policy choices that help explain both India's rapid economic growth and its growing inequality. With inequality growing, the poor do not benefit as much from growth as they might if inequality were stable. Of course, sustained growth has contributed to growing state revenue. As the ruling elites face electoral compulsions, some of this new revenue is finding its way into poverty eradication programs. However, the state's attention is focused on growth; a variety of these pro-poor programs are not implemented properly, further contributing to failures of human development.

As in the previous chapter, I first provide some historical background, summarizing key developments prior to 1980, including the Indian state's role in promoting import-substituting industrialization, the green revolution, and failed efforts at a variety of distributive programs, especially land reforms. This is followed by a core section on recent economic growth that emphasizes the late 1970s and early 1980s as a turning point for the Indian political economy – away from socialism and toward a closer alliance with business – and then traces the continuing economic impact of this pro-business shift on policies and growth outcomes over the next three decades. A final core section traces the distributional consequences of the narrowing state-business ruling alliance.

I. BACKGROUND

The economy that sovereign India inherited from its colonial past was deeply underdeveloped.[1] Agriculture was the mainstay of the economy, and the level of productivity was very low. Moreover, agricultural production had nearly stagnated during the first half of the twentieth century. Some industry had emerged, but mainly during the post-1930 period. As we move toward an analysis of the post-1980 period of high growth, it will be useful to keep in mind the deeply sluggish historical period that preceded the recent economic upsurge in India.

The Indian subcontinent has for a long time been characterized by a low-technology, low-productivity agrarian economy. The political stability of *Pax Britannia* also did not lead to spontaneous economic progress. The British in this nineteenth-century setting provided political unity, a "national" market, and infrastructure, but these contributions were insufficient for sustained economic growth of any type, including industrialization. Among the proximate factors militating against economic growth during the colonial phase were considerations of both supply and demand: low rates of saving and investment, primitive technology, and a poor economy with limited internal demand.

At a more distant level of causation, the negative role of the colonial state was significant insofar as it absorbed savings, failed to invest in such growth-promoting activities as technology development, and maintained an open economy that overwhelmed any indigenous dynamism that might have emerged. It is no accident that when indigenous capitalism and industry did emerge – mainly in the 1930s, though some existed earlier as well – it was primarily of the import-substitution variety, encouraged by a set of colonial policies whose rationale was more financial than industry-promoting. The consequences were, nevertheless, significant. While the role of industry in the overall economy at the time of independence, given India's large size, was extremely small, India emerged from colonialism with a significant group of indigenous capitalists involved in industry.

---

[1] In this section I am drawing on Kohli (2004), Chapters 6 and 7.

Equally important, these capitalists and India's nationalist political elite agreed that rapid industrialization would require protection and active state intervention.

As Nehru consolidated power, economic development was one of his priorities. However, early economic choices in India were deeply political.[2] Nehru's political preferences, expressed through the Congress Party, became India's dominant ideas and stressed the following: maintaining national sovereignty, the superiority of the state in steering progressive capitalist development, and the need for India's poor to share in the fruits of development. The nationalist commitments of India's leaders translated into suspicion of an open economy and a preference for heavy industry. In spite of low rates of domestic saving, foreign investors were by and large discouraged, mainly because they might have threatened hard-won national sovereignty. A variety of interests, including Indian business groups, benefited from these ideological choices; over time, they also helped sustain them. The Indian suspicion of an open trading regime, however, is more difficult to explain in terms of underlying nationalism. Protectionism was justified mainly in terms of prevailing economic ideas of "export pessimism" and "infant industry."[3] In the Indian case, there was also something deeply experiential and political about these choices. Economic openness during the colonial era had been interpreted by nationalists not only as killing nascent industries, but also as inhibiting the emergence of indigenous industrial capitalism. Indian businessmen and industrialists, who stood to benefit from a relatively closed economy in which competition would be limited, expressed these preferences openly. Protectionism, as well as an emphasis on heavy industry, was thus seen as serving the interests of nation building. How else, according to India's leaders, could such an enormous country, with its ancient civilization, reemerge as a powerhouse without being manipulated by external powers?

Belief in the state's ability to guide social and economic change was in any case widespread globally at the middle of the twentieth century. This view had a left-leaning tilt in India, reinforced by an admiration of the Soviet Union's developmental "successes" and by an affinity for the British Labour Party's type of socialism. These ideological proclivities

---

[2] Good studies of this topic include Hanson (1966), Bhagwati and Desai (1970), and Nayar (1989).

[3] A good discussion of the belief systems that have supported India's economic choices is found in Chakravarty (1988), Chapters 1 and 2.

were also consistent with the concrete interests of the Indian political elite, who could channel some of the fruits of development to themselves and their offspring. The statist model translated both into a direct economic role for the state – as in, for example, the widespread creation of public enterprises – and into a more indirect role in guiding the activities of private capital via the "license permit raj." What is surprising in retrospect is not so much India's affinity for statism, but how little open discussion took place concerning the type of state that could successfully undertake such ambitious economic tasks. A vague commitment to the poor and the downtrodden also permeated much of the nationalist political discourse. Gandhi and Nehru shared this commitment, though with different emphases. It found expression in socialist rhetoric and in policy choices such as land redistribution and the laws governing employment of urban labor. Unlike the commitment to nationalism and statism, however, the commitment to the poor was relatively shallow. India's upper-caste rulers may have meant well, but they were not even committed social democrats, much less revolutionary.

What was the impact of Nehru's economic approach, which was statist in intent and emphasized public investment in heavy industry? Any such assessment must keep in mind India's initial economic conditions. On the positive side, India had undergone some industrialization; a small but significant group of indigenous entrepreneurs was in place; banking and other financial institutions existed; and technically trained manpower, though not abundant, was not as scarce as it was in many African and Middle Eastern countries. The agrarian economy, by contrast, had not grown much over the previous several decades; internal demand was limited; rates of saving were low; experience with managing complex modern production was relatively scarce; and the health and educational conditions of the working population were abysmal. Given these conditions, how well designed was the developmental approach of sovereign India's leaders?

First, the agricultural sector: Nehru's approach to this sector was mainly "institutional" in the sense that he and India's economic planners hoped that, by tinkering with agrarian relations (via land reforms, for example) and by educating the peasantry (via extension programs, for example), they would improve India's agricultural production.[4] Thus, after some significant initial public investment, especially in irrigation,

---

[4] For a good discussion, see Myrdal (1968).

the agricultural sector was more or less ignored at the expense of industry. The results reflected this neglect. Agricultural growth was barely able to stay ahead of population growth. A more serious trend was that much of this growth was extensive and not intensive, that is, it was the result of bringing more land under cultivation, not of improving productivity.

The modest increases in agricultural production thus reflected increasing labor input – growing population – and the use of additional land, facilitated in part by new public investment in irrigation. Beyond this, the repeal of a variety of colonial-era taxes on agriculture may have created better incentives for agrarian producers, contributing to somewhat higher rates of production. Conversely, the state's downward penetration was minimal, and so was its capacity to alter agrarian relations. The relative neglect of public investment in irrigation and in encouraging the use of other agricultural products such as fertilizers further undermined the prospects for rapid increases in food production. By the mid-1960s, then, India's agricultural sector was on the verge of a crisis.

By contrast, Nehru emphasized heavy industry; he used the tremendous legitimacy at his command to pursue these priorities and to translate goals into outcomes. In truth, heavy industry was more readily influenced from the political apex than, say, agriculture or land redistribution. The imposition of substantial tariffs and quotas provided a protected environment in which industry could take root. The bulk of this growth, facilitated by rapidly growing rates of public saving and investment, was in the public sector: the further development of electricity, railways, communication, machinery, and steel.

The main source of growing public revenue was indirect taxation, especially of consumer goods. There were, consistent with India's socialist leanings, progressive income tax laws in place, but the government's capacity to collect them was limited – a problem that, over time, would become quite consequential. Indirect taxation sufficed during this early period because the government's expenditures on social provision were minimal: Nehru's government spent little on health and primary education, underlining the superficial quality of India's socialism. Moreover, Nehru's (and Congress's) legitimacy minimized the need to throw money at one group or another in order to buy political support. The level of political mobilization in India was also relatively low at this early stage, with much of the lower-class population deeply enmeshed in traditional patron-client relationships. Hence, public expenditures could stay focused on Nehru's priorities, especially the development of heavy industry, which generated substantial production growth.[5]

Critics of this strategy have documented that this growth was quite expensive, in the sense of being relatively inefficient.[6] Some of the underlying causes are inherent in the nature of the public sector – for example, investment in industries that are not immediately profitable and below-market social pricing of output. But others were specific to India: the role of generalist bureaucrats, ill-equipped to manage public sector industries, and growing political interference on the part of lower-level political elites who treated public sector industries as one more resource in their patronage networks. The highly protected environment within which these industries operated also contributed to the accumulating inefficiencies.

The Indian state's attempts to guide the private sector have also been roundly criticized. These criticisms,[7] however, need to be kept in perspective. Because the role of private capital in industry at this early stage was not all that significant, the prominent role assigned to the public sector is better understood as providing a substitute for a lagging private sector. After all, India's private sector had hardly flourished during the pre-independence period under nearly free-market conditions. That said, however, the socialistic Nehruvian state sought more to tame than to encourage private sector development. State intervention was definitely in a controlling mold, reflecting the belief of state elites that the state knew best: instead of asking business what the state could do and how the state could help, the state itemized what private business could not do and then created numerous barriers to the functioning of the private sector. Implementation, too, was haphazard and inefficient: for example, priority industries were not always the ones that enjoyed maximum protection, and overbearing bureaucrats in charge of licensing often discouraged private investors. Over time, the growing maze of bureaucratic obstacles to private sector development led to corruption and inefficient allocation of private sector resources.

As to distributional consequences, Nehru and his policies unfortunately failed to make any significant dent in India's poverty. The simple but powerful fact is that the overall growth rate of the economy was relatively sluggish during these years; the population grew at a

[5] For one good review, see Raj (1966).
[6] See, for example, Bhagwati and Srinivasan (1975).
[7] See Bhagwati and Desai (1970), esp. Part 6.

significant rate, and the number of poor in India grew steadily. Beneath this almost banal-sounding – but tragic – reality of India's slow suffering lay numerous questionable policy choices and poorly implemented policies.

Nehru's emphasis on heavy industry meant the neglect of agriculture, a set of policy decisions with serious negative consequences for India's poor, the majority of whom lived in the countryside, as they still do. It is no exaggeration to suggest in retrospect that there was no systematic policy to promote agricultural growth in Nehru's India. Much reliance was instead put on land reforms, a set of policies that were implemented very poorly. There was some success in eliminating the largest *zamindars* but much less in ensuring that land was redistributed to the rural landless. *Zamindari* abolition was thus mainly a political phenomenon (as distinct from a class phenomenon), in the sense that many *zamindars* were allies of the British, lost power as the nationalists gained, and posed an obstacle to Congress rulers as they sought to build political support at the periphery. Congress rulers thus pushed hard and succeeded in reducing the size of *zamindari* holdings. Those who gained were generally the "lower gentry" rather than the land tillers. In contrast to *zamindari* abolition, the several subsequent rounds of land reform (redistributing land above a certain "ceiling," or ensuring the rights of tenants) were mostly a failure.[8] There was some variation on this score across Indian states, a subject to be discussed further later. On the whole, however, land reform failed mainly because state authorities in India proved either unwilling or unable to confront powerful class interests in the countryside. Significant factors that contributed to the state's limited capacity on this score included the Congress Party's incorporation of landed interests as pillars of party support in the countryside; a federal structure in which land redistribution was the responsibility of state governments, where the power of the landed classes was especially significant; a less-than-professional lower-level bureaucracy that was readily co-opted by powerful rural interests; a legal system that was biased in favor of property owners; and a relatively low level of mobilization and organization among the potential beneficiaries.

During the Nehru period, the Indian economy grew at a modest rate, averaging 3.7 percent per annum (Table 2.1); the poor barely benefited from this growth. This was in part a function of the fact that growth was concentrated in heavy industry, which grew at almost a

[8] For details, see Herring (1983) and Appu (1996).

TABLE 2.1. *Basic Growth Data, 1950–2008*

Types of Growth	1950–64	1965–79	1980–90	1991–2008	1980–2008
GDP	3.7	2.9	5.8	6.4	6.2
Industrial	7.4	3.8	6.5	6.8	6.7
Agricultural	3.1	2.3	3.9	3.2	3.5
Service sector	4.9	4.1	6.6	8.0	7.5
Gross capital formation/GDP	13	18	22.8	24.8	24.1

Note: All figures are average percentage per annum.

Source: Author's estimates based on government of India, *Economic Survey*, various issues (http://indiabudget.nic.in).

7 percent annual rate during this period (Table 2.1) but created very few jobs. Most of the poor depended on agriculture, which grew at a sluggish rate (Table 2.1). Moreover, land redistribution programs were mainly a failure. These economic trends reflected governmental sins of both commission and omission. A focus on heavy industry paid off in terms of laying an industrial foundation, but, by the same token, agriculture and the poor suffered. The developmental outcomes were less socialist and more nationalist and elitist.

Indira Gandhi's economic policies were even more politicized than Nehru's, but with a difference. Whereas Nehru's policies reflected his deep political commitment to modernizing a sovereign India, Indira Gandhi was politically insecure, leading her to filter her policy choices through the prism of maintaining her personal grip on power. In retrospect, then, Indira Gandhi's era was unfortunately an era of missed economic opportunities in India, a period during which other countries exploited such opportunities. From the mid-1960s on, the global economy became more open to manufactured exports from developing countries,[9] and countries as diverse as South Korea and Brazil sought to take advantage of such global shifts. These countries, of course, came to be ruled by military dictators who prioritized economic growth and sought export promotion as an additional strategy. By contrast, India, after a brief flirtation with devaluation in 1966, moved almost in the opposite direction, becoming more and more obsessed with politics. Indira Gandhi's personalistic governance led India down a path whereby democracy was maintained, though tenuously, but economic policy was further politicized. And the

---

[9] See, for example, Lewis (1977), Chapter 6.

gap between the state's economic rhetoric and its capacity to implement policy only widened.

A set of agricultural policies adopted in the mid-1960s eventually produced India's "green revolution."[10] Insofar as these policies sought to concentrate production in the hands of landowning classes in some regions of India, they did not readily fit Indira Gandhi's populist designs. They are comprehensible, however, if one keeps in mind that they were adopted in the mid-1960s, just before Indira Gandhi's full embrace of poverty alleviation in the late 1960s. More important, India faced severe food shortages in 1965 and 1966, which made the country more open to seeking ways to boost food production and temporarily more dependent on food aid, especially from the United States. The United States favored green revolution policies and pressured India to adopt them in exchange for food aid. But the adoption of these policies was such a politically sensitive matter, in terms of both external dependence and possible distributional consequences, that policies were adopted by a handful of the political elite, essentially as executive decisions rather than through any open political discussion, a foretaste of future political and economic trends.

Various other social and economic policies adopted by Indira Gandhi in the 1970s were aimed at legitimizing populist politics. While the significance of some of these was mainly symbolic, others turned out to be quite economically consequential. Among the more symbolic – and thus politically consequential – was the removal of privileges that the Indian government had hitherto provided to Indian princes. More consequential economically, Indira Gandhi intensified the rhetoric about, but also to some extent the efforts to implement, land reforms. Land redistribution was a fairly central component of the new poverty alleviation strategy, though the actual impact was quite limited. Similarly, the nationalization of the banks was supposed to democratize lending and so was popular among Indira Gandhi's constituents.

Among the most consequential policy developments economically, the following had an adverse impact on economic growth. First, Indira Gandhi held her populist coalition together by channeling public resources to numerous interest groups – a case of largess that cut into public investment and hurt economic growth.[11] Second, the radical political rhetoric, some seemingly radical policies, and a new level of labor

[10] For good accounts, see Lewis (1995), Chapter 4; and Frankel (1978), Chapter 7.
[11] See Bardhan (1998).

activism alienated private investors, both domestic and foreign. Such policies included restricting the growth of private business and industry, the
nationalization of banks, and threats to nationalize other industries. And
third, India's closer political links with the Soviet Union, and a parallel
distancing from the West, made it difficult for the Indian economy to
derive the potential benefits of further integration with more dynamic
economies.

With Indira Gandhi's addition of populism to the statist model of
development, the gap between the state's ambition and its capacity,
which had already existed in Nehru's India, grew even wider, and the
Indian state became even less developmental. For example, Indira Gandhi
raised the expectation that her policies would help alleviate poverty – a
demanding task that would have required high rates of economic growth,
some effective redistribution, and the capacity to penetrate and reorganize
rural society. This demanding task, in turn, would have required a cohesive political party and bureaucracy. Indira Gandhi, however, achieved
nearly the opposite by further deinstitutionalizing the Congress Party,
further fragmenting the state's authority structure, and undermining the
professionalism of the bureaucracy. Rather than going to enhanced public
investment in agriculture, infrastructure, public sector industries, education, and health, the state's resources were increasingly directed at buying
political support. With growing politicization, the bureaucracy and public enterprises simply deteriorated. And finally, the state simply did not
support the private sector and became increasingly anticapital, with predictable negative results for investment and growth.

As is evident from the figures in Table 2.1 (p. 86), India's economy
did not perform very well between 1965 and 1979. Indira Gandhi's agricultural strategy, adopted under conditions of crisis and external pressure, concentrated agricultural investment in providing better seeds and
fertilizer to regions with assured irrigation, such as the Punjab. Price supports were also provided for food producers, thus shifting the terms of
trade somewhat in favor of the countryside.[12] While the distributional
consequences were decidedly mixed, the new policies did help improve
agricultural production.

On the face of it, the aggregate figures in Table 2.1 do not support this
view: the rate of agricultural growth between 1965 and 1979 was lower
than the earlier rate. However, much of this new growth was based on

---

[12] For a useful discussion of the politics of agricultural policy, and especially of issues
surrounding debates on terms of trade within India, see Varshney (1995).

higher yields. With the possibility of bringing more land under cultivation mostly exhausted – certainly without major public investment in irrigation – productivity-based food growth was essential to feed the growing population. Dramatic increases in wheat production undergirded this new growth, pulling India back from the brink of famine and mass starvation. The state intervened massively to support those property-owning elites who were most likely to generate economic growth, with benign consequences for production. While state intervention was a result of a crisis, and though the intervention was concentrated in the agrarian rather than the industrial sector, this alliance of the state and the propertied class was something new in India. Over time, even the industrial sector moved in this direction during the 1980s, but not before a significant populist interregnum and not without being pressed by yet another economic crisis.

Industrial growth in India decelerated sharply during the period 1965–79 (Table 2.1 and Figure 2.2, pp. 86 and 99), leading some observers to dub this an era of stagnation.[13] The underlying cause was mainly declining investment, but there was also accumulating inefficiency, and both of these, in turn, can be traced back to growing populism. While the rate of investment for this period (Table 2.1) was higher than the earlier rate, a more disaggregated picture clarifies the apparent contradiction. The higher aggregate rate mostly reflected savings (and thus assumed investment) in the household sector, where the majority of resources that are not consumed were maintained in the form of physical assets and were therefore not readily translated into investments with high rates of return. More significant was the behavior of public and corporate saving during this period, both of which decelerated.

The decline in public investment reflected both a failure to add to the revenue base (for example, by taxing new agricultural income or by generating surpluses in public enterprises) and growing public expenditure in such nondevelopmental areas as subsidies aimed at securing political support. This pattern was a direct function of Indira Gandhi's growing populism: she essentially threw public resources at the various social classes she sought to mobilize. As public investment declined, industrial growth was hurt on both the supply side and the demand side. Infrastructure development suffered, for example, creating serious supply bottlenecks for industrial production. On the demand side, too, given the weight of the public sector in India's industrial economy, reduced investment

---

[13] See, for example, Ahluwalia (1985).

shrank the demand for a variety of industrial products, thereby discouraging production.

Since public investment in India has not grown in recent years but industrial output has, it is also important to consider the role of corporate investment in the industrial deceleration during the Indira Gandhi era. Corporate investment also slowed down during this period, especially fixed capital formation. The underlying causes are difficult to discern but can be traced back to declining profitability. A decline in demand in the overall economy was probably partly responsible. Also at play, however, were more directly political factors. Populist politics led to steeper corporate taxes and to labor activism, industrial unrest, and higher wages, probably cutting into profitability. There is also the more diffuse impact on investor behavior of a seemingly leftward turn in national politics. While it is difficult to document decisively, investors may have been discouraged by the growing talk of nationalizing business (and the reality of nationalizing some banks), by new policies that sought to limit the size of firms and their areas of investment, and by the adoption of anti-business rhetoric.

Finally, whatever investment was taking place was not always efficiently allocated. Since there is little evidence that the rate of productivity growth during this period was lower than that during the Nehru period, much of the industrial deceleration under discussion cannot be attributed to issues of efficiency. Rather, the main culprit was reduced investment, both public and private. Nevertheless, continuing inefficiency was certainly a part of the overall economic scene. A poorly managed and inefficient public sector repeatedly failed to generate investable surpluses and thus contributed to a slowing down of industrial growth. A policy framework that did not encourage domestic competition led to misallocation of resources, hurting growth. Capital-output ratios, a rough indicator of efficiency, increased during this period, especially in manufacturing, underlining the fact that, in addition to the slowdown in investment, investment was simply not being utilized efficiently.

Leaving aside growth issues, Indira Gandhi's failures on the redistribution front were especially glaring because of the gap between promises and outcomes. The main achievement probably was to limit the growth of inequality, though, as critics will rightly add, this was more a matter of sharing poverty than of sharing wealth. Some of the money invested into such poverty-alleviation schemes as employment-generation programs probably did reach the poor, especially in states with committed leaders and better bureaucracies. By contrast, public education and primary health were ignored. In retrospect, the continuing neglect of primary education is especially perplexing in light of Indira Gandhi's commitment to the poor. Myron Weiner's provocative argument that the neglect reflected the exclusionary mindset of India's upper-caste elites probably has some merit.[14] However, even with the shift in national priorities on primary education that is currently under way, the fact is that numerous problems of implementation at the state level and below remain; this issue will be further discussed later.

Indira Gandhi's failures to redistribute agricultural land and to improve the contractual conditions of tenant farmers were truly notable.[15] All the rhetoric and some real legislation aside, the pursuit of land redistribution was left mainly in the hands of state governments. A few state governments made good use of the new, permissive political space, but these were seldom states with Congress governments. In the modal Congress-run state, which were the majority, the political structure consisted of two main hierarchies: a top-down, loyalty- and patronage-based chain that was the Congress Party, without a well-organized social base; and a bureaucratic hierarchy in which the quality of bureaucracy declined as you went down the hierarchy. Where these political hierarchies stopped in the countryside was where real social power – that is, the power of the upper-caste landowning elites – began. Neither the local-level party nor the bureaucratic elite were in a position to confront the landed elite; on the contrary, at times the party and the landed elite were the same people, and nearly always the local bureaucrats were deeply entrenched in local power structures. When on occasion some redistributive success seemed close at hand, tenants were either evicted by force or land ownership cases ended up in the courts, where they probably still languish.

To sum up, populism may be politically expedient, and on occasion even a political necessity to balance conflicting interests under conditions of weak political institutions, but its impact on economic growth and distribution is seldom benign. The Indian case fits this broader pattern. A more genuine social-democratic tilt in India, one that would have reconciled higher levels of growth and modest redistribution, would have required a well-organized social democratic party and a durable ruling coalition at the helm of a more effective state. Short of that rare pathway, a charismatic and popular leader promising radical redistribution – in the

[14] See Weiner (1991).
[15] See Appu (1996) and Kohli (1987).

Indian context of fragmenting political institutions and a largely private enterprise economy – was a recipe for failure.

II. POLICIES AND ECONOMIC GROWTH

As noted in the previous chapter, after returning to power in 1980, Indira Gandhi slowly but surely distanced herself from her earlier commitment to socialism and instead initiated a shift that has turned into a growing alliance with business groups.[16] In what follows, I analyze the pro-business economic policies that emerged from this political shift and trace the impact of these policies on the acceleration of economic growth in India. Of course, any full analysis of India's economic growth during the post-1980 period, which is not provided here, would also need to take account of the cumulative changes in the nature of the Indian economy since independence and of shifts in the global context. The emphasis here is on the state's pro-business interventions in the economy and on how these interventions have released economic dynamism in India.

One respectable interpretation of the recent Indian economic experience – let us call it the pro-market interpretation – emphasizes the process of economic liberalization in India that began in 1991.[17] India's earlier sluggish growth, according to this well-known line of thinking, was largely a product of a highly interventionist state and of a misguided import-substitution trading regime. In 1991, the argument might continue, India adopted a pro-market strategy that liberalized its internal regulatory framework, reduced tariffs, adopted appropriate exchange rate policies, and allowed foreign investors to play a significant role in the economy. As a result, rates of capital accumulation and the efficiency of the economy improved, propelling India into the ranks of the world's fastest-growing economies.

While widely embraced, this pro-market interpretation is unable to explain some important empirical anomalies in the Indian record and is plagued by some logical inconsistencies. First, economic growth in India started accelerating a full decade prior to liberalization of 1991.[18] Second, industrial production in India – a key object of reforms – did

---

[16] In this section I am drawing on my two earlier essays. See Kohli (2006a) and Kohli (2006b).

[17] For example, see Srinivasan and Tendulkar (2003) and Panagariya (2008).

[18] For example, see Nagaraj (2000), De Long (2003), Rodrik and Subramanium (2004), and Virmani (2004).

not accelerate in the decade following the liberalizing reforms,[19] though it has in recent years. And third, if a set of policies is supposed to work anywhere and at any time, why have some states within India responded well while others have not?[20]

I provide an alternate political economy account of India's recent growth acceleration that explains these anomalies. This account emphasizes the state's changing role since 1980, especially the abandonment of left-leaning anticapitalist rhetoric and policies, the prioritizing of economic growth, and a slow but steady embrace of Indian capital as the main ruling ally. Let us call such a strategy of development a pro-business strategy. In providing such an interpretation – let us call it the pro-business interpretation – I adopt a more general view that rapid industrialization in the developing world was promoted, not by minimal states that embraced the market, but by highly interventionist states that prioritized economic growth as a state goal, ruthlessly supported capitalists, repressed labor, mobilized economic nationalism in order to provide social glue, and channeled activities of firms to produce both for protected domestic markets and for export.[21] In light of such an analysis of "success," one can suggest, as I have earlier, that India's sluggish economic growth from 1950 to 1980 was a product, not mainly of the state's market distortions, but of a mismatch between the limited capacities of the Indian state and the highly ambitious statist model of development. Following 1980, I will now move on to argue, the acceleration of growth in India has mainly been a product of the state's embrace of economic growth as a priority goal and of business groups as the main political ally. Before developing this argument in some detail, however, it is important to lay out some abstract issues that set the framework for developing the more empirical argument. Those uninterested in theoretical concerns can readily skip the following brief detour and move straight to the Indian materials that follow.

Pro-market versus Pro-business State Intervention

Rare though the cases are, the experience of rapid and sustained economic growth in a developing country has repeatedly provoked scholarly debate. The underlying questions are familiar: how did country A or B

---

[19] See Chaudhri (2002) and Nagaraj (2003).
[20] See Ahluwalia (2000).
[21] I have developed this argument in detail in Kohli (2004).

(say, South Korea or China) get on the high-growth path, and does the experience of A or B provide a model, or at least lessons, for others? The main lines of the debate are also familiar: a high rate of growth resulted from the state's embrace of a pro-market strategy, namely, a move toward limited state intervention and an open economy; or, on the contrary, the country's success was a product of an interventionist state, especially of a close collaboration between the state and business groups aimed at growth promotion. Of course, in popular discourse on development, there is a tendency to treat all pro-business governments as pro-market governments. Even some scholars collapse this distinction, either obfuscating important analytical issues or, worse, providing an ideological cloak for what are clearly class issues.[22] Before interpreting the recent growth experience of India, therefore, it may be useful to sharpen the distinction between pro-market and pro-business strategies of state intervention; these development strategies vary in terms of the choice of typical policies, the logic and pattern of expected outcomes, and the underlying politics.

Whereas a pro-market strategy supports new entrants and consumers, a pro-business strategy mainly supports established producers.[23] A pro-market strategy rests on the idea that the free play of markets will lead to efficient allocation of resources, as well as promote competitiveness, hence boosting production and growth. This simple but venerable idea inspired the so-called Washington consensus on development during the 1980s and 1990s.[24] Shorn of numerous complexities, this development orthodoxy consisted of a few key arguments. First, the proponents of the orthodoxy were quite critical of the earlier state-interventionist, import-substitution model of development that was pursued by many countries in the 1950s and 1960s. Second, the suggestion was instead that economic growth in the developing world would improve if developing countries shrank their economic role and opened their economies to the external world. A failure to do so, the argument went, would produce fiscal and trade imbalances. Pressing policy issues thus involved bringing governmental expenditure more in line with revenues, on the one hand, and opening the economy with the hope of promoting exports, on the other. And finally, more specific policy suggestions that emerged included

---

[22] Panagariya, for example, holds that the distinction between pro-business and pro-market strategies is a "spurious distinction." See Panagariya (2008), p. 18.
[23] See Rodrik and Subramanium (2004).
[24] See Williamson (1990).

privatizing public sector enterprises, cutting public subsidies, reducing the public role in setting prices, currency devaluation, reduction of tariffs, and opening the economy to foreign investors.

All this is relatively well known and has by now been roundly criticized.[25] What needs to be reiterated is that advocates of a pro-market strategy logically expected a competitive, open, and efficient economy to lead to a number of additional benign outcomes: for the same amount of investment, a more efficient economy would lead to higher rates of economic growth; pursuing comparative advantage would create labor-intensive industrialization and thus rapid employment growth; competition would facilitate new entrants; terms of trade would shift toward the countryside, benefiting the rural poor; and since capital moves to capital-scarce areas in search of higher returns, regional inequality would diminish over time. The major anticipated problems in the pursuit of such a benign strategy would occur mainly in the short run, when the transition away from a statist, closed economy was likely to create disruption and recession. This also suggested that the pursuit of a pro-market strategy might be politically problematic. Since a pro-market strategy bets mainly on future winners, weak states of the developing world were likely to find few domestic allies in the short run. This is why external support for "reformist" developing country governments was deemed crucial by the proponents of pro-market strategies.

If the pro-market development strategy derived its inspiration mainly from some strands of neoclassical economics, the ideas behind a pro-business interpretation of economic success have developed more from real-world experience, especially from the rapid-growth successes of some East Asian economies. The key idea here is that success or failure is a function not so much of the degree but of the quality of state intervention. More specifically, identifying variation in how states are organized and in the institutionalized relationship between the state and the private sector is the key to understanding the relative effectiveness of state intervention in the economy. This relationship varies along a continuum stretching from considerable convergence in goals to mutual hostility between the state and the private sector. Other things being equal, the setting that has proved to be most conducive to (that is, that serves as a necessary but not sufficient condition for) rapid industrial growth in the developing world is one in which the state's near-exclusive commitment to high growth has coincided with the profit-maximizing needs of private entrepreneurs.

[25] See, for example, Serra and Stiglitz (2008).

The narrow ruling coalition in these cases has been a marriage of repression and profits, aimed at economic growth in the name of the nation. The developmental states of East Asia have generally created such political economies. Turning their countries into state-guided corporations of sorts, they have tended to be the fastest-growing economies in the developing world (e.g., South Korea and Taiwan, and in an earlier era, Japan).

Growth-oriented developmental states have pursued their commitment to high growth by developing trade and industry using well-designed, consistent, and thoroughly implemented state intervention. Specific policy measures have varied but have generally aimed at easing the supply-and-demand constraints faced by private entrepreneurs. Some of these interventions have been direct, and others indirect. On the supply side, for example, developmental states have helped facilitate the availability of capital, labor, technology, and even entrepreneurship. Thus the supply of capital was boosted at times by superior tax collection and public investment, at other times by using publicly controlled banks to direct credit to preferred private firms and sectors, and at yet other times by allowing inflation to shift resources toward private industrialists and away from agriculture and urban labor. Repression was also a key component in enabling private investors to have a ready supply of cheap, "flexible," and disciplined labor. Examples of less-direct interventions on the supply side have included the promotion of technology by investing in education and research and development, and/or by bargaining with foreign firms to facilitate technology transfer.

On the demand side, too, developmental states have pursued a variety of policies to promote their growth commitment. These have included expansionist monetary and fiscal policies, and tariff and exchange-rate policies aimed at boosting domestic demand. And when domestic demand was not sufficient, these states have just as readily adopted newer policies that shifted incentives in favor of export promotion or, more often, that helped promote production for both domestic and foreign consumption.

There has thus been significant variation in the specific policy measures undertaken by developmental states. Only some policies, such as labor discipline, have necessitated a repressive state. But what most policies adopted by developmental states reflected instead was a single-minded and unyielding political commitment to growth, combined with a political realization that maximizing production requires assuring the profitability of efficient producers but not of inefficient ones. Sometimes this has required getting prices right, but just as often it has required "price distortions," such as undervaluing exchange rates, subsidizing exports, and holding wages back behind productivity gains. The central issue has concerned the state's goals and capacities, expressed in the institutionalized relationship between the state and the private sector. Developmental states in successful late-late-industrializers have thus been pragmatically – and often ruthlessly – pro-business, more than they have been purely and ideologically pro-market.

The discussion of the contemporary Indian growth experience that follows, then, is framed by these general considerations: has India's recent economic growth resulted more from the embrace of the pro-market or the pro-business development strategy? To anticipate, the argument presented here is that, since 1980 or so, the pro-business political shift in India that I analyzed in the last chapter has led in the realm of the economy to the adoption of a pro-business development strategy. Of course, India is no East Asia: as a democracy, with considerable political fragmentation, India can't replicate the cohesion, effectiveness, or brutality of a Korean state; India's indigenous capitalism was also a lot more advanced by the 1980s as compared to, say, that in Korea around the mid-1960s, when a developmental state came into being there and needed to "pick winners" in order to create new capitalists; and labor in India remains well organized and protected. The new developmental state that India is thus in the process of crafting resembles the developmental states of yore mainly in terms of prioritizing growth and realigning closely with capital. The Indian state also remains activist in sofar as it continuously seeks to create a growth-oriented framework, supports capital as needed, and helps tame labor as far as possible within the constraints of a democracy. Many aspects of India's recent economic performance, in areas of both growth and distribution, are best explicable if one keeps in mind this pro-business standpoint adopted by the Indian state.

The Politics of Economic Growth in the 1980s

A glance at both Table 2.1 (p. 86) and Figure 2.1 clarifies the fact that economic growth in India accelerated noticeably around 1980. It is the case that the rate of growth of industrial production from 1980 onward (Table 2.1 and Figure 2.2) was not all that impressive, both by international standards and in comparison to India's own record in the 1950s.[26] Nevertheless, the growth of the 1950s began from a very low starting point, and the performance since 1980 has been a significant improvement over the 1970s, a decade dubbed the "decade of stagnation." Moreover,

---

[26] See Wallack (2003).

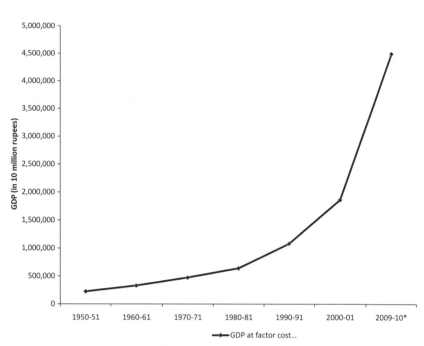

FIGURE 2.1. Gross Domestic Product in India, 1950–2010. *Source:* Government of India, Economic Survey 2010–11. *Quick Estimate

a number of economists have established, using a variety of more formal tests, that 1980 (or thereabouts) indeed represents a break from India's "Hindu growth rate."[27] So the first empirical puzzle is: what underlying changes might help us explain this break from the past?[28]

[27] See, for example, Rodrik and Subramanium (2004) and Virmani (2004).

[28] It should be noted that some of those sympathetic to India's liberalizing reforms in 1991 tend not to find the growth pickup of the 1980s all that puzzling, maintaining instead that this growth was not sustainable, e.g., Srinivasan and Tendulkar (2003) and Panagariya (2008). This view is not fully persuasive because the underlying fiscal problems toward the end of the 1980s were not of crisis proportions, and the pressure on the balance of payments was generated at least in part by unforeseen external circumstances. As to fiscal issues, note that interest payments on government debt constituted about 17 percent of government expenditures at the end of the 1980s, and 31 percent at the end of the "liberalizing" 1990s (Mohan 2000, Table 5b, p. 2029). The external debt service ratio in 1988 of 29.2 percent was high but was much lower than the 36.4 percent average of "all moderately indebted low income countries." India's short-term debt was also relatively low (Mookherjee 1992, Table 1). The pressure of maintaining payments on foreign debt was, in turn, exacerbated around 1991 by a sharp drop in remittances by nonresident Indians that at the time constituted nearly a third of India's export earnings (Kapur 2010, Figure 4.2). This drop (and the threat of a drop) was fueled by such unpredictable external circumstances as the disintegration of India's major trading

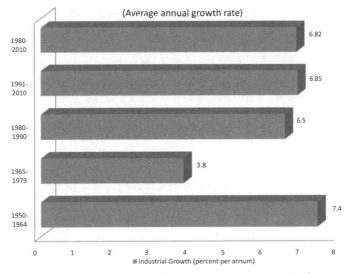

FIGURE 2.2. Industrial Growth in India, 1950–2010. *Source:* Author's estimates based on government of India, Economic Survey 2008–09, 2010–11.

A brief look at the more proximate economic determinants of the rapid increase in production sets the stage for a deeper analysis of the more distant causal variables in the broader political economy. In a rough-and-ready manner, economic growth accelerated because of improvements in the rate of both investment and productivity. As is evident from Table 2.1 (p. 86) and Figure 1.2 (p. 44), the overall rate of investment in the economy improved from 1980 onward (the trend actually began in the second half of the 1970s) and has shot up quite dramatically since 2005. The growth in investment in the 1980s was fueled by both growing public investment and private corporate investment, and in the 1990s, as public investment declined, by growing private investment (Figure 1.2); the role of foreign investment has also increased during the most recent period. As to productivity, especially total factor productivity in manufacturing, the literature generated by economists seems to suggest that there was a surge in the 1980s and then, though the economy still improved, some deceleration in the growth rate during the 1990s and beyond.[29] For

partner, the Soviet Union, and the first Iraq war and the related increase in oil prices, both creating a sense that devaluation might be imminent. So, while the macroeconomic problems were real, the government also used the occasion to do what it already wanted to do.

[29] See, for example, Virmani (2004a).

the purposes of a broad political economy analysis, then, leaving aside numerous related measurement and other problems that economists rightly debate, the first empirical puzzle translates into this: what political and policy changes during the 1980s help explain improvements in the rate of investment in and the efficiency of the Indian economy?

Before answering that question, however, two caveats are in order. First, it is important to reiterate that the higher rate of economic growth from 1980 on is at least in part a result of the changing composition of the national economic product. Over the last few decades, the contribution of the slow-growing agricultural sector to the national product has declined steadily, while the contributions of the more rapidly growing industrial and the service sectors, especially that of the latter, have grown; the fact that the overall economy now grows at a faster rate than it did when the agricultural sector dominated is to an extent simply a statistical artifact of the changing structure of the economy.[30] The outcome one is trying to explain, then – namely, improvement in the rate of investment and in the efficiency of the economy, especially of the industrial economy – is mainly of an order that brought to an end the earlier "decade of stagnation." And second, some component of the improvement in the growth rate from 1980 on was clearly a function of building on a good foundation a factor that is not readily quantified: accumulating technology, entrepreneurship, and management; trained workers; a sufficient tax base; dense supplier networks; and adequate demand in the economy.

What eventually triggered the upward shift in the growth rate of the Indian economy around 1980 was a slow but sure adoption of a new model of development. Instead of the statist and nationalist model of development of the Nehru era, which was then accentuated in a pop- ulist direction by Indira Gandhi during the 1970s, Indira Gandhi herself shifted India's political economy around 1980 in the direction of a state and business alliance for economic growth. This change was not her- alded loudly and has often been missed by scholars, especially because Indira Gandhi remains deeply associated with the politics of *garibi hatao*. Nevertheless, as analyzed in the last chapter, evidence shows that the post-Emergency Indira Gandhi was a different Indira Gandhi: she down- played redistributive concerns and prioritized economic growth; sought an alliance with big business; adopted an antilabor stance; put the brakes on the growth of public sector industries; and downgraded the significance

[30] See Wallack (2003).

of economic planning and of the planning commission. As suits a complex democracy, these changes emerged in fits and starts, and they were often camouflaged, helping maintain some of Indira Gandhi's credentials as the leader of the masses. The changes were nevertheless profound; they involved a shift from left-leaning state intervention that flirted with socialism, to right-leaning state intervention in which the ruling elites recommitted themselves to a more distinctly capitalist path of development. And important economic actors within India, especially big capital, understood these changes pretty clearly, expressing their satisfaction by increasing investment and helping India's economy grow rapidly.

The three components of the new model of development that Indira Gandhi adopted from 1980 on – and that for the most part has also been pursued by subsequent governments – were prioritizing economic growth as a state goal, supporting big business in order to achieve this goal, and taming labor as a necessary aspect of this strategy. The shape of the new model emerged slowly but quite, quite surely. First, let us take the issue of prioritizing growth. Within six months of coming to power, Indira Gandhi's government put out a new industrial policy statement that declared "maximizing production" to be its top priority.[31] Between then and 1982, a year she dubbed the "year of productivity," India's development strategy underwent a dramatic change: jettisoning redistributive socialism, a move hailed by the Indian press at the time, development was now to be pursued by a policy of "growth first," focusing on improvements in production and productivity.[32]

Indira Gandhi established powerful committees to study how this major transformation was to be implemented: among them were the L. K. Jha committee to study the overhaul of economic administration; the Abid Hussain committee to review trade; and the M. Narasimhan committee to consider financial reforms. These three senior bureaucrats were well regarded by the Indian business community. In addition to this long-term process, with its important signaling effect, numerous policy measures were also adopted to give concrete meaning to the "growth first" policy. As already noted, these all indicated considerable convergence of views between the government and Indian big business concerning the factors impeding growth: constraints on and lack of governmental support for business; labor activism; the inefficiency of the public sector; and the

[31] See Paranjape (1980).
[32] See Nayar (1989), p. 349.

decline in public investment, especially in infrastructure.[33] Notice also how the diagnosis within India of the factors impeding growth diverged from that offered by the emerging "Washington consensus" on development of the time. While there was some shared emphasis on deregulation and the inefficiency of the public sector, Indian business and government, for the most part, advocated a much more activist state, one that would spend more, control labor more, and support capital more actively. The shared elite policy preferences within India were thus clearly more pro-business than pro-market.

Starting in the early 1980s, then, Indira Gandhi's government initiated a series of pro-business policy reforms. First, the government withdrew some important constraints on big business and, going further, encouraged private firms to enter some areas hitherto reserved for the public sector. The Monopoly and Trade Restrictions Act (the MRTP act), which had effectively limited the growth of big business, was thus diluted, removing licensing restrictions and allowing big business to expand in such core industries as chemicals, drugs, ceramics, and cement. The government also encouraged the private sector to get into such areas as power generation. While small business was not always happy with such changes, big business welcomed them effusively.

Second, if expansion was to be encouraged, there was the question of financing the expansion. The government initially liberalized credit for big borrowers, but there was much back-and-forth on the policy.[34] Additional policies for the provision of finance were twofold. The government provided some tax relief to big business to encourage investment. More

---

[33] See, for example, the lead editorial, "All for Production," in *Economic and Political Weekly, Review of Management,* August 30, 1980. Reporting on Indira Gandhi's "two well-publicized meetings with selected group of industrialists and businessmen," the editorial noted that "it was ... made quite clear to the industrialists ... what the government was most concerned about just now was higher production. Of course, this precisely has been the industrialists position always.... [they] have been haranguing the government about the urgent need to remove alleged fetters on larger production.... the Prime Minister herself and her senior cabinet colleagues told the industrialists quite explicitly that the government accepted the position.... the government further accepted that industrialists needed to be given incentives to raise production." Also see B.M., "FICCI's Blueprint," *Economic and Political Weekly,* Jan. 26, 1980, p. 135, where the FICCI's policy preferences at the time are outlined.

[34] A few banks were nationalized during this phase. It would be a mistake to take this as a sign of continuing "socialism." The nationalized banks were losing money and were nationalized – bailed out, really – after mutual agreement. Bank nationalization and credit, however, did become a visible political issue; the government eventually tilted some of the credit towards the countryside, where the majority of the electorate lives.

important, the government altered the legal framework, as well as providing incentives, to encourage the private sector to finance new investment by raising resources directly from the public. As Pranab Mukherjee, the finance minister from 1982 on, commented:

An area of strength for the industrial sector today is the highly favorable investment climate, which has prevailed since 1980. This is a result of a series of policy measures implemented with the conscious objective of creating an environment conducive to industrial dynamism. Many of these measures have responded to the felt needs of the corporate sector.... the annual budgets for the years 1980–85 have a distinct philosophy. Incentives were provided to encourage savings and channel them into productive investment.... The Government has actively encouraged the corporate sector to mobilize the financial resources it needs for investment and modernization directly from the public. This policy has been highly successful. The total amount of capital issued by the private corporate sector increased from a little over Rs. 300 crores in 1980–81 to Rs. 529 crores in 1981–82, and further to Rs. 809 crores in 1983–84. This is an expansion of 170 percent in three years.[35]

Clearly, the government was consciously paving a pro-business path to higher growth and wanted to take credit for it.

Third, if private industry was to expand rapidly, both the national government and the business community felt that labor activism had to be tamed. This was difficult for Indira Gandhi in light of the fact that she was widely regarded as a leader on the left. Nevertheless, she put the "national situation" ahead of labor's interests and put labor on notice. Strikes, *gheraoes*, "go-slow," and "work-to-rule" movements were increasingly characterized by Indira Gandhi as "anti-social demonstrations of irresponsibility by a few" (*Times of India*, July 10, 1980). Special legislation was passed to discourage strikes, and labor and business were increasingly supposed to cooperate. While labor activism continued – India is after all a democracy – the die was cast for a new government attitude toward labor.

In addition to creating a new pro-business and antilabor context, one consistent with its growth-first policy, the Indian government also sought to restructure its own economic role. Of course, it is important to reiterate that what we are discussing here is India and not some well-constructed, cohesive, and brutal developmental state of the East Asian variety; Indian politics is not a world in which governments pick winners, corporatize interest groups, and balance budgets. Within the limits of India's

[35] See Mukherjee (1984), pp. 58–9.

fragmented state power, the scope of political reordering was nevertheless impressive. Unlike those following the "Washington consensus," the
Indian state in the 1980s never considered cutbacks in public expenditures
that could have been recessionary; there was instead widespread agreement that public investment in infrastructure "crowds in" rather than
"crowds out" private investment. Accordingly, Indira Gandhi sought
new revenue. Given the perceived political limitations (e.g., the inability
to tax more widely or effectively) and tax concessions to both investors
and well-off consumers – to keep up demand – the main source of new
revenue was indirect: excise and customs duties. With this new revenue,
and some borrowing at home and abroad, the government kept up the
pace of public spending (see Figure 1.2, p. 44), contributing to growth.

With revenues from direct taxes declining (because of tax concessions
to big business), on the one hand, and growing expenditures, including the
cost of modernizing defense and sustaining investment in infrastructure,
on the other, the fiscal pressure on budgets was significant. In line with
its new priorities – enhancing production mainly via the private sector –
the government sought to cut back some of its traditional expenditures.
Most significantly, it sought to limit new investments in public sector
enterprises; the new mantra instead was to improve their efficiency, in
part by better capacity utilization (read fewer labor strikes), and in part
by allowing them to revise upward the prices they charged for their output. The latter was also consistent with socialism taking a back seat.
Other changes of the same kind included cuts in subsidies to the public
distribution system and the abandonment of the Food for Work program in 1982. While budget deficits and the size of the public debt grew
during the Indira Gandhi years, that growth was downright modest in
comparison to what followed during the Rajiv period.

Finally, one should take note of some of the changes in India's economic relations with the outside world.[36] As an oil importer, the second

---

[36] Many observers of India, especially those outside of India, often judge the progress of
India's reforms or of liberalization mainly by this yardstick. This is understandable,
though for different reasons for different actors. First, some serious scholars, often
economists, are deeply convinced that global integration of an economy is the key to
improving efficiency and growth. Armed with this theory, they often look for evidence
of external liberalization – or the lack of it – as key events that will trigger meaningful
change. Second, there are those in the international business community, as well as their
spokesmen, whose primary interest is the opportunity for investment and trade in a
potentially large market like India. And finally, there are a variety of other observers –
associated with international development agencies or journalists – for whom some
combination of ideas and interests leads to rigid (or opportunistic) mindsets that one

petroleum price hike in 1981 increased India's import costs significantly. A commitment to increasing industrial growth was also going to require importation of machinery and other technology. Anticipating a foreign exchange squeeze, India entered a loan agreement with the IMF in 1981 for nearly $5 billion over a few years. India's pro-business policies had already been moving in a direction that the IMF found "encouraging," though not quite the "structural adjustment" package more commonly demanded. It is notable that the IMF did not insist that India cut back its public expenditures; in light of the fact that India did not owe any huge sums of money to foreign creditors, and given India's size and the leverage that that provides, Indian policy makers convinced the IMF of the need to keep up public investment in order to accelerate economic growth via the private sector.[37]

What India did do was to open up the economy somewhat, both to foreign investors and to foreign goods. Import liberalization in 1981, especially, was far from trivial, but also proved to be short-lived. The import bill rose sharply, without a commensurate increase in exports. Indian businessmen reacted sharply to the threat of cheaper imports and demanded protection.[38] The Indian government obliged; import restrictions were imposed again in the budget of 1983–4, around the same time that India terminated its IMF agreement, even before taking advantage of the full loan. If one ever needed evidence to support the claim that the primary commitment of the Indian state at this time was to established Indian businesses rather than to any general principle of creating free markets and a global opening, here it is. This was a pattern that would repeat itself during the Rajiv Gandhi years – more on this later – and that was not fully abandoned even during the more sharply liberal 1990s.

is tempted to label ideological. While the focus on the opening of the economy to the outside world is thus understandable (or at least comprehensible), it can also be myopic, especially if one wants to understand some of the key economic dynamics of such a large country.

[37] See Sengupta (2001), Chapter 2.

[38] By mid-1982, for example, FICCI was arguing against trade liberalization. The demands to restrict imports, however, were not universal. The Birlas were arguing against rayon imports and the Tatas against the dirt-cheap Bulgarian soda ash. Select public sector industries were also arguing against cheap imports of computer components. Those benefiting from cheap imports, however, also made some noise but did not prevail; these included some in the textile industry who wanted to import shuttle-less looms and glass manufacturers who wanted cheap soda ash. See "Clamors against Liberalization," *Economic and Political Weekly*, July 10–17, 1982, pp. 1135–6.

To sum up the discussion so far, Indira Gandhi during the first half of the 1980s abandoned a commitment to redistribution and recommitted herself to a "growth first" model of development. The political underpinnings of these shifting priorities were analyzed in the last chapter. These priorities, in turn, led Indira Gandhi to tilt the policy process in favor of big business and against labor, and to restructure the state's own role in the economy toward growth promotion. There were some halting efforts to open up the economy as well. While this model adopted some of the policies recommended by the "Washington consensus" on development, it was considerably more statist and more explicitly growth-oriented; it was also more pro-business than pro-market. Beginning in 1980, then, India's nationalist-capitalist model of development began to share some important traits with the East Asian model, in which highly interventionist states commonly ally with business and against labor and only selectively link their economies to the world, often more via trade than via capital.[39] Of course, state power in India is considerably more fragmented and checked by democratic forces than is the case in, say, a South Korea under Park Chung Hee. These differences were also consequential: budget deficits remained an issue as direct taxes were hard to collect and expenditures hard to limit; mercifully, labor could never be fully tamed; and the state itself remained "soft," creating numerous problems of inefficiency in the bureaucracy and public management. The shift in development strategy also created significant political problems, especially that of winning the support of a majority where the majority is poor, or near-poor, and the rhetoric of socialism and *garibi hatao* is being put on the back burner; these have already been discussed.

The growth-first, pro-business, antilabor shift initiated by Indira Gandhi basically continued under her successor, Rajiv Gandhi. Leaving aside a lot of rhetorical flourishes, as well as a fair amount of back-and-forth on specific policies, Rajiv Gandhi continued the policy changes initiated by Indira Gandhi, moving a little faster in some areas, a little slower in others. By the end of his rule some significant changes in the domestic political economy and a few changes that altered India's links with the world had been put in place. Most significantly, state controls on such activities of private Indian firms as entry into production, production decisions, and expansion in size were eased even further. Indian

---

[39] See Kohli (2009) for a discussion of the nationalist-capitalist model of development pursued in Asia in general.

business groups were also provided significant concessions on corporate and personal taxes, as well as assurances about future patterns of taxation. On the external front, some import barriers came down, though not dramatically; some import quotas were removed; and there was some currency devaluation. For the most part, however, the internal changes were more significant than the external ones.

Three important political economy observations concerning the Rajiv period need to be made.[40] First, irrespective of what actual reforms were implemented during this period, Rajiv Gandhi and his advisors decided from the outset to emphasize a break with the past. Whereas Indira Gandhi's growing embrace of big business was increasingly straining her commitment to socialism, as noted earlier, Rajiv Gandhi dropped the pretense of socialism altogether and openly committed his government to a new "liberal" beginning. Among Rajiv's important economic advisors at this time were individuals like L. K. Jha, Manmohan Singh, Montek Singh Ahluwalia, and Abid Hussain. These individuals had also been critical players during the post-1980 Indira Gandhi period, and some of them, especially Manmohan Singh and Montek Singh Ahluwalia, played a decisive role in the policy shift of 1991. Two conclusions thus seem warranted: stressing continuity or change was as much a political decision as one having to do with the substance of policy reforms; and more important, the decision to undertake major reform of the economy was already very much on the mind of key policy makers during the 1980s, who were then waiting for an appropriate political moment, which finally emerged with the "crisis" of 1991.

Second, it is clear from the policy changes adopted during this phase that the government's commitment was first and foremost to economic growth, and only secondarily to some abstract notion of "openness" or "laissez-faire." In spite of growing budget deficits, for example, the government kept up the pace of public investment, including investment in infrastructure. Public spending thus helped growth not only by boosting demand, but also by easing supply constraints. The government self-consciously lowered taxes on the middle class so as to boost demand, especially for consumer durables. Much of the new private investment flew into these areas, also improving the productivity of the hitherto heavy industry economy. And finally, the state got actively involved in promoting the growth of industries such as computers and electronics, providing them supply-side support and also maintaining pressure on

[40] For details, see Kohli (1989).

them to stay competitive by minimizing protection. For example, Rajiv Gandhi took a personal interest in the development of the computer industry. He encouraged collaboration among Indian computer specialists at home and abroad. Rules for entry were simplified; a variety of supports – such as technical parks – were provided; and collaboration with foreign companies was encouraged. Major Indian IT companies, such as Infosys and WIPRO, matured during these years, and such foreign companies as Texas Instruments and Microsoft established bases in India.[41] While problems of fiscal and balance-of-payment imbalances were building up, the government was also self-consciously promoting growth and succeeding.

Finally, it is important to note that the policy pattern was more pro-business, especially pro–big Indian business, than anything else. Much of internal policy reform – such as eliminating many licensing requirements, removing restrictions on the size of businesses, and opening up areas reserved for the public sector to the private sector – helped big rather than small or medium-sized private businesses. Moreover, whenever conflicts arose over external opening, especially on issues of foreign investment, but also on trade, the government accommodated the demands of Indian business groups. Spokesmen for FICCI, as well as government representatives such as L. K. Jha, often reiterated that the "pace of domestic liberalization" would continue but that "external liberalization was not really an objective of the policy."[42]

Indira and Rajiv Gandhi dominated the Indian political economy during the 1980s. This was also the decade in which India's economy made a breakthrough, moving beyond the "Hindu growth rate" to a more rapidly growing economy. One central suggestion here is that this shift in economic performance was triggered by the pro-business policy shift engineered by the two Gandhis. The new growth strategy produced both higher rates of investment and improvements in the efficiency of investment, contributing to higher growth rates, especially in the industrial and services sectors. The government's commitment to growth was evident, first, in sustaining relatively high levels of public investment during the 1980s (see Figure 1.2, p. 44). This investment helped ease a variety of infrastructural bottlenecks, such as those in coal, power, and railways; it might also have contributed to a higher growth rate by providing a

---

[41] See Ye (2007), Chapter 8. Also see Evans (1995).
[42] These quotes are from my interview with L. K. Jha. See Kohli (1989), p. 315.

TABLE 2.2. *Patterns of Capital Formation by Sector, 1970–2008 (averages as percentage of GDP)*

	Total Gross Capital Formation	Private Corporate Sector	Public Sector	Household Sector
1970–75	18.2	2.8	7.7	7.7
1975–80	22.5	2.3	11.0	10.0
1980–85	21.9	4.5	10.2	7.2
1985–90	23.7	4.5	10.5	8.7
1990–95	23.7	6.0	9.1	8.6
1995–2000	24.8	8.0	7.0	9.8
2000–08	30.5	10.6	7.1	12.8

Source: Author's estimates based on government of India, *Economic Survey*, various issues (http://indiabudget.nic.in).

boost to overall demand.[43] More important than the recovery of public investment was the changing behavior of the private sector.

Assuming that businessmen react to favorable opportunities for profit making, it is reasonable to suggest that the government's new pro-business policy regime in the 1980s was responsible for the rising share of corporate investment in GDP evident in Table 2.2 and Figure 1.2 (p. 44). Other evidence also supports the claim that private sector companies grew at a relatively rapid pace during the 1980s: whereas the paid-up capital of private companies grew at an average annual rate of 7.3 percent during the 1970s, the growth rate during the 1980s was nearly twice that, 14.3 percent; also, the number of private companies during the 1980s grew at an annual average rate of 13.5 percent, compared to a growth rate of 3.3 percent for public sector companies.[44] We also know that private investment in India tends to be more efficient than public sector investment. It follows that the state's pro-business tilt contributed to a higher rate of growth via the enhanced role of the private sector in the Indian economy. While the major beneficiaries were established big

[43] Rodrik and Subramanian (2004) find that public investment in the 1980s did not impact growth, though they do allow that the relationship holds with some time lag. Most economic analysts of India instead find a strong association between public investment and higher growth rates; see, for example, Nagaraj (2003). Even analysts considered pro-liberalization, but committed to growth, worry about declining public investment in India; see, for example, Mohan (2002).

[44] See Pedersen (2000), p. 268; and Virmani (2004a), p. 35.

business firms, the relative ease of entry also enabled new players to emerge as giants.

If the partial impact of the changing governmental commitment to growth can be traced via changing policies and enhanced investment, both public and private, our understanding of why and how the productivity and efficiency of the economy also improved remains rather diffuse.[45] Some of the underlying factors were probably unrelated to short-term policy changes; as noted earlier, these might include the building stock of technology and management in the economy, the establishment of a variety of producer networks, sufficient demand in the economy, an adequate tax base, and the presence of a sizable working class. Among policy-related changes, firms might have become more productive by the 1980s because many of them were producing more consumer than capital goods; technology imports were facilitated, and so was the availability of foreign exchange, enabling ready availability of a variety of scarce inputs and thus helping utilize industrial capacity at a relatively high level. Domestic competition also must have put pressure on some firms to economize, though for others a near-monopoly type of growth, and thus achievement of economies of scale, may have helped produce a similar outcome. The precise causal impact on productivity of such factors is hard to establish; what does seem clear is that the shift in governmental policies and the enhanced role of the private sector helped improve not only the rate of investment, but also the efficiency of the economy.

While the new pro-business strategy of the two Gandhis was indeed responsible for accelerating India's economic growth, it also created numerous other problems. The political problem of how to accommodate the excluded has already been analyzed. What is worth reiterating is a political economy problem. Given the nature of power in the Indian state, the embrace of a state-capital-alliance-for-rapid-growth model of development could never fully replicate the East Asian model; India's authority structure was and remains too fragmented, and given Indian democracy, the underlying class basis of state power could never be too exclusively pro-business. The clearest economic manifestation of these political traits

---

[45] Writing eloquently, and with an authority that he well deserves, I. G. Patel (1992) thus noted: "Efficiency, of course, is a dynamic concept and its best promoters, apart from entrepreneurship, skills and capital, are good information, competition with a level-playing field, transparency, relative stability of policies and improvements in technology. Once again, efficiency transcends the domain of micro-economics as narrowly and traditionally conceived, and requires something more than competitive market" (p. 43).

was the slow but steady building up of fiscal pressure; the inability to collect more revenue, on the one hand, and the inability to limit a variety of public expenditures, on the other. Even some of the external borrowing mainly fed internal fiscal imbalances. The growing fiscal and balance-of-payment difficulties, in turn, helped create the "crisis" of 1991. fiscal

The Politics of Economic Growth, 1990–2010

During the post-reform period, the service sector of the Indian economy has grown most rapidly. By contrast, agricultural growth has decelerated, and the growth rate in the industrial sector has been about the same as it was during the 1980s (Table 2.1, p. 86). In what follows I will analyze the political and policy underpinnings of these growth patterns, focusing especially on industrial growth because reforms have been aimed mainly at Indian industry. The stunning fact about recent industrial growth in India is this: in spite of all the noise about reform, the growth rate of India's industry has not been influenced all that greatly by the reforms (see Figure 2.2, p. 99). The real break in growth occurred around 1980. Since then nothing dramatic has changed, at least in terms of the aggregate outcomes. What have changed instead are the distributive outcomes associated with this growth, an issue to which I will return later. It is also notable that employment in manufacturing remained constant at around 12 percent of the workforce during the 1980s and then during the post-reform period.[46] How does one interpret this pattern as well as this rate of growth?

Once again, observing the more proximate economic determinants of these trends helps set the stage for a deeper political economy analysis. It is clear from Table 2.2 and Figure 1.2 (p. 44) that the overall rate of capital formation in the Indian economy did not alter significantly between the 1980s and the 1990s, though it did shoot up sharply during the post-2005 period. The composition of this investment has shifted throughout this period (Figure 1.3, p. 45); public investment has declined since the 1990s, and the resulting gap has been filled – nay, more than filled – by a variety of private investors. The growth rate of total factor productivity of the economy has not altered much, though labor productivity has improved. So the puzzle for analysis concerns the impact of the reforms on investment – especially on its changing composition – and on the rate of industrial growth, where the gains are not dramatic.

[46] See Nagaraj (2003), p. 3708.

That India in 1991 adopted a fairly significant set of economic policy reforms is well known. The economic reforms undertaken since 1991 have influenced both India's industrial policy and its external economic relations. The various industrial policy reforms – further loosening of licensing requirements, removal of MRTP constraints, tax concessions, further opening to private enterprise of areas hitherto reserved for the public sector, and taming labor – are best viewed as continuation of the "internal liberalization" well under way during the 1980s. These reforms also ought to be judged mainly as pro–indigenous business, enabling well-established businesses to grow and allowing some new ones to emerge and flourish. In light of the earlier discussion, none of these reforms should be all that surprising. Where there was a significant element of discontinuity was in the area of India's external economic relations, including trade, foreign investment, and financial relations. As is also well known, starting in 1991 import quotas were removed (fully only in 2001), tariffs came down slowly but surely, the currency was devalued, the foreign invest-ment regime was liberalized, and various restrictions on external financial transactions were eased. Some of these reforms helped Indian business; others put enormous competitive pressure on them. In adopting these external economic reforms, the Indian state was responding to a sharply changed world, as already discussed, and in the process attempting to establish a new social contract with Indian business: we will continue to put our full weight behind you, but you, in turn, must become more competitive. The underlying politics of these reforms was analyzed in the previous chapter.

While I move to trace the impact of India's economic reforms, the scope of external economic reforms must be kept in perspective. By India's own past standards, the changes were quite dramatic. In a comparative and global perspective, however, India's opening to the world remains rela-tively modest.[47] On the trade front, for example, tariffs did come down significantly, but the decline began in 1987, during the Rajiv Gandhi years, and toward the end of the millennium Indian tariffs still averaged some 30 percent, among the highest in the world. India's share of foreign trade, at some 25 percent of the GDP, was also among the lowest in the world in the early twenty-first century. The story on foreign investment is not all that different. While the inflows in the 1990s were huge com-pared to the past – averaging nearly $4 billion, including both direct and

[47] In listing the "modesty" of these reforms, I am drawing on Nayar (2001).

portfolio investment – on a per capita basis India remained one of the least exposed countries to foreign investment in the world; of course, FDI and portfolio investment shot up in India during the post-2005 period, but again declined during 2009 and 2010. And finally, it is well known that capital movement in India remains relatively restricted.

Of the major policy reforms initiated in 1991, then, internal deregulation has proceeded the furthest, and global opening has been real but slow and modest. By contrast, the attempts to trim current public expenditures, privatization of public enterprises, and labor reform face political obstacles and for the most part have not been pursued. As noted earlier, this pattern of reform underlines the pattern of power distribution in India: reforms that favor big business have been relatively easy to push through, but a variety of other interest groups are able to moderate any rigid ideological plan to turn Indian economy into a paradigmatic example of "neoliberalism."

A brief discussion of a specific case, the case of the automobile industry – a case that is far from atypical – will help explicate the pattern of these macro changes at a micro level.[48] Up until 1980 or so, India's auto industry was highly protectionist, dominated by two or three private business houses, including the Birlas and the Tatas. When Indira Gandhi introduced her important pro-growth policies in the early 1980s, a variety of controls on the entry of new firms and on expansion were loosened, leading to her son's effort to develop a new automobile manufacturing company, the Maruti Udyog. When these efforts faltered, collaboration with the Japanese auto manufacturer Suzuki Motors was the first major joint venture with a foreign company in the auto sector. The success of this venture put pressure on established automobile companies, many of whom entered into similar arrangements, leading to the entry into India of a number of Japanese automobile companies. While new products were introduced and supply bottlenecks eased, none of these changes threatened established, indigenous businesses in any fundamental way: tariffs and quotas on automobile imports remained, as did limits on the conditions under which foreign companies could enter India, generally as junior partners in joint ventures with established Indian companies.

As the Indian economy opened during the 1990s, the automobile industry came under further pressure. Industry associations lobbied

---

[48] In this discussion of the auto industry, I am drawing on the important research of Ye (2007), Chapter 8. Also see D'Costa (2005).

successfully to moderate the opening. Quantitative restrictions on imports remained in place during the 1990s, and foreign investors had to meet a variety of requirements such as minimum initial investment, export obligations, and obligations to use local inputs. In order to comply with WTO rules, India had to end quantitative restrictions on auto imports in the new millennium. The fear of imports again mobilized Indian automobile manufacturers. In line with the broader political economy analysis already developed, the Indian state again obliged, limiting the damage that unimpeded imports and foreign investment might cause to indigenous manufacturers. As quantitative restrictions were lifted, a variety of new customs duties on imports of new and old automobiles were introduced. Restrictions on foreign investors, including the need to use local inputs and export obligations, were institutionalized. By the mid-2000s, the Indian auto industry was a lot more open than it had been during the pre-1980 period, but the opening had been calibrated so as to preserve the interests of indigenous manufacturers. In the words of one analyst, global opening of the Indian auto industry "was allowed in areas that strengthened the competitiveness of Indian automakers and rejected when it threatened industrial interests."[49]

To return to the more macro issue of the rate of growth and the impact of reform, in the words of Montek Ahluwalia, a key policy maker in India, the reforms "were expected to generate faster industrial growth and greater penetration of world markets in industrial products, but performance in this respect has been disappointing."[50] With reform advocates themselves expressing disappointment, the real debate in the literature is about explaining the disappointing performance. The "disappointment," of course, has to be kept in perspective: at some 6 percent annual growth, India's is still among the world's fastest-growing economies; exports have grown steadily, and the balance-of-payment situation has improved considerably since the reforms. And yet industrial growth in the two decades following the reforms did not exceed the rate achieved during the 1980s; growth in total factor productivity during the post-reform period also did not improve dramatically as compared to the 1980s; export growth continued to be surpassed by growing imports; and the share of public investment declined, while the share of public debt continued to grow. Contending explanations, as one might expect,

[49] See Ye (2007), p. 241.
[50] See Ahluwalia (2002), p. 75.

tend to suggest either that the reforms have not gone far enough or that they have already gone too far, too fast.[51]

Focusing mainly on the political economy of growth, what requires discussion is why India's reforms did not lead to an acceleration of industrial growth – though, unlike cases of real neoliberalism in Latin America, they also did not hurt economic growth. As before, one needs to focus on issues both of rates of investment and of productivity. It is well known to observers of India that private investment, including corporate investment, has for the most part remained buoyant during the post-reform period but that public investment has declined (see Table 2.2 and Figure 1.2). Private corporate investment shot up rapidly after the reforms but peaked in the mid-1990s and has now again shot up during the post-2005 period. Capital formation in the household sector has also grown rapidly since the mid-1990s.

One must attribute the continued buoyancy of private sector investment to the various pro-business industrial policy changes introduced during the post-1991 period. The fact that the investment boom originated mainly in the "registered sector," especially in the first half of the 1990s, further suggests two observations: reform policies initially helped big business more than small business; and big business felt relatively comfortable with the slow pace of the external opening of the economy, at least until later in the 1990s, when continued imports and foreign-investor-produced goods brought forward protests and discouraged further investments. Since around 2005, supported by a business-friendly Congress government, the private sector has again accelerated its investment. The relatively high rate of private investment is also one of the main forces that has propelled the steady growth of industry during the post-reform period. The pro-growth and pro-business drift of the Indian state – which began in the 1980s and continued into the 1990s and beyond – is thus mainly responsible for the respectable performance of the industrial

[51] See, for example, Ahluwalia (2002) and Patnaik (1999) for these respective views. Advocates of more "liberalization" do not always clarify why they think what they think. Ahluwalia, for example, seems to suggest that further lowering of tariff barriers, further opening of the economy to direct foreign investment, and enhancing labor "flexibility" are the steps necessary to improve India's economic performance. Why he believes that these policies will do the trick is never made explicit; it is as if all sensible people must of course agree. An occasional reference is made to East Asia, with a suggestion that this is how East Asia did it. While my analysis too is influenced by East Asian successes, East Asia is a diverse place, and the fastest-growing states within that region, such as South Korea and Taiwan, during their peak-performing period were hardly models of open economies with "flexible" labor regimes. See Kohli (2004).

economy; I will return later to the issues of both why this growth has not been more impressive and the growth of the service sector.

Several related observations further support the point that the main dynamic underlying India's sustained industrial growth is not so much liberalization as it is the state's continuing pro-business orientation. First, contrary to what one might expect from further liberalization, the labor intensity of Indian industry decreased steadily during the 1990s.[52] Second, the unregistered sector of Indian industry – which one presumes to be more export-oriented and less capital-intensive – did not attract much new investment during the post-reform period.[53] Related to this, there is no clear evidence that exports of labor intensive goods grew sharply. Fourth, the level of concentration in private industry has increased since 1991: for example, the market capitalization of the top ten private companies increased from 2.2 percent of GDP in 1990 to 12.9 percent in 2004, and sales of the top ten companies during the same period grew from 2.3 to 9.3 percent of GDP.[54] And finally, the share of employment generated by the manufacturing sector has not kept pace with the rate of growth during the post-reform period.[55]

Leaving aside the issue of private industry, public investment in India as a proportion of total economic activity declined noticeably during the 1990s and beyond (Table 2.2, p. 109; Figure 1.2, p. 44). The underlying dynamics are not hard to understand. Given the fragmented nature of state power in India, public authorities find it hard to raise direct taxes – though some of this is now changing – in order to generate revenue. While direct taxes have gone up somewhat, a variety of tax concessions to the rich and the middle class have cut into the revenue pie, as has the decline of import duties. The service and agricultural sectors remain largely untaxed. The pressure on the expenditure side is merciless, especially the cost of

---

[52] See Chaudhuri (2002), p. 160.

[53] See Nagaraj (2003), p. 3711.

[54] These are my own calculations. Company data was taken from *Businessworld*, 22 August–6 September 1998 and 27 December 2004. The sales data for 2004 were collected from www.valuenotes.com. For one study that documents that further consolidation has been the main corporate response (along with growing use of foreign technology) to economic reforms, see Basant (2000). Another more recent paper that documents a similar trend is Mazumdar (2008). Yet another recent study, however, using a different data set, finds that the Herfindahl index of concentration has in recent years become more dispersed, especially if one includes the new entrants in the service sector. This study also finds that older business leaders continue to be leaders in the "post-liberalization" era; see Alfaro and Chari (2009).

[55] For an argument that this is a result of the skill-intensive nature of India's manufacturing growth, see Kochhar et al. (2006).

interest on the growing public debt and of providing for national defense. Faced with severe fiscal pressures in 1991, along with an IMF loan and the associated conditions, the Indian government sought to trim the deficit. While the successive governments have made some headway, they have been unable to control current expenditures. The budget deficit has thus been reduced mainly by cutting public investment, including investment in infrastructure. Among the various consequences, such vital inputs to industrial growth as the supply of electricity suffered during the period under discussion. Can anyone doubt that such state shrinkage is hurting India's economic growth? It is no wonder that various analysts, of a variety of persuasions, seem to agree that public investment in India needs to be stepped up.

The continued buoyancy of private investment and the decline of public investments constitute key elements of India's industrial growth "story" in the 1990s. An additional issue that deserves further attention is that the rate of productivity growth of the industrial economy during the post-reform did not improve over the 1980s. While the international opening of the economy has led to a fair amount of restructuring and consolidation of Indian industry, as well as to an increase in technology imports, somehow none of this is adding up to any sharp improvement in efficiency. Why? The answer of reform advocates seems to be that tariffs are still too high and that the labor regime remains rigid. While this may be the case, it is also possible that one should not expect too much from mere international opening, especially in a large economy with a relatively small role for international trade and investment. Moreover, the claim that trade opening will enhance economic efficiency may also have the causal sequence backward, at least for late-late-industrializers. If East Asian countries like South Korea are to be a model, note that state-supported improvements in industrial efficiency came first, and export success only later.[56]

In sum, while the Indian state indeed recommitted itself to private sector–led growth around 1980, India is no South Korea or Taiwan. The fact is that the Indian state has not done enough either to help improve the efficiency of the private industrial economy or to improve the life chances of its poor. First, India's dismal infrastructure continues to add to the cost of private industry. Second, while there is much talk of improving the labor situation, not only is the action limited, but the underlying model of change is poorly understood. Once again, if East Asia is to be the

[56] See Amsden (1989).

model, labor regimes in such rapidly growing countries as South Korea
have combined job security, training on the job, continuing skill improvements, and strict discipline, involving repression; such a "model" is thus
neither fully desirable nor likely to be replicated in India. Third, the state
has not done nearly enough to help improve the technological efficiency
of the Indian economy. Imports of foreign technology have helped somewhat. However, with declining R&D investment in the private sector,
and with the continuing cuts in the role of the public sector, the trend is
in almost the opposite direction. Fourth, the efforts to improve India's
human capital have been minimal. And lastly, both the incentives and
pressures on the private sector to boost exports have remained insufficient. This continuing inaction – some of it a result of political incapacity
and some due to a lack of imagination – may cumulatively help us understand why the productivity growth of India's industrial economy has not
improved during the post-reform period.

   If industrial growth during the post-reform period has been less than
spectacular, the main driver of overall growth has been the service sector. By now the service sector accounts for nearly half of India's GDP.
The category of "services" is something of a motley category insofar
as it includes such disparate economic activities as banking, public administration, hotels and restaurants, spending on education and health,
trade, communications, and business services. Data on services also
tends to be unreliable, posing problems for analysts.[57] Still, there is a
broad consensus in the scholarly literature, and official data supports
the claim, that India's service sector has led India's post-reform economic growth (see Table 2.1, p. 86).[58] Unfortunately, there is also a
consensus in the literature that much of this growth has not generated significant new employment opportunities. While scholars continue
to debate the causes of this jobless growth in services (as well as in
manufacturing, as noted earlier), it is likely that employment growth in
some subsectors is being neutralized by declining employment in other
subsectors.[59]

   While most services have grown at handsome rates, the truly impressive growth – double-digit per annum growth – has been concentrated
in only a few subsectors, especially business services, communications,
and banking. The most significant services – that is, significant in terms

---

[57] See, for example, Nagaraj (2009).
[58] See Gordon and Gupta (2004), Dasgupta and Singh (2005), and Banga (2008).
[59] See Banga (2008).

of their contribution to GDP – are trade (including wholesale and retail; nearly 14 percent of GDP), public services (including public administration, defense, education, and health; nearly 11 percent of GDP), banking (nearly 6 percent of GDP), and real estate (some 5 percent of GDP). Of these, only banking has grown at double-digit rates during the post-reform period. This is a result both of the growth of public banks in India, which have grown in tandem with the broader economy, and of relaxed new rules that have encouraged new private entrants, including foreign banks. The rapid expansion in services that has attracted most attention, of course, is the expansion in business services – mainly in the IT sector, including call centers, software design, and business process outsourcing – and in communications, mainly telecommunications, including cell phones. As I discuss these further, it is important to note that the much-publicized IT sector of India contributes less than 2 percent of India's GDP. While the growth of this sector is of great importance to India because of its balance-of-payment contribution via export earnings, the contribution it makes to the overall growth of GDP is limited. Nevertheless, the explosive growth rate of nearly 20 percent deserve some attention.

As India has emerged as a global leader in business services, many have wondered how India did it. The IT sector is relatively new in India, with its roots mainly in government-initiated programs begun in the 1970s. Unlike other major industries of India, there were no import-substitution-protected Indian giants in this area that would require a "calibrated" opening of the sector. The IT sector was thus never really regulated, and it globalized fairly rapidly. The links between Indians abroad with computer-related skills and similarly trained Indians in India helped the process of IT sector growth.[60] Unlike manufacturing, then, the case that economic growth in India is a product of liberalization and of new global links is stronger for some service sectors such as the IT sector. Even this claim, however, requires important qualifications.[61] First, the technically trained manpower that has fueled India's IT industry is a product of heavily state-subsidized technical institutions; these were established in an earlier era, when the ideology of statism and self-sufficiency prevailed. Second, the state has actively promoted the IT sector by providing a variety of supports, especially software technology parks, such as those outside Delhi (NOIDA) and in Bangalore. And third, the public funding

[60] See Ye (2007).
[61] I borrow these qualifications from D'Costa (2009). Also see Evans (1995).

of research, especially via defense industries, has fed the development of the private sector IT industry.

Finally, a brief discussion of India's poorly performing agricultural sector is in order. As was evident in Table 2.1, agricultural growth in India since 1991 has been relatively sluggish; production and income in the urban areas have grown some two to three times faster on a per annum basis than income in the agricultural sector. Sluggishness in agriculture not only is a drag on overall growth but also has serious distributional implications; the majority of India's working population continue to live in the countryside, but their incomes are growing at a much slower rate than those in the cities. While I will return to distributional issues later, it is important here to focus on the underlying causes of low rates of growth in the agricultural sector.[62]

Critics of India's "liberal" model of development have suggested that slow agricultural growth in India is part and parcel of India's global opening. The evidence to support this criticism is limited insofar as import penetration in agriculture has not been significant.[63] Much stronger evidence suggests instead that sluggishness in agriculture is associated with a decline in public investment in agriculture. It can be argued that this decline reflects the overall bias toward the private sector at the expense of the public sector that is part of post-1991 liberalization. While this argument is somewhat more persuasive, it is the case that public investment in agriculture started declining around 1980 and did not climb back to the 1980 level even toward the mid-2000s.[64] This decline in public investment is consistent with the suggestion that India adopted a pro–big business model of development around 1980. Relative neglect of agriculture, in turn, hurt agricultural growth via numerous links.

The most significant impact of low levels of public investment on agricultural production was probably mediated by the relatively slow expansion of agricultural areas under irrigation; important studies have documented the importance of irrigation for agricultural growth in India.[65] In addition, higher rates of public investment might have improved the quality of agricultural research and rural infrastructure. One analyst of Indian agriculture thus concludes: "deficiency in agricultural and rural infrastructure is the biggest problem for agricultural development. There

[62] For two good analyses on which I am drawing here, see Balakrishnan et al. (2008) and Dev (2009).
[63] See Balakrishnan et al. (2008), p. 17.
[64] Ibid., Table 6a, p. 22.
[65] See, for example, Vaidyanathan (2010).

is a need for massive increase in outlays (or public investments) for agricultural and rural infrastructure by simultaneously improving the delivery
system."[66] It is the case, then, that the attention of Indian leaders has been
focused on higher rates of growth, especially via promoting the industrial
and service sectors. The neglect of agriculture has contributed not only
to low rates of agricultural growth but also to negative distributional
outcomes, a set of issues to which I now turn.

Pro-urban policies, like elsewhere

III. THE STATE AND DISTRIBUTION

Pro-business growth in India has been accompanied by growing economic inequality. This inequality is manifest on several dimensions: across
regions; city versus the countryside; and across class lines, especially
within cities. I will now document this growing inequality and suggest
how government policies contribute to it. Among the important consequences of growing inequality is the fact that economic growth does not
alleviate poverty as rapidly as it might if inequality remained stable. Still, it
is the case that rapid economic growth in India over the last three decades
has helped reduce poverty. I document these trends, too, but qualify them
in two ways. First, assessing levels of poverty in India is a controversial
terrain, and much depends on how poverty is defined: depending on the
definition adopted, the number of poor in India can vary anywhere from
some 300 million to 500 million people. And second, beyond income
poverty, other indicators of well-being such as calories consumed, under-
nourishment among children, levels of illiteracy, and women's health
paint a depressing picture. While the size of the problem is truly daunting, the repeated failure of public policy formation and implementation
has also contributed to these outcomes.

Growing Inequality

Any discussion of the growing inequality in India must begin with the
caveat that some of these trends are par for the course. After all, even
with a relatively level field at the onset of rapid growth, inequality has
grown significantly in "communist" China. Capital and skills tend to be
scarce in economies like those of India and China, especially compared to
labor, and are likely to command higher rates of return in the process of
rapid economic growth. Moreover, some of the growth in inequality in

[66] See Dev (2009), p. 44.

TABLE 2.3. *Economic Growth in Rich, Medium-Income, and Poor States, 1991–2008*(all figures are average annual growth rate of net state domestic product)*

Rich States	Medium-Income States	Poor States
Gujarat 8.8	Andhra Pradesh 6.4	Assam 3.5
Haryana 7.5	Himachal Pradesh 6.9	Bihar 5.7
Maharashtra 6.7	Karnataka 7.4	Madhya Pradesh 4.8
Punjab 4.5	Kerala 6.7	Orissa 5.1
Tamil Nadu 6.6	West Bengal 7.2	Uttar Pradesh 4.3
	Rajasthan 5.8	
Average 6.8	Average 6.7	Average 4.7

* States are classified as rich, medium-income, or poor based on their per capita net domestic product for 1990–91.

Source: Author's estimates based on NSDP data from indiastat.com.

contemporary India does not have direct roots in pro-business patterns of public intervention; for example, wage hikes for public sector employees has accentuated rural-urban inequality. And yet it will become clear that a pro-business pattern of state intervention remains an important component of the "story" of growing inequality in India. It is also misleading to suggest, as some have, that growing inequality might not be a matter of concern;[67] growing inequality retards the pace of poverty alleviation and can be readily politicized, threatening democratic stability.

As already noted, economic inequality has widened along regional, rural-urban, and class lines. Let us take each in turn. Clear and strong evidence supports the claim that economic inequality across Indian states has grown during the recent period, especially since 1991. This inequality is evident in relative levels of income as well as in levels of consumption across states. Data for economic growth rates for major Indian states is provided in Table 2.3. These data are further classified into the growth rates of rich, medium-income, and poor states during the period 1991–2008. Several important trends are evident in Table 2.3 that are worth underlining.

The first thing to notice about the state-level income trends is the fact that India's rich and medium-income states grew at a much faster rate between 1991 and 2008 than India's poorer states. While the average rate of annual growth in the poorer states was 4.7 percent, the average for

[67] See, for example, Panagariya (2008), Chapter 8.

richer states was 6.8 percent. This compares to 5.5 and 5.0 percent average annual growth for the same set of poorer and richer states during the 1980s. The implication is clear: the richer states have grown faster than the poorer states, leading to widening income disparities. Since population growth rates tend to be higher in poorer states, the welfare implications of these growing disparities are even more serious. For example, in 1991 the per capita income of Bihar, India's poorest state, was about one-third that of Maharashtra, one of India's richest states; by the end of 2008, this differential had grown to one to four.[68]

The increase in inequality across Indian regions has been widely documented.[69] Economists use a variety of measures, such as "coefficient of variation" and "Gini coefficient," to assess relative inequality. One recent study thus concludes that the coefficient of variation across Indian states increased significantly between 1993–4 and 2004–5.[70] Another recent study, employing a variety of econometric techniques, concludes that "inequality in income levels between Indian states is rising over time."[71] These studies are based on national income accounts. Since such data is not without problems, it is worth noting that these patterns have also been confirmed by data based on surveys of Indian households. An important study thus confirms that consumption levels across Indian states have been growing more unequal.[72] Yet another study, based on a different data set, finds that levels of wealth across Indian states are growing more uneven, confirming the overall pattern of growing regional inequality.[73]

The issue of why some regions of India are growing faster than others is clearly a complex one. I have discussed this issue in some detail in an earlier study.[74] In that study I concluded that patterns of economic growth across Indian states seem to follow, not the free-market logic of capital moving to capital-scarce areas, but something more akin to a Matthew effect, namely, to him who hath shall be given. India's better-off states, I suggested, seem to attract most new investment and

<hr/>

[68] At the time of this writing in early 2010, there is evidence that the economic growth rate in Bihar has picked up. If this turns out to be an enduring trend, some of the arguments presented here will have to be rethought.
[69] Early statements include Ahluwalia (2000), Shetty (2003), and Bhattacharya and Sakthivel (2004).
[70] See Ramaswamy (2007), p. 55.
[71] See Nayyar (2008), p. 63.
[72] See Deaton and Dreze (2002).
[73] See Jayadev et al. (2007).
[74] See Kohli (2006b).

this, in turn, reflects the capacity of different state governments to create pro-growth conditions within their respective states. A more recent study confirms these trends: private investment in India flows disproportionately to the more affluent states; richer states also tend to have higher rates of public investment because of higher revenue and superior governmental capacity to collect such revenue; and intergovernmental transfers (grants from the national government to respective states) are not having a clear equalizing impact.[75] The main dynamic behind growing regional inequality thus seems to be differential growth rates across states and the main determinant of differential growth rates, in turn, appear to be the rate of private and public investment in these states. The states that are already better off seem to have an advantage in mobilizing both private and public investment, probably because of superior governmental capacity.

Initial conditions and the quality of state government thus appear to be the deeper determinants of why some states in India are growing more rapidly than others. With "liberalization," the related decentralization, and the reduced role of public investment in growth, conditions within each state have become even more salient for economic growth. It is important to reiterate, however, that varying initial conditions are themselves a product of past patterns of development, including the role of state governments and of state politics. I will return to some of these issues in greater detail in the next chapter. Suffice it to note for now that such important initial conditions as the quality of roads, the availability of electricity, levels of education, labor discipline, and law-and-order conditions – all factors that private investors take into account when deciding where to invest – can be traced back to the past developmental activities of state governments. The quality of state government is also important for mobilizing public resources within the state and for investing public resources – both from within the state and from the center – wisely. And finally, it matters greatly for private investors if state governments are pro-business or not; other things being equal, states that actively create pro-growth conditions and cater to business in a deliberate fashion are more likely to attract higher rates of economic growth.

The patterns of growth evident in Table 2.3 provide some support to these generalizations. The poor, slow-growing states of India tend to have such unfavorable initial conditions as poor infrastructure when compared

[75] See Nayyar (2008), pp. 64–65.

to India's better-off, rapidly growing states.[76] There can be little doubt that decades of misrule in states like U.P. and Bihar have contributed to these differential initial conditions. How does one judge quality of rule? While this is hard to assess accurately, the capacity to collect taxes is often a good indicator; on a per capita basis, then, India's richer states tend to collect much more in taxes, not only indicating the superior quality of governance, but also contributing to higher rates of growth via public investment.[77] Most specialists on Indian politics will also agree that states like Bihar or U.P. are governed rather poorly when compared to India's richer states. The fact that improvement in the quality of leadership in a state like Bihar may be responsible for rapid growth between 2005 and 2009 only adds support to the proposition that quality of governance helps economic growth.[78]

Finally, the content of governance matters for growth. The rapidly growing states not only are better governed but also tend to be pro-business and actively seek to create a favorable investment climate. I will discuss the case of Gujarat in the next chapter. For now, note that surveys of the investment climate across Indian states generally rate such states as Gujarat, Maharashtra, and Andhra Pradesh much higher than Bihar, U.P., or Orissa.[79] In sum, then, one may conclude that differing starting conditions, the quality of government, and the pro-business proclivity of state officials help explain differential growth rates across Indian states, and that these are some of the main factors responsible for growing regional disparities in India. In the past, India's more socialist government actively used public investment to moderate regional inequality. During the more recent period, by contrast, especially since 1991, state governments have become more important agents of growth promotion. In this new environment, state-level variables help explain the growing regional inequality.

India's federal structure is a work in progress. While accommodation of ethic identities within India is a huge political achievement, center-state

---

[76] For a ranking of India's states according to the quality of their infrastructure, see *India Today*, August 16, 2004, p. 20.

[77] During 2001–2, for example, the "per capita own tax revenue" of Maharashtra, Tamil Nadu, and Gujarat was 2,379, 2,251, and 2,089 Rupees, respectively, and of Rajasthan, Uttar Pradesh, and Bihar, 1,094, 777, and 303 Rupees, respectively. Data from online source, Indiastats.com.

[78] For example, a former senior government official of Bihar in a recent analysis attributes Bihar's growth acceleration "first and foremost" to "improved governance." See N. K. Singh, "Patna Unplugged," *Hindustan Times*, January 17, 2010.

[79] See, for example, World Bank (2004); and *India Today*, August 16, 2004, p. 21.

struggles in India have always involved economic issues. Whatever the
economic merits of past policies meant to minimize interstate inequality,
they have definitely contributed to the institutionalization of the Indian
federal structure. The political implications of growing regional inequality
have to be viewed against this background. Economic power in India is
increasingly shifting to the richer states of western and southern India. By
contrast, the power of numbers continues to be concentrated in India's
populous, poor states in the "heartland." It is impossible to predict how
these disparities will play out politically, but it would be hugely naïve to
believe that the political tolerance for such trends is infinite. Important
scholarly arguments suggest that a combination of economic deprivation
and identity politics can be politically explosive.[80] Recall that growing
regional inequality of this kind played an important role in the breakup of
Pakistan in 1971. In Nigeria, too, the power of numbers in the north and
the concentration of economic and other resources in the south has been a
continuing source of political instability.[81] With both logic and experience
pointing to the potential destabilizing role of regional inequality, these
new trends in India warrant concern.

Inequality across the rural-urban divide has also widened over the last
few decades. It was clear in Table 2.1 (p. 86) – and in the brief related
discussion above – that rural incomes have grown at about half the rate
of the overall national income in recent years. The determinants of these
differential growth rates, including the decline in the relative level of
public investment that is part of the new model of development, have
already been discussed. Since the majority of Indians continue to live in
the countryside, the slower rate of growth there is a major contributor to
the continuing high level of poverty, a subject to which I will return later.

Growing inequality across the rural-urban divide is manifest on several
dimensions. For example, levels of consumption in the cities are rapidly
outpacing those in the countryside. The government of India provides
survey results for what it calls "mean per capita expenditure" (or MPCE)
on basic consumption needs, including food. Based on this data, it is

---

[80] For example, an important argument explaining success of revolutions posits that the
roots are not so much economic deprivation alone as a combination of such deprivation
and nationalism, so that the "exploiters" can be identified as "them" or the "other." See
Johnson (1962). While I am not even coming close to suggesting that regional inequality
in India can create revolutionary conditions, I am proposing that a combination of
economic disparities and ethnic identity can be readily used as a source of political
mobilization.
[81] See, for example, Diamond (1988).

clear that in the early 1980s those living in the countryside tended to consume about two-thirds of what an average city dweller consumed. With growing inequality, by 2004–5 village dwellers were consuming just a little over half of what city residents consumed.[82] Data on wealth (as distinct from income and consumption) discussed earlier also confirms these trends: the net worth of rural households declined in proportion to the net worth of urban households between 1991 and 2002. However, the assets of rural households did not decline over the same period, suggesting that rural households have been acquiring debt at a faster pace than urban households.[83] The debt-related increase in farmer suicides, to be discussed later, is also consistent with this data.

What exactly will be the impact of such growing inequality across the rural-urban divide is again hard to predict. On the economic front, lower agricultural growth rates may lead to shortages of food and/or other commodities, leading to inflation, and to lower incomes in the countryside, leading to demand constraints on growth. If the cities continue to get rich more rapidly, this will inevitably hasten urbanization. The pattern of rapid growth in India so far has not been accompanied by a commensurate increase in employment. Migration to the cities, but without real jobs, will only exacerbate the problems of managing India's overcrowded and underserviced cities. As to politics, managing the politics of the city versus the countryside has so far not become a major challenge. In India the appeals of caste, religion, and regional identity tend to be more powerful, making it unlikely that a politics of "Bharat" versus "India" will precipitate. At the same time, however, the theme of poor villagers versus rich city slickers is seldom far from the political discourse in many states; various demagogues use some version of this appeal to propel themselves forward politically. Even the communists in West Bengal sustained their three decades of rule with their power base in the countryside.

Finally, it is important to note the growing inequality across class lines, especially in the cities. A variety of data have confirmed that urban inequality have grown since the early 1990s, though not rural inequalities. Since rapid growth has been mainly an urban phenomenon, these differential trends in the cities versus the countryside are not too surprising. Before delineating the dimensions of the growing class inequality in the cities, it is worth noting that inequality in the countryside, though

---

[82] The figures for the rural MPCE as a percentage of urban MPCE were 66 percent in 1983 and 56 percent in 2004–5. See Dev and Ravi (2007), p. 519.
[83] See Jayadev et al. (2007).

relatively stable, is fairly serious. About half of all rural households own
no or little land, and some 2 percent of households own more than a quarter of all the land. Nearly 80 percent of rural households own no land
or own less than a hectare (about 2.5 acres).[84] These landless households
and smallholders are generally tribals and members of lower castes who
suffer the double indignity of poverty and social marginality. If and when
growth in the agricultural sector picks up – say, via large-scale capitalist
agriculture engineered by the state and the corporate sector – these vast
majorities will likely remain excluded, picking up only the crumbs of the
growth process.[85]

A variety of data support the claim that class or class-type inequality
is widening in urban India. First, the Gini coefficient of expenditures on
consumption went up from 34.06 in 1983 to 37.51 in 2004–5.[86] Estimates of income based on tax return data show that the shares of the
top one percent, the top 0.1 percent, and the top 0.01 percent of earners
shrank substantially during the 1960s and 1970s, but then increased in
the subsequent decades, climbing back by 2000 to where they had started
in 1956.[87] To put this in a comparative perspective, India's richest top
1 percent commanded some 9 percent of total income in 2000; by comparison, the 1 percent in the United States commanded some 15 percent,
and in France some 8 percent. What is especially useful about the income
tax data is that they document the growing share of income of India's rich,
which is in turn consistent with the central thesis of this study, namely,
that since about 1980, India's political economy has become pro-business,
which helps explain the forces that are simultaneously generating higher
rates of economic growth and widening inequality.

Wealth inequality in India has also widened fairly sharply over the
last two decades.[88] Based on survey information about the net worth of
households, wealth data gives us a sense of the dimensions of the class
type of inequality in India, as well as of how it is widening. The first thing
worth noting is the magnitude of the wealth inequality: the top 10 percent

---

[84] The 2003–4 land ownership data is reported in Government of India (2009), Table 7,
    p. 22.
[85] Of course, large-scale capitalist agriculture is not the only route to higher rates of
    agricultural growth. Much depends on public policy. A more forward-looking state could
    increase public investment in such agricultural inputs as irrigation and create incentives
    that encourage employment in agricultural production, leading to shared growth.
[86] See Dev and Ravi (2007), Table 3, p. 510. Also see Himanshu (2007).
[87] See Banerjee and Piketty (2005).
[88] The information in this paragraph draws on Jayadev et al. (2007).

of individuals own over half of all of India's wealth, and the bottom
50 percent own less than 10 percent of the wealth; India's wealth Gini in
early 2000 was 0.66, compared to the United States at 0.78 and to 0.55 in
China. The second thing to note is that this inequality is widening rapidly.
Between 1991 and 2002, for example, the wealth Gini went up by two
percentage points, a significant jump. What this means more concisely
is that, if you were fortunate enough to be among India's wealthiest
5 percent in 1991, your wealth at the time was 758 percent of that of
a median individual; by 2002, your wealth when compared to that of a
median individual had grown to 814 percent.

India's new world of development has privileged those with access
to capital and skills. Higher rates of return on these scarce factors are
probably at the root of the growing inequality in urban India. Substantial
pay increments for public sector workers – which are motivated at least
in part by the desire to ensure some parity with private sector gains –
also contribute to the growing inequality. While workers in the organized sector remain part of a "labor aristocracy," wage shares have
declined, and, more important, jobs in the organized sector have not
grown in proportion to the growing economy.[89] This leaves a vast majority in the urban sector as members of the "informal economy," barely
managing on the margins of urban life. Such disparities, in turn, feed a
variety of social and political trends: activism and strikes; gangsterism
and crime; a growing nexus between crime and politics; gated communities for the rich; growing slums; and a variety of other forms of "urban
decay."

To sum up the discussion in this section, economic inequality in India
is widening along several dimensions: across regions; across the rural-
urban divide; and across class lines, especially in the cities. While some
of this inequality may well be an inevitable part of the growth process,
the role of public policy in creating a pro-business political economy, and
thus in generating this inequality, is also clear. Some of this inequality is
already having a political impact or is likely to in the near future. In a
mobilized democracy like the Indian one, it is quite naïve and irresponsible
to propagate the view that widening inequality ought not to be a matter
of concern. Not only can this inequality become a source of political
instability, but, as discussed in the previous chapter, growing economic

[89] The government of India defines the organized sector as factories that use power and
employ more than ten people or factories that do not use power but employ more than
twenty people.

inequality generates new patterns of social stratification and of power inequity that, in turn, are likely to become self-perpetuating.

Poverty and Human Development

It is well understood that inequality in the context of rapid economic growth may widen while the incidence of poverty is declining at the same time. The underlying dynamics are straightforward. Economic growth implies – by definition – rising income in a society. As long as the gains are not totally appropriated by the rich – which happens only rarely – all incomes rise with growth, leading to a decline in poverty. If the rich appropriate the lion's share of growth – which is often the case – the incomes of different strata rise at different rates, leading to growing inequality. This is basically what has been happening in India in recent decades: along with rapid growth and growing inequality, poverty has been declining. I document these trends here but also put them in a broader context of well-being, of which income poverty is only one component, albeit an important one. I also discuss the failure of public policy to accelerate the process of poverty alleviation and of creating a healthy, educated, and gainfully employed population.

The study of poverty in India is a vibrant and controversial field. The stakes are high: not only does the fate of a substantial segment of the Indian population depend on a correct assessment of what works and what does not, but the legitimacy of governments and of the economic policies they pursue also depend on emerging poverty trends. The government of India periodically establishes commissions to study the problem of how best to assess the extent of poverty in India; as we will see, since the identification of who is really poor has an element of arbitrariness to it, much depends on which views prevail.[90] As to poverty trends, no sooner does new data become available than scholars rush to analyze it and to publish their results, taking sides on whether the situation for the poor is improving, not improving, or most likely, not improving enough.[91]

The government of India has so far chosen to define poverty in terms of the income necessary for subsistence, especially to provide the nutrition

[90] For two recent such reports, see Government of India (2009a), popularly referred to as "the Saxena Report" and Government of India (2009b), popularly referred to as "the Tendulkar report."

[91] For one preview of scholarly debates, especially on more technical issues, see Deaton and Kozel (2005). For most recent essays that analyze the latest data available, see Dev and Ravi (2007) and Himanshu (2007). Many of these poverty debates are carried out in the pages of India's great and unusual magazine, *Economic and Political Weekly*.

necessary to survive, work, and reproduce the next generation. The official norm used to be that a daily caloric intake of some 2,400 calories was necessary to stay above poverty line in the villages and that 2,100 calories was needed in the cities (the logic being that agricultural work requires more physical labor). If a household's income allowed family members to consume more than the minimum number of calories, they would qualify as being above the poverty line; if not, they were below the poverty line (BPL). A public organization in India, the National Sample Survey (NSS), periodically surveys the Indian population in order to assess their consumption patterns, which in turn become the basis for calculating what percentage of the population lives below the poverty line. Unlike more advanced countries, where income data may be readily available, in a low-income economy like the Indian one, income data is imputed from levels of consumption. Since determining what was consumed depends on memory, and since prices vary – both over time and across states – there is room to debate the reliability of the data, which scholars and policy makers do, leading to numerous controversies.

Over time in India, the caloric norms have been weakened in estimating the official poverty line. At times this redefinition is for sound reasons, but at other times it is nearly arbitrary. There has been a growing dissatisfaction with India's official poverty line because scholars and policy makers believe that it minimizes the number of poor people in India. The two recent reports cited earlier, namely, the Saxena Report and the Tendulkar Report, have both suggested modifications, the former reasserting the need to measure poverty in relation to caloric intake and the latter arguing for a shift to a basket of consumption goods as more appropriate for measuring poverty. As distinct from these debates within India, the World Bank generates its own definition of poverty in order to facilitate cross-national comparisons, though these can be problematic. The World Bank has recently redefined its per capita poverty measurement upward, from an income of $1.00 per day to $1.25 per day. The World Bank also provides estimates for the size of the population living below a per capita income of $2.00 per day.[92] The United Nations Development Program has recently provided (in *Human Development Report*, 2010) yet another approach to the study of poverty by creating a Multi-Dimensional Poverty Index (MDPI), an index that includes income poverty but broadens it to include other indicators of well-being such as education and health. As we will see, estimates of how many poor people there are in India vary quite a bit depending on which definition of poverty one adopts.

[92] See, for example, Chen and Ravallion (2008).

Irrespective of whether one accepts the government of India's official definition of poverty or that of the World Bank, it is the case that the level of poverty in India has declined steadily during the high-growth era that began around 1980. Estimates based on the official definition suggest that the percentage of poor in India has declined from 45 percent in 1983 to some 29 percent in 2005.[93] If one adopts the World Bank's definition of poverty, per capita income of $1.25 per day, poverty in India has declined from some 60 percent in 1981 to 42 percent in 2005, and for income of $2.00 per day, from 87 percent in 1981 to 76 percent in 2005.[94]

While poverty in India is clearly declining, the rate of decline varies according to the definition of poverty one accepts, and, more important, estimates of the number of people living under conditions of poverty in India at present can vary enormously. Since $2.00 per capita income is probably too high a standard to set for a country like India – though by global standards, an income of $2.00 per day appears pretty low – current plausible estimates of the number of poor in India vary anywhere from about 29 percent (official estimate) to 42 percent (the World Bank's lower estimate). According to the United Nations' MDPI, some 55 percent of Indians live under conditions of poverty.[95] Arguing for assessing poverty in terms of a basket of consumption goods, the Tendulkar Report estimates that some 37 percent of Indians live in conditions of poverty. The Saxena Report, however, arguing for a definition of poverty based on caloric intake (say, a minimum intake of 2,100 calories), estimates that nearly 50 percent of Indians consume less food than this minimum and thus live under conditions of poverty. While these disagreements on definitions and related estimates cannot be settled in a study like the present one, two conclusions seem warranted: poverty in India has been declining steadily; but some one-third to one-half of India's population continues to live under conditions that must be judged unacceptable, irrespective of the definition of poverty one embraces.

While an understanding of trends based on the percentage of the population living in poverty is important, so is the absolute number of people living in poverty. Given India's relatively high rate of population growth, the absolute number of poor in India has hardly declined; if anything, their numbers may have increased. Even by the official definition of poverty,

[93] See Dev and Ravi (2007), Table 2.
[94] See Chen and Ravallion (2008), Tables 7 and 8.
[95] Reported in the *Times of India*, July 15, 2010. For details, see United Nations Development Program, *Human Development Report*, 2010.

the number of poor in India went from 324 million people in 1983 to 315 million in 2005, which is a negligible change.[96] By the World Bank's definition of poverty of $1.25 per day, the number of poor in India increased from some 420 million people in 1981 to 455 million people in 2005, which is again a fairly small change.[97] The fairest conclusion is probably that the absolute number of poor people in India has not declined. What is more important in normative terms is to focus on the numbers: they are staggering! Whether one accepts 315 million or 456 million people as the correct estimate, the number of poor people living in India exceeds the population of most countries in the world. (After China and India, the United States is the third-largest country at some 300 million people.)

Most of India's poor live in India's villages, where the majority of Indians live in any case, but where the population of poor people far exceeds that in the cities. Most of the rural poor tend to be village dwellers who own no land and who belong to lower castes or to one tribal group or another. The urban poor are generally part of the "informal economy," somehow surviving on the margins. India's poor are also concentrated in India's poorest states: for example, four states of India – namely, Bihar, Madhya Pradesh, Orissa, and Uttar Pradesh – accounted for nearly 60 percent of India's poor in 2005. The fact that the poor are concentrated in states with low economic growth rates and in the countryside – where, again, agricultural growth has lagged well behind the growth of industry and services – underlines the importance of growth for reducing poverty. If one keeps in mind the earlier discussion on growing disparities across regions and across the rural-urban divide, it ought to be clear that poverty would have declined faster had public policy helped to mitigate growing inequality. Moreover, careful econometric work has established that, beyond economic growth, a variety of direct interventions such as public expenditures, levels of human development, infrastructure, inequality of assets, and levels of inflation all significantly modify the impact of growth on poverty.[98]

A focus on contrasting developments across Indian states on the dimension of poverty reduction helps point to possible deeper political variables that may help us understand why poverty is declining more sharply in some regions than in others. What are discussed here are only some cross-regional trends that help shed light on the broader national picture; I will

[96] Dev and Ravi (2007), Table 2.
[97] Chen and Ravallion (2008), Table 7.
[98] See Nayyar (2005), p. 1638.

turn to some state–specific analyses in the next chapter. Over the years, the states in which poverty has come down the most include Kerala, West Bengal, and Tamil Nadu (see Figure 3.5, p. 152, in the next chapter). By contrast, poverty has declined the least in such states as Jammu and Kashmir, Madhya Pradesh, and Himachal Pradesh.[99] While rates of economic growth are a significant predictor of these trends, equally interesting is the fact that, for a unit of economic growth in various Indian states, poverty has come down much more rapidly in some states than in others. Thus, for example, one unit of growth in Kerala or West Bengal has been four times more "efficient" in reducing poverty (as indicated by what economists call the growth elasticity of poverty) than one unit of growth in, say, Bihar or Madhya Pradesh (see Figure 3.4, p. 151, in the next chapter).[100] More concretely, this means that it will take four times the growth rate of Kerala or West Bengal to reduce the same amount of poverty in Bihar or Madhya Pradesh. How does one best understand such different capacities to reduce poverty across Indian states?

The two states that have reduced poverty the most, West Bengal and Kerala, have long had experience with left-leaning governments. Three of the four southern states – Kerala, Andhra Pradesh, and Tamil Nadu – are among the states that have reduced poverty the most (Figure 3.5) and have a high capacity to reduce poverty (Figure 3.4). (While Karnataka does not do so well on these measures, it is important to note that the percentage of poor in Karnataka also remains below the Indian national average.) By contrast, all the Hindi-heartland states – Bihar, Uttar Pradesh, and Madhya Pradesh (also Rajasthan) – are among the bottom states, either on the dimension of capacity to reduce poverty or in terms of the actual decline in poverty or both. Leaving proximate determinants of such patterns aside (for example, irrigation infrastructure, growth of farm yields, access to credit), the deeper explanation of such a pattern probably lies in the nature of social and political power in these states and, related to that, in different policies whose results have accumulated over decades. Put as a general thesis, it may be suggested that poverty has been reduced the most in states where effective governmental power rests on a broad political base; in such cases, rulers have minimized the hold of the upper classes on the state, successfully organized the middle and lower strata into an effective power bloc, and then used this power to channel resources to the poor.

[99] See Besley et al. (2007). Also see Datt and Ravallion (1998).
[100] See Besley et al. (2007), Table 3.1.

This simple thesis can be used to explain the varying capacities to reduce poverty across Indian states. First, let us consider the cases of India's two left-leaning states, Kerala and West Bengal. Poverty in Kerala has been reduced sharply, and its human development indicators are far superior to that of the rest of India.[101] And all this has been accomplished while economic growth rates in Kerala have been close to the Indian average. Underlying these redistributive achievements are complex historical roots, including the political mobilization of lower castes and classes well before independence. This broadened political base then facilitated the rise to power of a well-organized communist party.[102] A more pro-poor regime interacted with a more efficacious citizenry, creating what some scholars have rightly called a virtuous cycle.[103] This created both a supply of and a demand for a variety of successful pro-poor public policies, including land reforms, higher levels of investment in and better implementation of education and health policies, and greater gender equality. The fact is that, when compared to other Indian states, cultivated land in Kerala is now distributed the most evenly, and the wages of landless laborers are the highest in India.

While the case of West Bengal is more mixed[104] and I will return to it in the next chapter, the main dynamics of poverty alleviation again seem to be that a well-organized regime with a broad political base has been relatively effective in pursuing tenancy reform, helping push up minimum wages (though only somewhat), and implementing some centrally sponsored antipoverty programs more effectively than other states. Land inequality in the countryside in West Bengal is also among the lowest in India, though the wages of agricultural laborers are only marginally above the Indian average. There is also some evidence that tenancy reforms – via enhanced security and bargaining power – have helped agricultural productivity, thus making growth in West Bengal more inclusive.[105]

If India's social-democratic states have effectively leveraged superior party organization and a broad political base to pursue modest redistributive reforms, how does one interpret the fact that all of India's southern states are above average in their poverty alleviation capacities? To begin

---

[101] See Dreze and Sen (2005), section 3.8.
[102] See, for example, Heller's chapter on Kerala in Sandbrook et al. (2007).
[103] Dreze and Sen (2005).
[104] See Kohli (1987) and Mallick (1994) for two contrasting views. Harriss (1999) and Dreze and Sen (2005), section 3.7, provide nuanced perspectives.
[105] See Banerjee (2002).

with, one should not exaggerate the sense that all southern states are similar. They include Kerala at one extreme and Karnataka and Andhra at the other, which at times do not fare much better than Uttar Pradesh on some dimensions of poverty alleviation. And yet it is the case that poverty in three of the four southern states has come down relatively rapidly, and the human development indicators of all of them are better than the Indian average.[106] Economic growth rates across the southern states, though above average, vary quite a bit. So what other characteristics, besides growth, do they share that distinguishes them from, say, the Hindi-heartland states and that might help explain their superior capacity to alleviate poverty?

India's southern states share two sets of distinguishing political traits, one well researched and the other much more in need of research. The well-established fact is that the narrow domination of Brahmins was more effectively challenged in all the southern states relatively early in the twentieth century.[107] Since independence, the political base of power in these states has generally been the middle castes and classes, and in some instances even the lower classes. This is quite distinct from the Hindi-heartland states, where Brahmanical domination has been challenged only relatively recently. The other fact is that the quality of the state-level bureaucracy in the South has generally been superior. While this "fact" needs to be documented by further scholarly research, over years of fieldwork I was repeatedly struck by a sharper sense of professionalism among state-level bureaucrats, especially in Tamil Nadu, more akin to the IAS than to prevailing practices in the Hindi heartland.

How might prolonged rule by a government with a broader political base and a more effective bureaucracy influence poverty alleviation? Leaving Kerala aside, land redistribution has not been very effective in the southern states. The main policy instruments of poverty alleviation have instead been somewhat different. Over the last several decades the southern states have invested more heavily in education and health than in the Hindi-heartland states.[108] Another study notes that, on the whole, the southern states have benefited more from subsidized public distribution

---

[106] See Dreze and Gazdar (1997), Table 1, p. 38. It is worth noting that on this dimension Andhra Pradesh tends to be an underperformer compared to the other south Indian states. For example, the illiteracy rates in 2004–5 in Kerala, Tamil Nadu, and Karnataka were 7.5, 22.6, and 29.5 percent, respectively; while the rate in Andhra Pradesh was 36.1 percent (the average for all other major states of India was 34.3 percent). For data, see National Family Health Survey (III), Chapter 2.

[107] See Frankel and Rao (1990).

[108] Singh (2010).

of wheat and rice;[109] populist leaders and a superior bureaucracy must get the credit. With a more effective bureaucracy, other poverty alleviation programs (such as a variety of employment-generation programs) have also been better implemented.

The contrast with the Hindi-heartland states of northern India is striking. Of course, these states have experienced low growth rates. However, the contrasts in the social and political structures are also notable. Well into the late twentieth century, the main mode of politics in these states was Congress Party rule that rested on a narrow political base of upper castes and classes. With patron-client ties as the key defining unit of the political society, factional bickering among the patrons was the core trait of state politics. This personalistic bickering detracted from any constructive use of state power in promoting either growth or distribution. With long traditions of *zamindari* or *taluqadari* rule (forms of indirect rule), the quality of state-level bureaucracy that these regions inherited was also generally low. Virulent patronage politics politicized the bureaucracy in the post-independence years, further diluting the state's developmental capacity. For some three to four decades following independence, then, a narrow political base, personalistic factionalism, and a less-than-professional state-level bureaucracy characterized state power in this region of India. Land reforms were also poorly implemented in the Hindi-heartland states. With upper-caste landowners wielding considerable power – both in the state and in the society – and with a readily corruptible bureaucracy, this failure was not surprising. A variety of other state interventions that might have helped the poor were also ineffective.

In recent decades, the political base of state power in all of these states has broadened, though the social power of upper-caste landowners remains significant. Over time, this broadening of state power may lead to some greater benefits for the poor, as has recently been evident in Rajasthan and Madhya Pradesh. Meanwhile, factional bickering and a politicized bureaucracy have nearly been institutionalized in the Hindi-heartland areas, leading to policy ineffectiveness. Decades of malign neglect and policy ineffectiveness have thus accumulated, creating the largest concentration of the poor within India.

So far the focus of the discussion has been mainly on income poverty. While adequate income is essential for well-being, a fuller understanding of well-being also requires that we pay attention to such other indicators as literacy, health, and education. The concept of "human development" introduced by the United Nations – a concept influenced by the writings

---

[109] See Harriss (2003), p. 225.

of A. K. Sen[110] – is one such broader indicator that combines income measures with literacy and life expectancy. The main point of the Human Development Index (HDI) is to underline the fact that income measures do not fully account for other components of well-being such as health and education. As in the case of income poverty, India's HDI has improved steadily, from 0.42 in 1980 to 0.61 in 2007. To put these figures in perspective, the HDI for Niger in 2007 was 0.34, the worst HDI score of all the countries in the world, and the figure for Norway was 0.971, the best HDI score in the world; the score for China in 2007 was 0.772, well above India's. Out of some 182 countries, with many African countries clustered toward the bottom of the HDI hierarchy, India ranked 134 – a fairly low rank for a country aspiring to be globally significant. What is also important to note is that India's HDI lags behind what its per capita income would predict, whereas – for the sake of a comparative perspective – China's HDI rank is better than its income rank.[111] What this suggests is that, as bad as India's poverty indicators are, some other indicators of well-being, such as caloric intake and indicators of the health of children, are even worse.

In spite of declining rates of poverty, the share of the Indian population that consumes less-than-adequate calories (2,400 in rural and 2,100 in urban India) has been going up. If some 65 percent of the population consumed less-than-adequate calories in 1983, by 2005 this figure was as high as 76 percent.[112] The situation is worse in the rural areas than in the cities. It is difficult to understand why declining poverty is not leading to a better-fed population. Possible interpretations are numerous: it may be – though this is not persuasive – that steady economic growth is reducing calorie requirements in India; or it may be that families are devoting larger shares of their growing incomes to other needs, such as the education of their children; or it may be that larger shares of growing incomes are being appropriated by adult male members of the family – buying a watch, a bicycle, better clothes, or consuming more alcohol – leaving women and children worse off. The evidence to support one or another of these interpretations is not readily available. What is clear is that the number of Indians who are consuming fewer calories than are considered adequate by nutritionists has been growing.

[110] Sen's "capability" approach to development is well known to scholars of developing countries. See, for example, Sen (1999).
[111] These figures on HDI in this paragraph are taken from online data provided by the United Nations Development Program in its *Human Development Report* (2009).
[112] See Deaton and Dreze (2009).

The health indicators for children and women are truly depressing. While the overall trend is again positive insofar as infant mortality and the proportion of underweight children are declining steadily, there is much room for concern, especially about the current levels, but also about trends. It appears that the rate of decline in infant mortality and in the population of underweight children slowed from 1990 onward.[113] While the reasons are again not obvious, the trends are consistent with the discussion here on average food consumption trends. The current numbers are staggering: most of India's children remain underweight and anemic, and nearly one-third of women suffer from a low body mass index. As two scholars of such trends conclude: "These are appalling figures, which place India among the most 'under nourished' countries in the world."[114]

Finally, we should take note of the literacy situation in India. On this dimension the trends are somewhat more positive. The last round of the National and Family Heath Survey (2005–6) provides the most recent and most reliable data; they conclude that "literacy has increased substantially over time."[115] Since the concept of "literacy" remains fuzzy, it is important to note that about one-third of Indians of all ages have no education at all (with literacy at nearly 66 percent) and that another 19 percent have less than a fifth-grade education; this suggests that nearly half the population has either no or minimal education.[116] The number of women without education has declined from 55 percent in 1992–3 to some 42 percent in 2005–6, and for men from 29 to 22 percent. While the trend is clearly moving India toward a more literate population, the survey also concludes that the rate of change is slow.[117] As to variations across India, the survey confirms what is well known: states like Kerala have the fewest uneducated women (10 percent) and states such as Bihar the most (60 percent).[118]

Looking to the future, the survey found that 72 percent of primary-school-age children attended primary school in 2005–6. This bodes well

---

[113] Deaton and Dreze (2002), p. 37. Also see Himanshu (2007), p. 505.

[114] See Deaton and Dreze (2009), p. 50.

[115] See Government of India (2007), "Summary of Findings," p. xxx. As this book goes to press, the results of the 2011 census have just come out and they, too, broadly support this conclusion.

[116] Ibid., Table 2.6, p. 28.

[117] Ibid.

[118] Ibid., Table 2.7, p. 30. For a useful discussion of the factors that might drive these trends, see Dreze and Sen (2005), Chapter 5. I will return to some related explanatory issues later.

for future literacy. However, this should be qualified by information that is also well known, namely, that the mere fact of being enrolled in a school tells us very little about what children are actually learning; problems of poor infrastructure, teacher absenteeism, poor motivation, and the low quality of education have been well documented.[119] It is not surprising that there is a sharp drop in enrollment between primary and secondary school. Only about half of secondary-school-age children attend secondary school. If these trends continue, it suggests that the present situation – nearly half of India's population has no or little education – is likely to continue, at least into the next generation. There are numerous reasons why children do not attend school at all or drop out. The survey results suggest that the main reason for not attending school was "not interested in education" followed by "it costs too much" and children are "required for outside work."[120] These survey results support earlier studies that have sought to debunk the notion that lack of parental interest in education is the main culprit behind the dismal state of primary education in India, arguing instead for stronger public action.[121]

The failure to provide adequate levels of health and education to India's poor is ultimately a colossal political failure. As in the case of income poverty, higher rates of economic growth are clearly helpful – as is clear from the earlier discussion, they are contributing to modest improvement – but, in the final analysis, such public goods need to be delivered by an effective state. The failure to do so is in part a failure of political will and in part a failure of political capacity to reach down into the society. Given a federal system, the failure is also in part a national failure, but for the rest, numerous ineffective state governments make the task doubly difficult. Moreover, unlike redistributive issues that direct attention mainly to class and power, the provision of public goods in India also seems to be influenced by the mindset of the country's rulers and by low administrative capacity. A variety of arguments have been put forward to explain the poor public goods provision in India; these include factors as diverse as callous rulers, caste iniquities, patterns of electoral competition, and historical inheritance.[122] Many of these explanations implicitly or explicitly focus on the issue of "political will," that is, on why rulers do or do not prioritize health and education as policy priorities. This is clearly an important issue to understand. As important in

---

[119] For a good overview and for numerous other references, see ibid., Chapter 5.
[120] Government of India (2007), p. 34.
[121] See Dreze and Sen (2005), Chapter 5.
[122] A good discussion of these rival explanations is available in Singh (2010).

contemporary India, however, is the issue of political capacity, especially the low administrative capacity to implement policies that might benefit the poor in terms of employment, income, health, and education.

Electoral pressures in a poor democracy like that of India repeatedly push political parties – whether in or out of power – to commit to "inclusive growth." This was discussed in the previous chapter. Rapid economic growth and, related to that, growing public revenue have enabled state elites in recent years to devote more resources to such policy areas as health, primary education, and employment generation via public works programs. A primary issue, then, is this: can these resources actually achieve what they are intended to achieve? Can the Indian state actually help improve health and educational opportunities and/or create better income opportunities for the poor via public works in India's vast rural hinterland? Chances are that without improving the quality of the lower-level bureaucracy in India, only a small proportion of these resources will actually reach their intended beneficiaries.

The example of the flagship program of the Indian government to help India's poor, the National Rural Employment Guarantee Act (NREGA), will help both to substantiate this last claim and to bring this discussion on the politics of poverty and human development to a conclusion. In 2005, India launched a program to provide 100 days of employment on demand via public works projects in rural India. Over time, this program has spread to nearly all of India. If well implemented, the program can generate additional income for the poor of nearly $2.00 per day for 100 days; as such, it has the potential to make a sharp dent into the worst of India's rural poverty. Unfortunately, the quality of implementation remains relatively poor. While the program has been generally well implemented in a few states, such as Rajasthan and Andhra Pradesh, implementation problems involve diversion of funds by local leaders and bureaucrats, poor-quality projects, opposition by land owners who fear upward pressure on local wages, and a sense of inefficacy among the intended beneficiaries.[123] Of these, the one area in which state elites can intervene directly is in improving the quality of local bureaucracy. Poor-quality local bureaucrats remain a major obstacle to implementing a variety of pro-poor schemes – not only NREGA, but also efforts to improve the delivery of health and education in India's villages.

---

[123] I noticed these problems in a field visit to villages in Uttar Pradesh (near Lucknow) in January 2009 and presented my findings to a seminar on NREGA organized by the government of India, Ministry of Rural Development, New Delhi, January 21–3, 2009. Two good analyses of NREGA are Dreze and Khera (2009) and Ghate (2009).

IV. CONCLUSION

In this chapter I have analyzed emerging economic trends in India, both growth and distributional, emphasizing their political and policy determinants. In the previous chapter I analyzed political changes in India, focusing on the emerging alliance between state elites and business groups as a key feature of the new Indian politics. The economic impact of this changing political context has been the subject of the present chapter. The argument is that the pro-growth and pro-business policies of the Indian state help to explain the growth acceleration that began in India in the early 1980s and has continued since. The pro-business pattern of state intervention also helps to explain the growing inequality in India along regional, rural-urban, and class lines. Growing inequality, in turn, has reduced the positive impact on bringing down poverty that growth might otherwise have had. While poverty in India is declining, much of this cannot be attributed to successful state intervention. Beyond short-term electoral considerations, India's pro-growth state is barely concerned about India's poor; this is most clearly manifest in a near-total neglect of the issue of improving the state's capacity to implement pro-poor policies. The results include poorly implemented policies in such areas as education, health, and employment creation, leading to a dismal human development record.

Not all the available evidence fits neatly into this argument; it never does. For example, first, the pro-business interventions of the Indian state are hardly of the East Asian variety, where governments chose economic winners and then channel resources and support to them. The pro-business role of the Indian state is instead more that of a facilitator than of a direct doer. And even as a facilitator, elements within the Indian state can still make the lives of businessmen quite difficult. Second, while the growth record in industry and agriculture can indeed be best explained with reference to a pro-business pattern of state intervention, the patterns in the service sector are more ambiguous; some service areas have grown precisely where the role of the Indian state has been more akin to that of a "night watchman" state. Third, some kinds of inequality, such as rural versus urban, have also been accentuated by public sector pay hikes, which are really not an aspect of pro-business policies. And finally, the failure to make a dent in India's poverty and poor human development record was as much a part of "socialist" India in the past as it is an aspect of "pro-business" India today.

In spite of such anomalies that detract from a coherent account, much of what is happening in the contemporary Indian political economy can be

explained in terms of the state-business alliance, which drives both policies that are pursued and policies that are neglected. Economic growth
in India started accelerating during the early 1980s, following the pro-
growth and pro-business shift initiated by Indira Gandhi. Ever since then,
changing governments have maintained this commitment. The results
include the fact that private investment has now become the main driver
of growth in India. Following the opening of the economy in 1991, and
especially in the new millennium, foreign private investors have also been
welcomed, and their role has grown. The relative decline of public investment has meant that sectors and regions that are most dependent on
such investment, such as the poorer states of the Indian heartland and
the agricultural sector, have been left behind. Notable outcomes include
the handsome growth of the industry and service sectors, a laggard agricultural sector, growing income inequality, and relatively slow gains for
those at the bottom of the social hierarchy.

The issues of persistent income poverty for large numbers and of the
inability to provide health and education to India's poor pose a formidable
challenge for the Indian state. To be fair, the problems are daunting
and predate the modern era; to restate a well-known adage, poverty has
always been there, it is wealth that really requires explanation. What also
requires explanation in modern India is why rapid economic growth is
not helping the poor more rapidly. What excuse can there be for India
to remain one of the most undernourished countries in the world? If not
an excuse, an explanation at least emerges when we focus on the fact
that economic growth in India has been highly elitist, propelled by a
democratic state that repeatedly promises inclusion but seldom delivers.
Among the reasons for this political failure is the fact that state elites are
focused more on growth and less on improving the state's capacity to
deliver jobs, income, and services to the poor. With nearly a third to a
half of the population living under conditions of poverty, illiteracy or low
levels of education, and poor health, including serious malnourishment
among children – India's next generation in the making – the state's
repeated failure to reach the poor ought to be a matter of great concern
and even outrage.

3

Regional Diversity

To Him Who Hath

The focus of the discussion so far has been mainly at the national level. In Chapter 1, I analyzed political changes since about 1980, emphasizing the tight nature of the state-business alliance that now governs India and the problems that this ruling alliance creates, especially the recurring problem of how to gain the support of the excluded masses in the democratic process. The focus in Chapter 2 was on the impact of the state-business alliance on patterns of economic growth and distribution; I suggested that policies pursued by India's pro-business rulers since the 1980s have generated both rapid economic growth and growing economic inequality, the latter especially during the post-1991 period, leading to only modest gains for those at the bottom of Indian society. While the issue of regional diversity has been touched upon all along, a national-level discussion masks enormous political and economic variation across Indian states. In what follows I introduce the reader to some of this variation, though only in a highly abbreviated fashion, focusing on the political and social determinants of economic outcomes.

India's federal system provides a fair amount of political and policy autonomy to its constituent states. For example, agriculture, land rights, law and order, education, and health are some of the important policy areas that are mainly under the control of state governments. Since the shift in the industrial policy regime in the early 1990s, state governments are also in a position to actively promote new industries in their respective states. Recall that the largest of India's states – say, Uttar Pradesh (U.P.) at nearly 200 million people, or Maharashtra and Bihar at nearly 100 million each – could easily be among the largest countries in the world. The populations of these and other Indian states are organized in

complex and diverse social structures that are products of varied historical pasts. Since many of their people speak different languages, regional
identities are often strong. Of course, none of this is to minimize the fact
that India is a relatively centralized political system in which the national
government not only controls taxation and finance, defense, and foreign
policy, but also sets the overall framework of politics and of economic
policies. The center and the states often jockey for influence. Any understanding of India's political economy would thus be incomplete without
some understanding of its regional diversity.[1]

The roots of India's regional diversities often originate in the distant
past, especially in how these regions have been governed and in the types
of economies that have developed within them. Authority structures and
socioeconomic forces have conditioned each other, often locking in long-
term patterns of change. In addition, other factors such as location –
say, coastal versus inland – and resource base have contributed to such
diversity. During the post-independence period, India's rulers used public
resources to minimize the developmental inequity that might arise from
such inherited regional differences. By contrast, over the last two to three
decades patterns of development across Indian states have come to vary
quite a bit. In what follows I seek to explain this developmental diversity
across Indian regions. The main analytical theme that continues in this
chapter is that varying political and authority structures across Indian
states, especially the underlying state and class/caste relations, are a key
determinant of regional developmental dynamics.

Three political tendencies compete for ascendency in India's states:
neo-patrimonial, social-democratic, and *developmental.* While most
Indian states exhibit all of these tendencies, some states during some periods have emerged more clearly as neo-patrimonial or social-democratic or
developmental, with discernible developmental consequences, especially
when these political tendencies persist over decades rather than years.
For example, where neo-patrimonial tendencies are ascendant and come
to dominate the state over a prolonged period, state-level governments
simply lack public purpose. Instead of using state authority and resources
to pursue the broader public good, ruling elites use their power either
for personal gain or to benefit a narrow political community that they
define as their "own." Repeated private appropriation of public goods in
these states has accumulated into poor economic performance, on both

---

[1] A good study of past diversity across Indian states is the two-volume collection Frankel
and Rao (1990).

the growth and distributional fronts. States such as U.P. and Bihar during recent decades typify India's neo-patrimonial states. Among other Indian states where social-democratic politics has emerged as a dominant tendency, the power of state-level rulers rests on mobilized lower castes and classes. The power of the rulers may be well organized (e.g., through parties) or may be more diffuse, as in the case of states with populist rulers. While both left-wing-parties and populist rulers can hurt economic growth, democratic pressure limits their follies. When institutionalized, social-democratic rule tends to be best suited to improve the conditions of the poor within India. Such states as Kerala and West Bengal, and also some of India's other southern states, typify these tendencies. Finally, a few of India's states have started moving toward becoming developmental states of sorts, in which the government works closely with business groups to promote economic growth. While these states generally do well on the dimension of economic growth, politics within them tends to be volatile, with exclusionary characteristics. Gujarat and Maharashtra typify this emerging tendency across Indian states.

After providing an overview of the regional diversity across India, I analyze why differing political tendencies have emerged across India's states and the developmental consequences of such variation in governing structures. I use the example of U.P. to discuss the ascendance of neo-patrimonial politics, West Bengal as an example of prolonged rule by a party that has prioritized redistributive outcomes, and Gujarat as a case in which a developmental coalition is currently at the helm. All along I also comment on a few other states that conform to or diverge from these patterns.

I. OVERVIEW

For a political economic analysis, one of the more significant dimensions of regional diversity across India is the varying standard of living across Indian states. It was noted earlier and is evident clearly in Figure 3.1 that per capita incomes across India's states vary enormously; for example, India's richest state, Haryana, is nearly four times wealthier than India's poorest state, Bihar.[2] India's poorer states also tend to be the larger states, with nearly one-third of all of India's population living in three of the poorest states – Bihar, U.P., and Madhya Pradesh (M.P.). It is also clear

---

[2] As a comparison, the difference in median household income between Mississippi and New Hampshire, the poorest and the richest U.S. states in 2009, was less than 1:2.

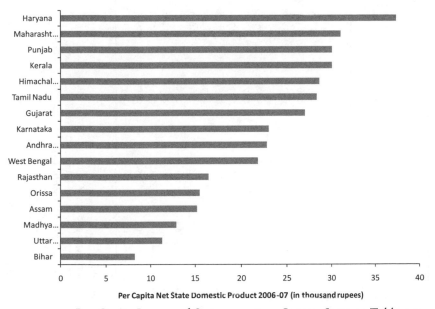

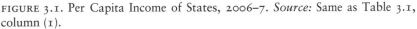

Per Capita Net State Domestic Product 2006-07 (in thousand rupees)

FIGURE 3.1. Per Capita Income of States, 2006–7. *Source:* Same as Table 3.1, column (1).

from Figure 3.2 that the percentage of poor tends to be higher in India's poor states than in the better-off states. This is not surprising because, other things being equal, higher average income suggests, by definition, that there will be fewer poor households. Other indicators of well-being such as literacy and a broader composite indicator, the HDI (discussed in Chapter 2), also covary with state incomes (see Table 3.1).[3] What should also be underlined about Figure 3.2, however, is that the relationship between income and poverty is far from perfect. Notice, for example, that a state like Maharashtra has a much higher percentage of poor than its income level would predict, and that states like Punjab and Himachal Pradesh have a much lower percentage of poor than their income levels might suggest.

A positive association between income and a variety of indicators of well-being – even if not perfect – can lead to a sanguine view that, as

[3] For those interested in statistical association, note that when HDI is regressed on per capita state product for India's major states (for 2000), the R-square is significant and is 0.77. Some of this is suspect because the literacy data, which is part of HDI, and which is generated by the Ministry of Education, tends to be inflated. However, even the better-quality literacy data that is reported in Table 1 (from National Family Health Survey – III) produces a significant R-square of 0.477, clearly suggesting a positive association.

TABLE 3.1. Selected Indicators of Major Indian States

State	(1) Per Capita Income 2006–7 (thousand Rs.)	(2) Average Growth Rate, 1980–2008 (%)	(3) Average Growth Rate, 1990–2008 (%)	(4) Population, 2011 (millions)	(5) Poverty Elasticity	(6) Poverty Head Count, 2004–5 (%)	(7) Human Development Index, 2000	(8) Illiteracy, 2005–6 (%)
Andhra Pradesh	22.8	5.8	6.4	84.7	−0.76	14.8	0.57	36.1
Assam	15.2	3.7	3.5	31.2	−0.38	20.5	0.53	23.1
Bihar	8.2	5.5	5.7	103.8	−0.3	41.5	0.45	47.8
Gujarat	27	7.7	8.8	60.4	−0.66	16.8	0.61	25.2
Haryana	37.3	7.2	7.5	25.4	−0.57	13.9	0.62	29.6
Himachal Pradesh	28.6	6.6	6.9	6.9		11.6		19.2
Karnataka	23	6.9	7.4	61.1	−0.53	27.1	0.61	29.5
Kerala	30	5.9	6.7	33.4	−1.23	14.5	0.72	7.5
Madhya Pradesh	12.9	4.9	4.8	72.6	−0.39	37.2	0.52	37.3
Maharashtra	31	6.4	6.7	112.4	−0.4	30	0.66	20.8
Orissa	15.5	5.4	5.1	41.9	−0.69	47.1	0.52	32.3
Punjab	30	4.7	4.5	27.7	−1.03	8.1	0.65	26.9
Rajasthan	16.5	6.3	5.8	68.6	−0.43	21.5	0.56	40.7
Tamil Nadu	28.3	6.5	6.6	72.1	−0.59	28.3	0.64	22.6
Uttar Pradesh	11.3	4.9	4.3	199.6	−0.64	33.3	0.49	37.6
West Bengal	21.8	6.5	7.2	91.3	−1.17	25.7	0.59	29.1
All-India average	22.6	6.2	6.1		−0.65	28.3	0.58	31.7

Sources:

Column (1): Per capita net state domestic product for 2006–7 in thousand rupees from indiastat.com.

Column (2): Author's estimates of average annual growth rate of state domestic product between 1980–2008 using data from indiastat.com.

Column (3): Author's estimates of average annual growth rate of state domestic product between 1990–2008 using data from indiastat.com.

Column (4): Population in millions from Census 2011, Provisional Population Tables (www.censusindia.gov.in); accessed on May 3, 2011.

Column (5): Elasticity of poverty calculated for the years 1960 to 1998 from Besley et al. (2007), Table 3.1.

Column (6): Poverty head count ratio (official poverty line) for 2004–5 from Dev and Ravi (2007), Tables 8, 18, 19.

Column (7): Human Development Index 2000 from indiastat.com.

Column (8): Percent of population age six and above with no education from International Institute for Population Sciences (2007), National Family Health Survey 2005–6, Table 2.7, p. 30 (http://www.nfhsindia.org).

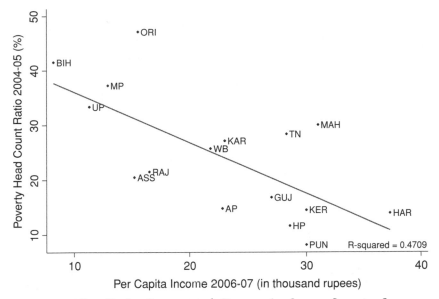

FIGURE 3.2. Per Capita Income and Poverty in States. *Sources:* Same as Table 3.1.

India's states get richer, well-being within them will continue to improve. While this is true to some extent, the impact that rising incomes will have on reducing poverty and on improving literacy in the near term ought not be exaggerated. First, to repeat a point made earlier, it is clear from Figure 3.3 that over the last two decades India's richer states have, on the whole, been growing at a faster rate than India's poorer states. While this does not deny the possibility that growing incomes in a state like Bihar will eventually help Bihar's poor, what it does underline is a point made in the last chapter, namely, that India's richer states are pulling even further ahead and that growing inequality will retard the poverty-reducing impact of growth. Second, there is no strong relationship between rates of economic growth and the decline in poverty across Indian states in recent years.[4] A third and even more telling qualification on the proposition relating income and well-being is evident in Figure 3.4: for

---

[4] The figures for the decline in poverty across Indian states are depicted graphically in Figure 3.5. When the decline in poverty was regressed against economic growth over more or less the same time period (1980–2008), the results were not significant (R-square was 0.0374). The results hold even when one controls for initial levels of poverty.

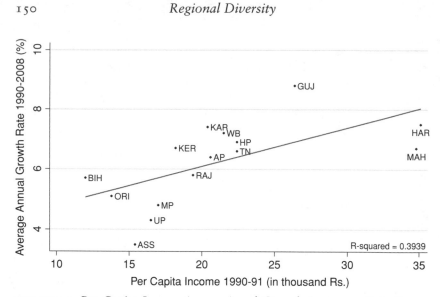

FIGURE 3.3. Per Capita Income (1990–1) and Growth (1990–2008) in States. *Sources:* Same as Table 3.1. Punjab is excluded here because it is a real outlier in terms of high per capita income and very low rates of growth during this period. If Punjab is included, the R-square is 0.1175.

a unit of economic growth, the capacity of Indian states to reduce poverty varies enormously. Notice, for example, that the capacity of Indian states like Kerala and West Bengal, with strong social-democratic politics, to reduce poverty is much greater than that of a variety of other states. I will return later to a fuller discussion of the underlying dynamics.

As far as economic diversity across India's states is concerned, then, the following patterns are worth reiterating. First, some of India's poorest states today – Bihar, Uttar Pradesh, and Madhya Pradesh – were India's poorest states two decades back and have grown at a relatively sluggish rate since (Figure 3.1); they also continue to have the highest percentage of poor across Indian states (Figure 3.2). Second, at the other end of the wealth and growth spectrum, India's richer states – Gujarat, Maharashtra, and Haryana – have grown most rapidly over the last two decades (Figure 3.3). And finally, as far as distributional issues are concerned, there is no doubt that levels of income influence poverty (Figure 3.2). What is equally interesting to reiterate is the fact that some states – for example, Kerala and West Bengal – have a higher capacity to reduce poverty than other states (Figures 3.4 and 3.5).

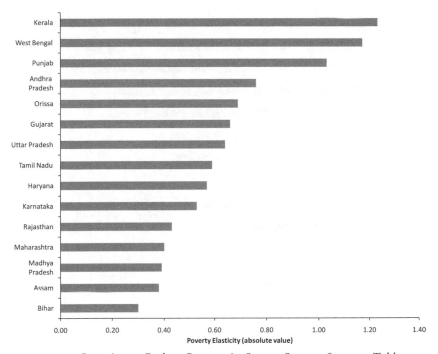

FIGURE 3.4. Capacity to Reduce Poverty in States. *Source:* Same as Table 3.1, column (5).

How can one best explain some of these broad regional patterns? What might be the underlying mechanisms that retard development in some states and generate wealth and prosperity in others? Similarly, why are some states more capable than others of reducing poverty? While the underlying causes are clearly complex, my suggestion in this chapter is that the nature of politics in India's states helps us understand some of the underlying dynamics. Of course, if political patterns fluctuate, the impact of politics and policies on economic development is not likely to be predictable. Instead, the suggestion here is that if discernible political tendencies emerge and persist, then their economic impact is likely to be significant. For example, states where neo-patrimonial political tendencies are dominant will tend to perpetuate underdevelopment; developmental coalitions, by contrast, will tend to reinforce inherited advantages in order to generate economic dynamism; and states in which social democratic political forces are ascendant, especially if these forces are broad and well organized, are capable of intervening to create pro-poor growth.

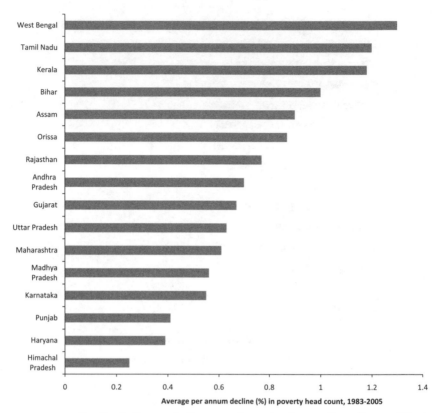

FIGURE 3.5. Decline in Poverty in States, 1983–2005. *Source:* From Dev and Ravi (2007), Tables 8, 18, and 19.

Bihar and Uttar Pradesh typify Indian states in which neo-patrimonial politics has dominated in the recent decades. Politics in these and few other Indian states, such as Madhya Pradesh and Orissa, tends to lack institutional moorings. Since forces that might provide cohesion (e.g., robust political parties, regional nationalism, and organized class politics) tend to be missing in these states, a variety of politicized social cleavages, often cleavages based on ascriptive identities, readily fragment the body politic. In such a setting, state-level politics seems to be characterized by some typical tendencies: the fragmented political arena is dominated by a single leader, surrounded by loyal minions; modal political relationships are vertical, of a patron-client type; the bureaucracy is politicized, based more on loyalty to the leader than on merit; symbolic appeals are used regularly to build diffuse political support; the zero-sum quality of politics makes those excluded from power feel totally excluded; and instead of carrying out any systematic public policy, leaders channel public resources for personalistic and narrow sectional gains. The core characteristic of neo-patrimonial states that differentiates them from other Indian states is that they lack public purpose. States with developmental or social-democratic politics at the forefront, by contrast, are motivated by some public purpose, albeit with differing definitions of who in the "public" counts the most: business groups for the more growth-oriented leaders, the lower and middle classes for social-democratic leaders.

When political authorities intervene heavily in the economy, as they do in all of India's states, it matters a great deal what motivates state action. The tragedy of the neo-patrimonial states of India is that public action is often not motivated by a concern for the public good, however defined. Public action is instead either motivated by the personal interests of ruling elites or aimed at building support networks via patronage politics. In order to understand why state action in these settings lacks public purpose, it helps to think about the political forces that are simply missing in these states. As I have argued in some detail elsewhere, nationalism, the emergence of political parties, and modern social classes are some of the more important agents that historically have transmitted a sense of public awareness to the politics of developing countries.[5] In India, anti-colonial nationalism and the emergence of the Congress Party were the historical catalysts for motivating the national-level state to undertake a variety of developmentally oriented interventions. Across Indian states, too, as will be noted later, the rise of business groups and the role of the communist parties and of regional nationalist movements have put limits on the personalistic abuse of state power.[6] In states with strong neo-patrimonial tendencies, unfortunately, such social or political forces that might promote more publically oriented interventions are either missing or have eroded. Instead, politics in these states has long been dominated by traditional landowning, upper-caste groups that have bequeathed to the state personalistic and patrimonial tendencies, a set of tendencies that now continue even as the social base of the ruling parties has evolved. Later I will discuss the case of Uttar Pradesh in order to trace the origins and persistence – at least in one case – of neo-patrimonial political traits.

---

[5] See Kohli (2004). While the argument is interspersed throughout this book, especially in the more historical chapters, for my discussion of the Indian case along these lines, see Chapter 6.

[6] In emphasizing the significance of regional nationalist movements, I have been influenced by Singh (2010).

When states with neo-patrimonial rulers intervene in the economy, they typically hurt economic performance, especially economic growth, as well as redistribution and poverty alleviation. It is not surprising that in Figures 3.2 and 3.3, Bihar, U.P., Madhya Pradesh, and Orissa are clustered at the bottom end of performance on both the growth and poverty-alleviation fronts. The underlying mechanisms are not hard to understand. On the growth front, given a highly personalized state, including the bureaucracy, public intervention seldom achieves its goals: infrastructure projects are poorly implemented; major public sector firms become patronage tools; and education and health are poorly delivered. All this not only hurts growth directly but also discourages private investment by creating a poor "investment climate." Private investors are further discouraged by the uncertainty and lack of predictability created by mercurial leaders with considerable discretionary power. The fact that India's central government has cut back on public investment especially hurts these states because of their inability to attract private investment. The poor in these states suffer not only because of sluggish economic growth, especially in the agricultural sector, but also because most of the resources aimed at poverty alleviation seldom reach the poor. These resources are instead captured by a variety of "big men" in long chains of patronage that provide some semblance of support to the leader, at least until a competing leader promises to support an alternative set of excluded "big men," who then help bring her or him to power. The cycle of corruption and waste then begins yet again.

It is important to note that these neo-patrimonial tendencies exist in nearly all of India's states. They happen to be dominant in the states currently under discussion. Even in these states, it is important to qualify the discussion by underlining the fact that historical inheritance is not deterministic. A new leader, such as Nitish Kumar in Bihar in recent years, can help break inherited patterns; how long such initiatives to break the vicious, self-reinforcing cycles of neo-patrimonial politics can be sustained, however, remains an open question. Moreover, even in the neo-patrimonial states of India, there remain pockets of success. And finally, the problems of India's neo-patrimonial states need to be kept in perspective; India is no Congo or even a Zimbabwe. India's neo-patrimonial states are part of a stable democratic-capitalist national structure. The economies of these states are growing, and their rates of poverty are coming down. The problem is that the absolute number of poor people in these states continues to grow, and numerous socioeconomic problems not only remain unsolved but are accumulating, making it more difficult to break out of the low-level trap these states are caught in.

As distinct from Indian states with strong neo-patrimonial tendencies, a handful of other states have actively sought to promote economic growth by encouraging private sector development. These states not only mirror the national-level trend in India toward prioritizing growth and supporting private capital but are also beginning to perform some of the functions that one associates with the developmental states of East Asia. Indian states with developmental leaders at the helm have a clearer public purpose, even though that purpose is defined fairly narrowly in terms of the promotion of economic growth. This commitment facilitates a ruling alliance with producer and business groups, whom the leaders consider best suited to be agents of growth promotion. Leadership priorities bequeath some sense of efficiency to the state-level bureaucracy, especially in those pockets within the state most relevant to growth promotion, such as the economic ministries. A variety of pro-business incentives are then put in place, including taming labor activism. The focus of growth-promoting interventions may vary, especially because of differing initial advantages: for example, governments in such states as Gujarat and Maharashtra have often promoted manufacturing; in Karnataka and Andhra Pradesh, service industries; and in Punjab and Haryana, agriculture and agriculture-related industries. The common political-economic theme that gives these states some coherence as a "type" is a political commitment to growth via support for the private sector.

It is relatively easy to notice that developmental tendencies are emerging in some of India's states but more difficult to explain why this is so. The first thing to note is that in none of these states is developmentalism the only tendency: periodic riots and killings of Muslims are very much a part of Gujarati politics; corruption and gangsters are common in the politics of Maharashtra; nearly feudal clan politics characterize Haryana's leaders; fragmentation and cronyism is rampant in the Punjab; and populism is never too far from the developmental commitments of leaders in such southern states as Andhra Pradesh. And yet, since political proclivities are a matter of degree, governments in these states do focus on growth more than those of other Indian states and tend to form partnerships with business groups in order to achieve this goal. As to why they do so, it helps to keep in mind the social and political conditions in these states when the era of high growth began. For a variety of complex historical reasons, entrepreneurial groups were already prominent in these states when the national government created the framework for private sector–led growth. States with already advanced private sectors were thus well suited to take advantage of the new "liberal" political economy.

As to why some states had already developed more robust private sectors prior to the "liberal" era, it may be useful to recall some well-known historical developments. For example, western India was of course where indigenous Indian capitalism took root in the nineteenth and the early twentieth centuries, especially in such industries as textiles. Cities like Bombay and Ahmadabad have long been centers of industry and commerce. That governments in Gujarat and Maharashtra were well attuned to private sector needs, and best suited to take advantage of policy shifts over the last few decades, is then understandable. Other states like Punjab and Haryana did not have any industrial advantage but did have a vibrant capitalist agriculture. Because of such historical advantages as a good irrigation system – created by the British in the nineteenth century in order to settle former Punjabi soldiers – which was subsequently reinforced by the state-supported green revolution in the 1960s, political elite in these states were often closely tied to an entrepreneurial strata, albeit a strata composed of numerous smaller agrarian entrepreneurs. The initial advantages of some of the southern states were not so much the early development of capitalism, but rather other advantages: higher rates of literacy; better-quality state level bureaucracies inherited from the more direct colonial rule practiced by the British in these parts of India; and, related to both of these factors, the early political mobilization of middle and lower strata that, at a minimum, weakened the traditional, landowning patrimonial elites. In sum, states in which developmental tendencies are now emerging had early "modernizing" advantages, mainly in the direction of earlier development of a private sector, or at least an earlier weakening of "antimodernizing" forces.

It is not surprising that, at the onset of India's "liberalization," such developmental states as Gujarat, Haryana, and Maharashtra were already India's wealthiest states and have since grown most rapidly (Figure 3.3). Inherited advantages, of course, do not guarantee future success; for example, with its fragmented, contentious, and corrupt state apparatus, Punjab may well lose some of its initial advantage of a vibrant capitalist agriculture. Leaders in most states with robust private sectors, however, are attempting to consolidate developmental coalitions so as to take advantage of India's economic decentralization. Managing these narrow coalitions is not easy in the face of electoral pressures. Nevertheless, high rates of growth provide some legitimacy. A variety of other political experiments – some of which were previewed in the context of national politics in Chapter 1 – are also under way at the state level to manage pro-business ruling coalitions. Later I will examine the case of Gujarat in order to investigate some related issues that arise in at least one case.

Leaders in India's better-off states are combining inherited advantages with deliberate strategies to promote rapid growth. Among the inherited advantages are better infrastructure, a more literate workforce, more buying power among the population, and of course a more robust private sector. As state elites forge growth-oriented coalitions with private sector elites, it is typical for pro-business policies to emerge. These include eliminating bureaucratic obstacles to investment, provision of a variety of subsidies – especially cheap land, tax holidays, and reliable access to electricity – and favorable labor laws. More important than specific policy priorities is the general sense that a state welcomes business and that state elites are ready to help overcome any and all bottlenecks faced by private producers. The results have included higher levels of private investment – both national and foreign – moving into these states. Ironically, rapid growth has enabled even state revenue to grow more rapidly in these states, leading to higher levels of public investment as well. Over time, rising wages, a scarcity of land, and the difficulties of maintaining narrow growth-oriented coalitions in a poor democracy may become significant obstacles to the developmental ambitions of political rulers; for now, however, the richer states of India are getting even richer with the help of activist states.

Finally, one should take note of social-democratic tendencies in some of India's states. Since some related issues have already been discussed in the previous chapter in the context of a discussion of the differential capacity of Indian states to reduce poverty, the present discussion can be relatively brief. The main point worth reiterating is that power is distributed somewhat more equally in states with strong social-democratic politics than in states where neo-patrimonial or developmental tendencies dominate. Whereas narrow coalitions of political and economic elites are attempting to consolidate power in some states, and power hierarchies are managed by personalistic leaders via patronage chains in yet other states, mobilized lower-middle and lower strata play significant political roles in states with strong social-democratic tendencies. Where this power of the lower classes and castes is well organized via political parties, such ruling parties are in a position to implement modest redistribution, adding an egalitarian bias to the growth process. As already noted, West Bengal and Kerala are two such cases in India. In these states poverty has come down rapidly since the early 1980s (Figure 3.5); rates of economic growth over the same period are close to the high Indian average (Table 3.1, column 2); illiteracy is either close to the Indian average (West Bengal) or, as in Kerala, well below what income levels might predict (Table 3.1, column 8); and rural land inequality is the lowest in India.[7] While the record is far from perfect – for example, Kerala has a high level of consumption inequality produced by overseas remittances; the CPM in West Bengal has not done nearly enough to improve the health and education of poor Bengalis; the level of poverty in West Bengal remains close to the high Indian average; and economic growth in these states rests on a fragile base – these states still come closest to implementing a deliberate strategy of inclusive growth.

There are other states in India where the middle and lower-middle castes and classes – though only to a lesser extent the real lower strata – have also been politically significant for quite some time but where this mass power is not well organized. Tamil Nadu is a clear example of this kind, though other South Indian states like Andhra Pradesh and Karnataka also exhibit similar characteristics insofar as Brahmanical domination in them was successfully challenged rather early on, truncating the power pyramid. Without strong parties, however, mass politics in these states has typically given rise to populist leaders who have mobilized support, not along class lines, but through regional nationalism. While such leaders are just as capable as neo-patrimonial leaders in a state like Uttar Pradesh of wrecking their state economies, as already discussed, several factors limit their destructive tendencies: mass pressure from a mobilized electorate, better-quality state bureaucracy, and the political weakness of feudal-like *zamindars*. The result is that politics in these states tends to be infused with a sense of public awareness, at least more so than in states like U.P. and Bihar, and the content of this public awareness is often antielitist.

While the "welfare" achievements of these southern states are decidedly mixed, they all tend to do better than India's neo-patrimonial states. They have all made some notable advances: Karnataka, Andhra Pradesh, and Tamil Nadu are all middling performers in terms of rates of economic growth (Table 3.1, column 2); poverty has come down rapidly since the early 1980s in Tamil Nadu (Figure 3.5), and illiteracy is well below the Indian average (Table 3.1, column 8); Andhra Pradesh has both a high capacity to reduce poverty (Figure 3.4) and very low levels of poverty,

---

[7] I measured the land inequality of Indian states as a ratio of the amounts of land operated by large and marginal farmers in 1995–6; this data is readily available online at Indiastats.com.

nearly equal to Kerala's (Table 3.1, column 6); and Karnataka performs a little better than the Indian average on levels of both poverty and literacy (though this level of performance would be well predicted by both per capita income and rates of growth).

The roots of the early emergence of antielitist mass politics in some of Indian states with strong social-democratic politics are clearly complex. I will later use the example of West Bengal to provide some case-specific analysis. What all of these social-democratic cases seem to share are weaker structures of caste domination, certainly weaker than in the Hindi heartland, where such domination is only now being challenged. A number of historical factors help to explain why caste domination in these states was challenged rather early: some of these states were already on the periphery of the core areas of Brahmanical domination in India; Brahmins were a small minority in many of these states; and forces such as the influence of missionaries, coastal metropolitanism, early urbanization, and religious revival movements battered caste hierarchies. Weaker caste hierarchies, in turn, did not provide as fertile a soil for the patron–client type of politics that flourished in U.P. and Bihar; instead, politics based on horizontal association – nationalistic or communist – came to the fore. Whether and why such mass politics came to be well organized is another historical puzzle to which I will return later, but only in the specific case of West Bengal. To sum up this discussion for now, the early emergence of mass politics, which is of course the flip side of weaker structures of caste domination, has bequeathed social-democratic tendencies to some of India's states. These tendencies are strongest where class politics emerged and became well organized via political parties; even without a coherent political outlet, however, mass politics has over time made some visible welfare contributions.

The impact of mass politics on patterns of development operates through different mechanisms when such politics is well organized as opposed to when such politics is expressed mainly through populism. When state governments have been ruled by well-organized parties, as in West Bengal and Kerala, state elites have succeeded in insulating the state machinery from direct capture by landowning and other societal elites. The ruling elites have, in turn, used this power to alter land rights, implement land redistribution legislation, and help raise the wages of workers. Such interventions have made the growth process more inclusive. Populist leaders, by contrast, have seldom succeeded in redistributing assets or in altering the growth pattern; the power of populist rulers is too diffuse to permit such state interventions. To the extent that populist rulers in states like Tamil Nadu have succeeded in deliberate pro-poor interventions, it is either through encouraging equality of opportunity, say, by promoting basic education, or via well-implemented, targeted pro-poor programs that do not challenge the basic power hierarchies of society.

To sum up, the regional diversity across India is at least as significant as that encompassed, say, within the European Union. The clearest manifestations of this diversity is divergent standards of living. While some indicators of well-being covary with income, quite a few do not, making for a complex mosaic. I have sought to give some order to this complexity by imposing a typology of the political tendencies that tend to dominate Indian states and that, in turn, produce these different economic outcomes. Like all typologies, this one overgeneralizes at times and undergeneralizes at other times. Still, I hope that categorizing the dominant political tendencies across Indian states as more neo-patrimonial, developmental, or social-democratic provides, first, a manageable intellectual map for situating differing political economies of Indian states and, second, the possibility of discussing in greater detail the causes and consequences of differing state-market links that emerge when one type of politics emerges and persists rather than another.

II. NEO-PATRIMONIALISM IN INDIA: UTTAR PRADESH

I use the example of Uttar Pradesh in this section to deepen our understanding of a set of Indian states in which neo-patrimonial politics has emerged dominant. Unfortunately, given constraints of scope and space, this effort to deepen the analysis will not be deep enough. As India's largest state, Uttar Pradesh is a complex regional polity with considerable internal diversity; those wanting more details should consult one or more of the sources cited later. For purposes of this study, Uttar Pradesh serves as an example of one of India's worst developmental performers. It is clear from Table 3.2 that when juxtaposed with the all-India record or the record of four southern Indian states, Uttar Pradesh lags behind on all development indicators that might be considered consequential, including growth and poverty. The economic performance of Uttar Pradesh has been especially lagging since 1990. The suggestion presented here is that this poor performance is in part a function of the manner in which economic decentralization since 1991 has left India's poor states to fend for themselves,and in part a result of the poor quality of governance that makes it difficult for a state like Uttar Pradesh to fend for itself. Since national-level issues of liberalization and decentralization have already

TABLE 3.2. *Some Developmental Indicators of Uttar Pradesh in a Comparative Perspective*

	Uttar Pradesh	South India[a]	All India
Per capita income, 2006–7 (in rupees)	11,334	26,038	22,580
Economic growth, 1980–2008 (average annual %)	4.9	6.3	6.2
Economic growth, 1990–2008 (average annual %)	4.3	6.8	6.1
Poverty head count, 2004–5 (official poverty line) (%)	33.3	21.2	28.3
Decline in Poverty,[b] 1983–2005 (%)	0.6	0.9	0.8
Illiteracy,[c] 2005–6	37.6	23.9	31.7
Human Development Index, 2000	0.49	0.63	0.58

[a] I borrowed the idea of comparing Uttar Pradesh to South Indian states from Dreze and Gazdar (1997). The four South Indian states are Andhra Pradesh, Karnataka, Kerala, and Tamil Nadu.

[b] Average per annum percentage decline in head count ratio between 1983 and 2005 from Dev and Ravi (2007), Tables 8, 18, and 19.

[c] Illiteracy is defined as the percentage of the population above the age of six with no schooling.

Sources: Same as in Table 3.1.

been discussed, I emphasize here a personalistic and corrupt state-level politics that lacks public purpose as a significant contributor to the poor development performance of Uttar Pradesh.

Background

In colonial India, Uttar Pradesh was called United Provinces, a large administrative unit that the British slowly created over the nineteenth century from fairly diverse subregions.[8] Mostly in the Gangetic plains, eastern Uttar Pradesh was fertile and heavily populated. The British settled lands in central and eastern Uttar Pradesh, turning de facto Thakur and Brahmin landowners of the Mughal era into de jure *zamindars* and *taluqadars*, that is, mega upper-caste landowners who were to become allies of the British, squeezing the peasantry for rents and sharing them with the British in exchange for legal protection. While substantial landowners were plentiful in western Uttar Pradesh too, this

[8] In this section, I am drawing on Hasan (1990), Srivastava (1976), Brass (1965), and Kudaisya (2007).

part of the state also had many owner-cultivators. Proximity to Delhi reduced the need for intermediaries, and relative labor scarcity inclined even the "clean castes" of the area to take up agriculture. Along with a variety of cultivating castes, such as the Jats, agriculture in western Uttar Pradesh from fairly early on had a more commercial cast. Efforts to annex parts of central Uttar Pradesh – especially the subregion of Awadh – led to a major riot by the local aristocracy in 1857, following which the British demilitarized the nobility of Uttar Pradesh further but also gave them greater control over their respective domains, not only providing an enhanced share of revenues but also preserving domination over traditional hierarchical social relations.

The post-1857 *Pax Britannia* in Uttar Pradesh led to political stability and economic stagnation. In this, of course, Uttar Pradesh was not alone; as noted earlier, this was the pattern in much of India. Where Uttar Pradesh was distinct was in the character of the underlying social structure, a set of traits that would prove to be of long-term consequence. While upper castes have dominated Hindu society for a very long time, this domination in Uttar Pradesh – as in Bihar – was nearly complete, a situation due at least in part to the numerical significance of the "clean castes." Whereas Brahmins in a southern Indian state like Tamil Nadu constituted some 3 to 4 percent of the regional population, in Uttar Pradesh they were 9 to 10 percent of the population.[9] Along with some other upper castes such as Thakurs, the "clean castes" comprised nearly 20 percent of the state's population. In eastern Uttar Pradesh, Thakurs and Brahmins also owned nearly 60 percent of all the land. Many of these members of the "clean castes" were the *zamindars* and *taluqadars* mentioned earlier, who also enjoyed perks of power due to both local custom and proximity to the colonial state. Numerical significance, then, combined with economic, political, and status superiority gave Brahmins, Thakurs, and other "clean castes" near hegemonic control over local society.

A variety of middle and backward castes constitute more than 40 percent of the local population in Uttar Pradesh, and the scheduled castes another 20 percent. While some of the middle and backward castes were family farmers, most were deeply entrenched in a hierarchical social structure of economic dependence – via a variety of forms of tenancy – and status inferiority. Also notable is the fact that nearly 15 percent of the

---

[9] These and the following figures are from the 1931 census and taken from Hasan (1990), p. 154.

regional population was Muslim. Some Muslims were landowners, but most were not. During the Mughal period Muslims had enjoyed a sense of superiority in local society, which declined during the colonial period, leading to simmering dissatisfaction; this too would prove to be of long-term significance.

It would be difficult to make the case that Uttar Pradesh was an especially backward region during the colonial period. Of course, the economy consisted mainly of low-productivity agriculture, but that was true of much of India. As a landlocked region, Uttar Pradesh did not enjoy any of the commercial development of such port cities as Bombay, Calcutta, and Madras. Nevertheless, agriculture in western Uttar Pradesh was already commercialized by the late colonial period; small handicraft industry flourished in urban centers; some textile and sugar industry was interspersed throughout the state; and reputable institutions of higher learning existed in such cities as Lucknow, Allahabad, and Banaras. At the time of independence, then, the level of development in Uttar Pradesh, especially as manifest in per capita income, was close to the Indian average or even a little higher.[10]

As is well known, Uttar Pradesh has been central to India's political life for much of the twentieth century. The Nehru-Gandhi family has its political base in Uttar Pradesh. Numerous prime ministers of India have also come from Uttar Pradesh. Even before the rise of the anti-colonial Congress movement in the 1920s, this north central region of India was hardly acquiescent: the 1857 revolt against the British was centered in Uttar Pradesh; and in the early part of the twentieth century, a variety of peasant demands for lowering taxation and securing tenant rights were organized by the Kisan Sabha. Gandhi and other Congress leaders sought to incorporate these demands into a broader nationalist movement. While the Congress was quite successful at this mobilization, Gandhi co-opted and/or marginalized the more radical elements of the local political movements.[11] Congress's proximity to pro-Hindu groups and simmering local resentment of Muslims also combined to encourage the emergence of the Muslim League as a rival to the Congress, a movement that would eventually be decisive in the creation of Pakistan.

To simplify complex political developments, the Congress in U.P. built a strong nationalist movement during the 1930s and 1940s. The emerging

---

[10] See Singh (2007), p. 274.
[11] See Pandey (1978).

educated groups in urban centers provided the political base for nationalists. In the countryside, however, where most of the people lived, Congress sought to differentiate mega landowners, who were allies of the colonial states and were to be treated as enemies, from a variety of other substantial landowning groups, who were potential allies in the nationalist cause. While this political strategy eventually led to Congress's demand to abolish all *zamindaris* – and thus to the Zamindari Abolition act of 1952 – such demands were periodically softened and seldom pursued with any vigor. While the largest *zamindaris* in U.P. were indeed abolished following independence, property-owning members of higher castes – whether former *zamindars* with reduced properties, or other landowners who benefitted from the abolition of *zamindaris* – entered the Congress Party in a big way. Following independence, then, the Congress in U.P. very quickly became a party dominated by landowning Brahmins and Thakurs who, in turn, were able to mobilize the support of their dependants, especially the landless poor and the scheduled castes, for the Congress.

At the time of independence, it would have been difficult to predict that U.P. was destined to become one of India's most backward states. As already mentioned, the regional per capita income was roughly equal to that of the rest of the country. On the political front, U.P. was described as "one of the best governed states" of India.[12] Many politicians from the state played important roles in national politics, including Nehru, who fairly quickly emerged as India's undisputed leader. With this as the starting point, it would be much easier to understand had U.P. performed well on a variety of developmental fronts. Unfortunately, that is not what happened. By 1967–8, the per capita income of U.P. was already some 20 percent below the national average. Between then and 1990–1, the economic performance of U.P. continued to lag, but not by a great amount: as late as 1990–1, per capita income in U.P. was only 25 percent below the Indian average. Since 1990–1, however, the gap between U.P. and other states has grown rapidly. For example, the per capita income of U.P. by 2006–7 was 50 percent below the Indian average. This suggests that, whereas it took forty years following independence for the per capita income of U.P. to fall some 25 percent behind the Indian average, since 1990, U.P. has fallen another 25 percent behind in only twenty years; that is, the gap is now growing twice as fast. What requires explanation, then, are both the factors that retarded the developmental performance of U.P. during the first forty years and, even more important, especially for this

[12] Pai (2007), p. xvi.

study, the factors that explain the recent incapacity to take advantage of a new political and economic environment.

The Era of Congress Dominance

Well before the national economic policy shifts of the 1980s and 1990s, U.P. had already started lagging behind the rest of India: agriculture growth remained sluggish during the era of Congress dominance and new industry did not take root. Moreover, a variety of redistribution programs, such as land reforms, were poorly implemented. The results included slow rates of economic growth and high rates of poverty. The proximate causes of this poor economic performance are easy to list: relatively low levels of public investment; poor infrastructure; inability to attract private investors; a variety of inefficiencies related to land tenure and to poor quality of human development; and a dysfunctional lower-level bureaucracy.[13] To get a fuller sense of the root causes, however, one needs to understand the political and social context within which economic processes unfolded.

For nearly four decades following independence, U.P. was ruled by the Congress Party. While this rule was challenged periodically, the challenges succeeded only intermittently, at least until the late 1980s. Since then, the Congress in U.P. has been reduced to a minor political player, a set of developments to be analyzed later. During the era of Congress dominance, Congress in U.P. ruled the state while closely allied with the upper castes, especially the Brahmins and Thakurs. The historical antecedents of this pattern have already been noted. Following independence, Congress was of course India's nationalist party and thus enjoyed broad-based support. In U.P. this support was solidified by channeling the fruits of power to Brahmin and Thakur elites, who, in turn, used their influence to mobilize their dependents to vote for Congress. By far the largest number of officeholders under Congress rule during the 1950s and 1960s were Brahmins or Thakurs.[14] While competing elites jockeyed for power, creating factional conflicts, long chains of patronage, grafted onto a rigid caste structure, characterized the ruling arrangement in the state.

Three other characteristics of how authority was exercised within U.P. at this early stage are important to keep in mind because they help us

---

[13] A fairly comprehensive analysis of Uttar Pradesh's economy is available in two volumes: Government of India (2007). While the focus of this report is on the more recent period, much can be learned from it about earlier developments too.

[14] See Srivastava (1976). Also see Brass (1965) and Hasan (1990).

understand how state politics influenced the economy. First, the state-level Congress elite were mostly first-generation nationalists.[15] This leadership class transmitted to state politics a sense of public purpose that was significantly less personalistic and corrupt than what followed. And yet, as second-tier leaders, the horizons of these state leaders were limited. The grander aspirations in India to use state power to foster development were mainly national-level aspirations of the likes of Nehru. Politics for the state-level elite, even relatively enlightened elites, thus quickly became less a means to developmental change and more an end in itself. Second, though factional conflicts among upper-caste Congress leaders in the state were mainly personal or caste-oriented (Brahmins versus Thakurs), there was also an element of ideology in these conflicts. Whereas the national Congress was increasingly leaning left of center under Nehru, state leaders in U.P. tended to be more conservative. Closely allied with landowning groups, their policy preferences – to the extent that such preferences existed – were mainly focused on diluting the land reform initiatives of the national center. And third, factional conflicts within the state were kept within limits by the Congress "high command" in Delhi. While Congress leaders in U.P. very much had their autonomous political bases within the state, unlike the situation in many other states, especially the southern states, state politics in U.P. was deeply intertwined with national politics.

During the 1950s and 1960s, economic growth in U.P. already began to lag behind the national average. The causes of this sluggishness are not easy to understand, especially because most growth-promoting policies at this early stage, especially industrial policies, were conceived in New Delhi and applied to all the Indian states. It is the case that central assistance to U.P. during these years lagged behind the national average, and relatively few central projects found their way into U.P.[16] This is ironic because, given its size, U.P. carried a disproportionate weight in national politics. The explanation is probably that most central assistance went to states that were difficult to manage politically; by contrast, U.P. was a secure bastion of the Congress Party and could thus be taken for granted. The per capita plan outlay of U.P. also consistently lagged behind the average

---

[15] Here I am thinking of such leaders as Purshottam Das Tandon, G. P. Pant, Sampur-nanand, Kriplani, K. P. Malviya, Rafi Ahmed Kidwai, and eventually even C. B. Gupta.

[16] For example, per capita central assistance to all states in the first, second, and third five-year plans was 25, 27, and 56 rupees, respectively. By contrast, the figures for U.P. during the same periods were 14, 18, and 47 rupees, respectively. See Srivastava (1976), Table 15.1, p. 326.

outlay of other Indian states.[17] This is because the state's economy was mainly agricultural and because taxation of agriculture was abolished following independence. The capacity of states like U.P. to raise their own revenue thus lagged behind, contributing to lagging public expenditure within the state. Due to the relative scarcity of both central resources and the state's own, then, public investment in U.P. lagged from early on, contributing to slower growth, not only directly but also indirectly – and more devastatingly, because of the long-run impact – via the relative neglect of infrastructure, health, and education.

Private investment did not fare much better. As noted in earlier chapters, the national government during these early years had no policy to stimulate investment and growth in agriculture. Within the state, a number of factors militated against private investment in agriculture: *zamindari* abolition transferred land, not to tillers, but often to noncultivating castes, who became absentee landlords, with few incentives to invest; a variety of onerous tenancy arrangements discouraged tenants from investing; and without public support, family farmers shied away from investment, at least until the second half of the 1960s, when the publicly subsidized green revolution altered the relevant incentives. Poor infrastructure and the low quality of human capital also discouraged private industry. The cumulative impact of sluggish private and public investment was relatively low rates of growth. As far as one can determine from the record, the Congress leadership in U.P. was relatively oblivious to these emerging trends. They tended to assume instead that "development" was something that was initiated in New Delhi. The focus of state-level politics was mainly on jockeying for power, consolidating factional support via channeling patronage, resisting redistributive change, and courting favor with the "high command" so that New Delhi might tilt the power balance in their direction.

If this was the first Congress phase in U.P., the second phase began with the embrace of the green revolution by farmers in western U.P. during the second half of the 1960s. The higher incomes of commercialized family farmers led to demands for greater political representation. In the deeply caste-oriented politics of the state, many of the middle-caste farmers resented their exclusion from power by the Brahmin and Thakur leaders of Congress. By the late 1960s, the Congress was in any case

---

[17] Again, whereas the average per capita plan outlay for all Indian states during first, second, and third five-year plans was 40, 52, and 92 rupees, respectively, the figures for U.P. were 24, 34, and 68 rupees. See ibid.

in decline across the country. The growing economic clout of middle-caste farmers, especially the Jats, then led to the first significant challenge to Congress's rule in U.P. The emergence of the Jat leader Charan Singh most clearly represented this political shift. A variety of backward castes in eastern U.P. had for some time supported parties other than the Congress; for example, many had been sympathetic to a type of socialism preached by Ram Manohar Lohia. Over time, these two political streams – the green-revolution-bred middle-caste farmers from western U.P. and the backward castes of eastern U.P. – merged, mainly because of a shared antipathy to upper-caste and Congress-party dominance in the state. Between 1967 and 1970, and again following the emergency of 1977, backward-caste parties posed brief but serious challenges to the Congress. However, these challenges became decisive only during the 1990s. Prior to that, Indira Gandhi found a new legitimacy formula to shore up the sagging fortunes of the Congress Party, both in U.P. and in India as a whole.

When Indira Gandhi split the all-India Congress Party in 1969, many of the conservative Congress leaders in U.P., along with much of what passed for the organizational structure of the Congress Party, chose to ally themselves, not with Indira Gandhi, but with the "old" Congress. As is well known, this faction of the Congress lost popularity all over India, including in U.P., during the subsequent years. By contrast, Indira Gandhi reestablished the hold of her populist faction of the Congress all over India during the 1970s, including in U.P. Indira Gandhi's Congress ruled U.P. for much of the 1970s and 1980s, though hardly unchallenged. Some of the core political characteristics of this second phase of Congress rule in U.P. are now worth underlining.

First, Congress leaders in U.P. increasingly came to be appointed by Indira Gandhi, and they were often rewarded less for their political base within the state than for their loyalty to the leadership. Over time, this undermined the popularity and the legitimacy of Congress leaders in U.P. Second, the support base of the Congress in U.P. did not undergo any major changes, though some subtle changes were quite consequential. The caste/class base of Congress continued to be a somewhat strange alliance of upper and lower groups, along with support from the Muslim minority, with a variety of middle groups groping for an appropriate alternative to the Congress.[18] Unlike the situation in some other states,

[18] See Brass (1981).

such as Gujarat (to be discussed later), Congress in U.P. never became an alliance of middle and lower castes. This reflected in part the slow pace of economic change in U.P. There was hardly any big capital in U.P. to pressure either the Congress Party or the U.P. state government to undertake purposive policies. The lower classes were not mobilized; unlike the situation in yet other states such as West Bengal (also to be discussed), there was no pressure from the lower classes or the left in U.P. Mired in factionalism and patronage battles, run from New Delhi, Congress in U.P. remained popular owing mainly to the popularity of the Nehru-Gandhi family. Increasingly, however, this popularity was not automatic. It had to be "bought" instead by channeling public resources to a variety of groups. The strategies included allowing upper castes to occupy state offices; channeling input and output subsidies to family farmers; offering symbolic gains to the more traditional Muslim elites; and allocating resources to poverty alleviation programs so as to secure the support of the lower strata. This, then, was the third important characteristic of the new Congress. While it was still a party of the upper and lower castes and of the Muslims, all of these groups were beginning to develop stronger identities, and their support could not be taken for granted.[19]

U.P. increasingly became a central battleground in the numerous power struggles faced by Indira Gandhi. Indira Gandhi knew that she needed the support of U.P. to maintain national control. Ironically, or maybe not so ironically, this position of strategic centrality within a more turbulent national polity worked to the economic advantage of U.P. Resource transfers to U.P. increased, leading to a significant jump in plan expenditures in U.P. during 1975–90 (Figure 3.6). It is also notable from Figure 3.6 that economic growth in U.P. closely parallels the trend in plan expenditure. This relationship stands to reason: first, public investment goes toward investment in irrigation and provides a variety of other kinds of support to agriculture, helping agricultural growth; and second, public investment also helps initiate major new industrial projects, along with improvements in infrastructure that may also help attract private investment. Some such causal links seem to underline the relationship evident in Figure 3.7, where it is clear that the higher the rates of plan expenditure

---

[19] On the changing character of factions within U.P., especially as they increasingly became "lobby groups" organized around competing identities during the 1980s, see Stone (1988).

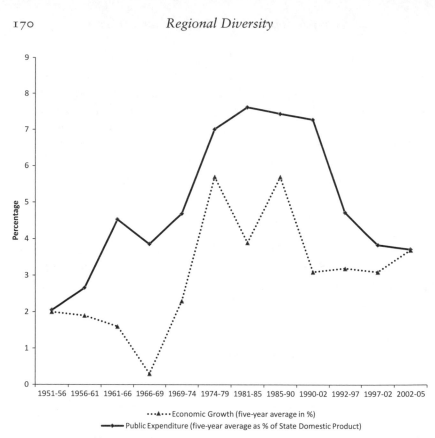

FIGURE 3.6. Public Expenditure and Economic Growth in Uttar Pradesh, 1951–2005. *Source:* Government of India (2007).

in U.P., the higher the rate of economic growth over the entire period under discussion.[20]

The economic performance of U.P. during 1975–90 reflected trends all across India. As already noted, a part of this growth resulted from increased central transfers to U.P., which in turn reflected the political calculations of Indira and Rajiv Gandhi. Some additional factors were at work, too. The green revolution spread to parts of central and eastern U.P. This not only boosted productivity and growth in agriculture, but also served to thaw frozen social structures, mobilizing backward-caste family farmers across all of U.P. (more on this later). Industrial growth in U.P. during these fifteen years was also respectable, averaging nearly 7 percent per year. Much of this was focused on agro-processing, such as the sugar industry, but also on the textile, chemical, and engineering sectors. According to the government's own analysis,

[20] Note that the R-square of 0.46 was significant at the 0.014 level.

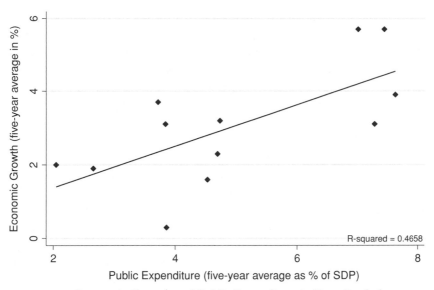

FIGURE 3.7. Economic Growth and Public Expenditure in Uttar Pradesh, 1951–2005. *Source:* Same as Figure 3.6.

"through the late 1970s and the 1980s, large doses of public investment (both Central and State) stimulated private sector participation in the state's industrial growth and kept Uttar Pradesh ahead of the national average."[21]

The Post-1990 Political Economy

A variety of indicators underline the fact that Uttar Pradesh's economy during the post-1990 period has not performed well: economic growth has been well below the Indian average (Table 3.2); nearly a third of the population still lives below the poverty line (Table 3.2), and the decline in poverty has been below the mean of Indian states (Figure 3.5); and the Human Development Index, including literacy, remains well below the already low Indian average (Table 3.2). Some of these indicators reflect continuity with past trends, and thus their causes are deeply rooted in the past; I have referred to these in the earlier discussion. However, it is also clear that the new, post-1990 "liberal" era has been very hard on India's poor states, including U.P.

[21] See Government of India (2007), V. II, p. 62.

Post-1990 politics in U.P. has evolved in a manner that has further undermined the government's developmental role within the state and thus the state's capacity to compete in the new environment. There is no doubt that the power of the upper castes and of the Congress Party has been challenged decisively during the post-1990 period; it is understandable that many celebrate this apparent deepening of democracy. At the same time, however, the new political forces – including backward-caste parties, lower-caste parties, and communal parties – have failed to create politics with a public purpose. Economic scarcity accentuates the tendency to view the omnipresent state as a ready route to upward mobility. Since access to the state has in the past been monopolized by the upper castes, newly mobilized groups rightly believe that it is now their turn. Unfortunately, it is not easy to satisfy the aspirations of the many simply by opening access to the state; that would require a growing economy and much more inclusive socioeconomic programs supported by the state. Absent that, leaders manipulate mass sentiment, focusing on such token gains for their respective communities as "reservations" (affirmative action) and such symbolic gains as building statues of community leaders. Without organized parties that might link leaders and followers, and without a robust business class to check abuses of power, the political situation encourages demagogues who excel at manipulation of public sentiment while personalizing power. Such personalistic use of state power further undermines the possibility of its constructive use, perpetuating the low-level equilibrium trap created by the emergence of neo-patrimonial politics as the dominant political tendency within the state.

In order to put some flesh on this skeletal argument, it may help to begin the discussion with a quick overview of the post-1990 political changes in the state. As a caveat, it is important to keep in mind that not all of the developmental shortcomings of U.P. are a product of its recent governance problems; some of the problems are of earlier origin, and the new, winner-take-all national economy definitely handicaps India's poor states. And yet poor governance within the state distinguishes U.P. from other, more dynamic states of India. So it is the recent governance patterns within the state – a period during which neo-patrimonial tendencies came to the fore – with which we must begin.

As already noted, up until the late 1980s, U.P. was mainly a Congress-run state, and the Congress in U.P. was mainly a party of the upper castes that won state elections with the additional support of the lower castes and Muslims. Over time, this ruling pattern came to be challenged by excluded groups, especially the backward castes. This challenge had already emerged in the late 1960s, reemerged following the emergency, but again failed because of competing leadership ambitions and the inability of the backward castes of western and eastern U.P. to work together. As the Congress Party became weaker nationally during the late 1980s, backward-caste parties in U.P., now led less by the Jat leaders from the western half of the state and but more by Yadav leaders from the east, came to the forefront. Thus began a new era in U.P. politics, now without the Congress Party at the helm.

With the Congress Party diminished, three sets of political forces have taken turns governing U.P. over the last two decades: parties with backward-caste leaders; the Hindu nationalist party; and, most recently, a party with leadership from among the untouchable castes, the *dalits*.[22] None of these parties has been capable of offering stable government with a focus on long-term development. The focus of the political class has instead been on how to win elections, how to maximize personal or sectional gains when in power, and on the pursuit of a variety of gimmicks that leaders hope will influence electoral sympathies but leave the socioeconomic ills of U.P untouched.

Parties led by and ruled in the name of backward castes came to power in U.P. during the late 1980s. While this was a national trend, it put down real roots in U.P., where middle castes had been kept out of political office by the Congress–upper caste combine. First the Janata Party and then the Samajwadi Party (SP), led by Mulayam Singh Yadav, have since been in and out of power.[23] With its core support in Yadav and a few other backward-caste groups, the SP is able to muster some 20–25 percent of the popular vote in U.P., but seldom much more. A constant preoccupation of leaders like Mulayam Singh is thus coalition politics: before coming to power, with whom to reach electoral arrangements; and when in power, who should become a minister, or who will support the ruling minority government, or which policy gimmicks might help consolidate support for the next election. Even when there is an overt commitment to development, which Mulayam Singh has periodically espoused when in power, fending off challenges to power has consistently trumped the pursuit of systematic policies. Moreover, the SP is hardly much of a party, bequeathing to any government under Mulayam Singh a sharp neo-patrimonial character: within the SP, "there is no second line of leadership"; policy

---

[22] For a good overview, see the useful collection by Pai (2007).
[23] See Verma (2007).

decisions emerge from "the whims and fancies of the leader"; and "at the most, the [SP] is being run as a family business ... [with] many members of Mulayam's family [exerting] – considerable influence."[24]

The main challenge to the SP during the 1990s in U.P. was of course the BJP. With the destruction of the mosque in Ayodhya (a city in U.P.), U.P. was in many ways the epicenter of the rise of Hindu nationalism in the early 1990s. And yet the BJP's popularity in U.P. declined just as rapidly as it had emerged.[25] If the SP sought to build an electoral base on caste mobilization, the BJP sought to unite all Hindus by mobilizing anti-Muslim sentiment. This proved to pay only short-term dividends. First, the significant Muslim minority in U.P. started supporting the more secular SP, creating a powerful opposition force. Second, while the BJP attracted the support of upper-caste Hindus, that was not sufficient to win elections. The BJP also courted the support of the backward castes by projecting a member of that caste – Kalyan Singh – as the party leader in U.P. While this attracted some support, it also backfired. Kalyan Singh was just as personalistic as most other leaders in U.P., diluting the BJP's reputation as a well-organized party with a public purpose (though with a fairly communal definition of the relevant public). Moreover, personalistic gains by other backward castes during Kalyan Singh's rule alienated BJP's core support among the upper castes. The mobilized cadres of the BJP were also disappointed with the party's pragmatic bent when in power. With only minority support, the BJP in U.P. sought coalition partners with all and sundry, leaving behind a lackluster record of governance.

Finally, among the post-1990 political developments in U.P., one must take account of the Bahujan Samaj Party (BSP) and its enigmatic *dalit* leader, Mayawati.[26] In and out of power during the period under discussion, Mayawati is very much in control in U.P. as I write this in 2010. Considering that *dalit* women still can rarely uncover or raise their heads in front of upper-caste men in U.P. villages, Mayawati's emergence is a singular achievement of Indian democracy. At least as far as the politics of dignity is concerned, democracy in India is enabling even the lowly to hold high political office.[27] The importance of the psychic gain that comes from witnessing "one's own" in power should not be underestimated.

[24] Ibid, pp. 185–6.
[25] See the useful essays by Abhay Kumar Dubey, Smita Gupta, and Badri Narayan Tiwari in Pai (2007).
[26] A useful study is Chandra (2004). Also see essays by Nicolas Jaoul, Sudha Pai, and Vivek Kumar in Pai (2007).
[27] A favorable assessment of Mayawati and the BSP in U.P. is available in Kumar (2007).

And yet such gains can be short-lived if they are not followed up by real broad-based socio-economic policies. Unfortunately, on this dimension, Mayawati has much in common with other aspirants to power in U.P.: relentless pursuit of power as an end in itself; personalization of power; and little or no concern for development of any type, pro-growth or pro-distribution or some combination.

A few examples from Mayawati's short period in power will highlight the neo-patrimonial character of her rule; these examples were gathered during fieldwork.[28] First, shortly after coming to power in mid-2005, Mayawati met Manmohan Singh, India's prime minister, who congratulated her and urged her to pay attention to U.P.'s development. Mayawati agreed, even accepting the idea of creating a high-level committee to offer advice, but then went her own way, staffing the committee, not with experts, but with those loyal to her. Second, India's foremost industrialists, the Tatas, were apparently interested in investing in a major power project in U.P. and needed a large chunk of land on which electricity-generating plants could be built. An appropriate piece of land was identified in the Bundelkhand region. The U.P. government needed to facilitate access to this land. The deal fell through, in part because political support for the project from Mayawati was missing (she did not even attend key meetings), but also because Mayawati's brother, who attends all such meetings concerned with land allocation, apparently reasoned that greater returns on providing this land could likely be found elsewhere; part of the project was eventually given to a business house in U.P., Jaypee, with close personal links to Mayawati. And third, it became clear in visiting rural U.P. that NREGA has not been pursued with any vigor. This is surprising insofar as the main beneficiaries of NREGA are likely to be members of the lowest castes, in the name of whom Mayawati rules. Upon inquiry it emerged that Mayawati was concerned about the electoral impact of NREGA. Given the "National" in the title of the program (subsequently amended to include the name of Mahatma Gandhi), she might have reasoned that the program was more likely to benefit the Congress than her own party; hence the near-absence of pressure from the top to implement this significant pro-poor program in U.P., at least up until 2009.

During the post-1990 period, politics in U.P. has become deeply fragmented. While the state elite were never all that developmental in U.P.

---

[28] These examples are drawn both from my conversations with senior government officers in Lucknow and from my visits to villages, mainly during 2009–10. It is the case that as this book goes to press, Mayawati has started putting more emphasis on NREGA.

to begin with, caste-based competition for electoral support has further accentuated the tendency toward pursuing power as an end itself. None of the competing parties in U.P. really has a clear developmental agenda that it pursues while in power. The results include the worsening of U.P.'s relative economic situation within India. As already noted, economic growth in U.P. has decelerated since about 1990, not only in relation to other, faster-growing states of India, but also in contrast to its own past performance during the late 1970s and 1980s. The proximate cause of this deceleration is of course a lower level of investment, both private and public, but especially public, because it was higher levels of public investment that had earlier created moderately high rates of growth (Figures 3.6 and 3.7).

How does one explain the relatively low level of new investment in U.P. since 1990? While the poor quality of governance within the state has been a key cause, it is also important to underline the ways in which the new national political economy is systematically biased against India's poor states, especially because it has led to a decline in public investment.[29] First, as was noted in earlier chapters, India's agriculture has suffered since 1990, due in part to a lower level of public investment from the national government. For a poor state like U.P., which depends heavily on agriculture, this has meant lower overall growth and a diminished capacity to expand the state's revenue base. Second, as the national government has forsaken the objective of promoting equality across Indian states, a variety of central resources that formerly supplemented U.P.'s developmental efforts have declined: between the mid-1980s and the mid-2000s, for example, grants from the central government to U.P. declined from 15.5 percent of U.P.'s total expenditure to 8.2 percent, and loans fell from 19.8 percent to 7 percent.[30] Third, in spite of the avowed economic decentralization, there has been considerable centralization of Indian finance over the last two decades. Reminiscent of the "structural adjustment" programs imposed on debt-ridden developing countries by international development institutions in the heyday of the "Washington consensus," Indian national government now imposes conditions on India's poor states, which are often debt-ridden, stipulating how to spend and when to spend. These policies, along with the high interest rates on state debts that have been triggered by the new "market-oriented" national policies, hurt public spending within states. The cumulative impact is a significant

[29] The comments and data on this issue are drawn from Jha and Das (2007).
[30] Ibid., p. 316. Also see Government of India (2007), V. 1, section 2.4, p. 40.

deterioration in the fiscal health of some of India's poor states, especially U.P.[31]

Seeing that some Indian states are doing much better than others in the new Indian political economy, clearly factors within states are also important in explaining the relatively poor performance of states like U.P. The poor quality of governance just discussed is one such important factor. Successive governments in U.P. have simply not been focused on development, irrespective of whether one conceives of development in terms of growth, or redistribution, or human development, or building institutions, or infrastructure. The more state politics becomes fragmented and personalistic, the less it is used to pursue the public good; all manner of development suffers. The impact of a lack of a developmental focus is evident in patterns of both revenue generation and expenditure.

On the revenue side, there is no doubt that reductions in central support are one key culprit in the fiscal constraints now faced by states like U.P. However, it is also the case that the capacity of the U.P. government to raise taxes within the state is among the lowest in India.[32] This is in part a function of the fact that the core economic sector, agriculture, is largely untaxed, and the industrial base of the state is not sufficient to provide ample taxes. Most taxes, such as sales taxes, are indirect. Taxes are also collected inefficiently, with corruption a major problem. A more developmentally oriented leadership could certainly find ways to improve the mobilization of resources within the state.

A related issue is that a large portion of public resources is not invested in core developmental tasks. It is used instead either to pay interest on the mounting debt or on a variety of political gimmicks like building statutes and parks. As already noted, "plan expenditure" in U.P. – the portion of public resources of which development resources is a part – has diminished steadily since 1990 (Figure 3.6).[33] And finally, the lack of a developmental focus among leaders is clearly manifest in the fact that the U.P. government does not even spend all of the resources it has

---

[31] Ibid., p. 308.
[32] For example, while the per capita tax revenue collected by such Indian states as Maharashtra, Punjab, Tamil Nadu, and Gujarat in 2001–2 was more than 2,000 rupees, in U.P. and Bihar it was 777 and 303 rupees, respectively. Toward the end of the decade, this situation began to alter somewhat with the introduction of some new indirect taxes.
[33] Toward the end of the period under discussion, there appears to be an upward shift away from this diminishing trend. If this continues, either due to some changes in central policies or because of enhanced resources collected via new indirect taxes, the future results may be different from those of the recent past.

at its disposal and seldom negotiates with the central government for more.[34]

With the state's political class focused on everything but the state's development, a variety of socioeconomic problems continue to accumulate: poor infrastructure; the decay of major public institutions, including universities; the deterioration of law and order; and widespread corruption. This is not a context conducive to attracting private investment. Over the last three decades, private investment has increasingly become the main driver of growth in India. States like U.P. are being left behind because private investors would rather invest in other Indian states with better "initial conditions" and with more developmentally oriented political leaders. There is ample evidence to indicate that U.P. lags well behind in attracting private investment.[35] The government's own reports suggest that the key problem is governance and that the "dynamism has to percolate from the top."[36]

In addition to the problems of economic growth, the redistributive failures of various U.P. governments are well known. More than two decades back I attributed the failure to implement land reforms and to pursue a variety of pro-poor programs in U.P. to the role of landowning castes in the state apparatus, weak political parties, and a corrupt lower-level bureaucracy.[37] As noted earlier, the social base of ruling parties has since changed, especially with the rise of the BSP. However, the BSP, in spite of its lower-caste base, remains a leader-dominated party, with very limited downward reach. Without organizational cohesion or penetration, it is unlikely that any of the competing parties in U.P. can implement pro-poor programs. More important, antipoverty policies are hardly a priority in U.P. Scholars have thus documented with care the "comprehensive failure of social provisions in a wide range of fields, including basic education, land reform, child immunization, public distribution, maternal health, social security, public works, environmental protection [and] anti-poverty programs," attributing this failure to both an apathetic state and an undermobilized society.[38] The state's role looms especially large when one focuses on developmental failures, including issues of both growth and distribution, and when one compares U.P. to other states in India.

[34] See Government of India (2007), V. 1, section 2.4, p. 41.
[35] Ibid., p. 40.
[36] Ibid., p. 43.
[37] Kohli (1987), Chapter 5.
[38] See Dreze and Gazdar (1997). The direct quote is from p. 56.

III. DEVELOPMENTAL TENDENCIES AT THE HELM: GUJARAT

If U.P. is one of India's worst economic performers, Gujarat is among its best. I use the example of Gujarat here to underline the emerging developmental role of some of India's regional governments. With a population of some fifty-five million in 2006, Gujarat approximates the size of Britain or France. While Gujarat's per capita income is above the Indian average and well above that of the Hindi-heartland states, what is truly notable about Gujarat is its recent rate of economic growth: it has been India's fastest-growing state since 1980, and especially since 1990 (Tables 3.1 and 3.3). Gujarat is also one of India's most highly industrialized states, with industrial growth driving the overall growth. Of course, all is not well in Gujarat: agricultural growth is lagging; the rate of poverty has not come down as rapidly as one might have expected, given Gujarat's East Asian growth rates; and caste and ethnic violence, especially violence against Muslims, casts a long shadow on any depiction of Gujarat as "shining." In the analysis that follows I trace the links between the "good" and the "bad" in Gujarat.

I will argue that Gujarat's rapid economic growth is propelled by a close working alliance between the region's political and economic elite. A robust private sector emerged early in Gujarat. While governmental stability has been rare, for the most part, upper castes and classes have controlled the levers of power. As this power has been used to support business and commercial interests, the private sector has flourished. Given a narrow ruling alliance, however, consolidating electoral majorities has proved a formidable challenge. A variety of strategies have been used to mobilize electoral majorities, including ethnic and religious violence. For now, the BJP has used Hindu nationalism as a strategy to win elections and to provide a pro-business, pro-growth government in Gujarat. The durability of an electoral alliance based on religious nationalism has yet to be tested.

Background

Following the principle of linguistic states, Gujarat became a state of Gujarati speakers in 1960. The broader western region of India, including Gujarat, was part of the Bombay Presidency during the colonial period. As its name suggests, of the three major Presidencies of India – Bengal, Madras, and Bombay – this one centered on the commercial port city of Bombay. Consolidated in the late nineteenth century, following the defeat

TABLE 3.3. *Some Developmental Indicators of Gujarat in a Comparative Perspective*

	Gujarat	Hindi-heartland[a] States	All India
Per capita income, 2006–7 (in rupees)	27,027	10,794	22,580
Economic growth, 1980–2008 (average annual %)	7.7	5.1	6.2
Economic Growth, 1990–2008 (average annual %)	8.8	4.9	6.1
Poverty head count, 2004–5 (official poverty line) (%)	16.8	37.3	28.3
Decline in Poverty,[b] 1983–2005 (%)	0.7	0.7	0.8
Illiteracy,[c] 2005–6	25.2	40.9	31.7
Human Development Index, 2000	0.61	0.49	0.58

[a] The three Hindi-heartland states averaged here are Bihar, Uttar Pradesh, and Madhya Pradesh.
[b] Average per annum percentage decline in head count ratio between 1983 and 2005 from Dev and Ravi (2007), Tables 8, 18, and 19.
[c] Illiteracy is defined as the percentage of the population above the age of six with no schooling.
Sources: Same as in Table 3.1.

of the indigenous Maratha rulers, colonial rule in the Bombay Presidency provided a framework for some commercial and industrial development. Not only the premiere city of Bombay, which is now part of the state of Maharashtra, but also the corridor from Bombay to Ahmadabad – now the major city of Gujarat – experienced economic development, including industrialization. Unlike the case of the Bengal Presidency, where British commercial and industrial interests were dominant, indigenous capital took root in western India, including in the important textile industry in Ahmadabad.[39] And in contrast to U.P., the present state of Gujarat was historically more highly industrialized at the time of independence, though given the industrial hub of Kanpur in U.P., the contrast should not be exaggerated.

The nature of the land system in the Bombay Presidency should also be outlined, especially because of its long-term political and economic consequences. Unlike the situation in the Bengal Presidency, as well as in

[39] See, for example, Bagchi (1972).

parts of old U.P., the British did not rule Bombay by "settling" *zamindars* as mega-landlords, revenue collectors, and local chieftains. Bombay was instead ruled more directly, and the modal land tenure system was centered around peasant property, or what in Indian history was popularly known as the *ryotwari* system, a *ryot* being a peasant who owns the land he cultivates. While there were plenty large landlords in the Bombay Presidency, including princely states here and there, peasant owners dominated the land tenure system. In addition, many of the larger land holdings were broken into smaller holdings during the post-independence period, creating a large stratum of peasants who owned small to medium-sized pieces of land, generally less than fifty acres.[40] As will be discussed later, many of these middle and upper-middle landowners in Gujarat belonged to the caste of Patidars. The Patidars, many of whom share the last name Patel, have in turn been a dominant force in Gujarati society and politics, especially in the countryside.[41]

Brahmans and Banias are among the important upper castes of Gujarat; they tend to be concentrated in the cities.[42] During the late colonial and early post-independence years, Brahmans and Banias played prominent political and economic roles. Commerce and industry were dominated by Banias. Many of the first-generation nationalist leaders in the region and the state's earlier chief ministers – such as Morarji Desai (Brahman), Jivraj Mehta (Bania), Balwantrai Mehta (Bania), and Hitendra Desai (Brahman) – belonged to these groups. The dominant community in the rural areas was the Patidars. They constitute some 12 percent of the state's population and tend to be concentrated in the central part of mainland Gujarat; most of them tend to be medium (five- to fifteen-acre) and large (sixteen- to fifty-acre) landowners and agriculturalists. The Patidars were mobilized into nationalist politics by Sardar Vallabhbhai Patel, who rose to be independent India's second most important Congress leader, second only to Nehru. That gave the Gujarati Patels a powerful role in the politics of the region. In alliance with Banias and Brahmans, the Patidars have remained a major political force in Gujarati politics.

[40] See Sheth (1976).
[41] See Pocock (1972).
[42] For the discussion on caste structure and early politics in Gujarat, I am drawing on my own chapter on Gujarat (Chapter 9) in Kohli (1989). See the references in that chapter for a variety of other source material.

The Kshatriyas are the main backward caste of the region. They comprise nearly a quarter of the state's population. Under the leadership of upper-caste Rajputs, many of whom were princely rulers allied with the British, the Kshatriyas were mobilized into the region's politics with the approach of independence, when it became clear that numbers would influence who rules.[43] The Kshatriyas, however, are a disparate group; their political unity has waxed and waned, as has their influence. Below the Kshatriyas in the caste hierarchy are of course the scheduled castes and tribes. What is notable is that the tribal population of Gujarat is quite significant in terms of numbers. Concentrated in the eastern part of the state, often poor and illiterate, they constitute nearly 15 percent of the state's population. The scheduled castes of Gujarat, however, are somewhat more "advanced" than those in the rest of India, due in part to pockets of progressive educational policy in the past, but due mainly to the role of Mahatma Gandhi, who after all was a native of Gujarat. And finally, Muslims constitute another 8 to 9 percent of the state's population. Occupying a region bordering Pakistan, Gujarat's Muslims hold an uneasy political position in the state, often viewed with suspicion for holding dual loyalties, and especially vulnerable in recent decades with the rise of the Hindu nationalists.

Before Gujarat became a state in 1960, the region's economy had already developed pockets of dynamism. Most prominently, there was the Bania-controlled textile industry around the city of Ahmadabad. Many Patidar landowners were also commercially inclined; cash crops such as ground nuts were prominent, as were dairy production and dairy cooperatives. While in per capita terms Gujarat's position in India was nothing exceptional around the time of independence, the significance of pockets of economic dynamism lay deeper. Most importantly, even before it came into being as a state, a nascent commercial–capitalist class was emerging. Some of these were Bania industrialists, and some were Patidar economic elite with roots in agriculture. As important, the region's political elite belonged to the same communities – notice Mahatma Gandhi and Sardar Patel, a Bania and a Patidar respectively – and when they did not, like some Brahmin leaders such as Morarji Desai, they learned to work closely with the economic elite. From early on, therefore, Gujarat's politics was "commercial in style and technique."[44]

[43] See Shah (1975).
[44] See Sheth (1976), p. 68.

The Era of Congress Dominance

As in the rest of India, the Congress Party was and remains a major political force in Gujarat. A variety of Congress governments ruled Gujarat for
more than three decades between 1960 and the early 1990's, when the
BJP finally emerged as the new ruling party. The era of Congress dominance was of course not seamless; for example, the Congress of the 1960s
in Gujarat was very different from the Congress of the 1980s. In spite of
significant political shifts – to be discussed later – governments in Gujarat
have repeatedly been pro-production, especially pro-industry. The results
have included economic growth rates in the state that tend to be above
the Indian average. More dramatically, industrial growth in Gujarat has
been well above the national rate; if in 1960 Gujarat was the eighth most
industrialized state of India, by 1980, it was already the second most
industrialized state, second only to neighboring Maharashtra.[45]

The Congress Party in Gujarat during the 1960s was under the sway of
the regional leader Morarji Desai, who in turn represented the more conservative wing of the national Congress Party. As already noted, Gujarat
politics during this early period was dominated by the upper castes. The
upper caste–led Congress Party provided good, albeit highly elitist, government in Gujarat. For example, Myron Weiner described local Congress
units in Gujarat during the 1960s as "well organized," staffed by "ded-
icated party workers," with "little internal dissension" and exhibiting a
"tone of reliability and modernity."[46] Pravin Sheth described the Gujarat
Congress Party as providing "good government performance" with the
help of a "strong party organization" with "very little factionalism"
under the leadership of Morarji Desai.[47] In terms of policy preferences,
Congress leaders were very much "right of the center."[48] The fact that
Congress leaders championed business and commercial interests is understandable in light of the fact that the regional economy was already relatively advanced by Indian standards, that economic elite of the region
were politically active, and that the political and economic elite shared
ascriptive bonds of caste origins.

The early leadership of Congress in Gujarat was mainly in the hands of
Bania and Brahmin elites. The Patidars increasingly came to control local

[45] See Mehta (1989), p. 220.
[46] See Weiner (1967), pp. 69 and 86.
[47] Sheth (1976), p. 84.
[48] See Mahadevia (2005), p. 309.

governments, cooperatives, and eventually even higher elected offices. The backward castes of the region were beginning to assert their political presence under the Kshatriya leadership, but this challenge materialized only during the 1970s and succeeded only in the 1980s. Various lower castes remained marginal at this early stage. Unlike the situation in many other Indian states, the upper-caste leaders of Gujarat prioritized industrial development, including private sector–led industrial development: "Development strategy in Gujarat has been very clear and unambiguous ever since its inception in 1960 in according a high priority to industrialization. . . . the state has made a clear choice of encouraging the secondary sector over the primary and territory sectors."[49] A number of factors help explain the pro-industrial leanings of Gujarat's political leaders. First, the political elite were already socialized into serving economic interests. Second, anti-industrial interests were relatively weak in the region: there was no traditional *zamindari* system, and the well-off Patidar landowners were happy at this early stage to control local economic bodies like dairy cooperatives and patronage resources via the control of local governments. Third, under Gandhi's influence, the trade union movement in the state was relatively tame.[50] Finally, and most importantly, "right from the beginning the industrial lobby was an important influence in shaping government actions and policies" in Gujarat.[51] In sum, unlike the situation in many other Indian states, politics in Gujarat from the beginning was less an end in itself. Industrial capitalism had already established a toehold; labor was tame; and a right-leaning political elite chose to work with the industrialists and businessmen. Over time, this alliance of the political and economic elite gave Gujarat a considerable advantage in terms of attracting private investment and facilitating growth.

State government also prioritized the building of infrastructure from the very outset.[52] These efforts were concentrated in the Bombay-Ahmadabad corridor, where privately controlled industry already existed, and underlined the public commitment to further support private sector–led industrial development. More direct support for industrial development came in the form of a number of public organizations created to encourage industrial development and in the form of publicly subsidized construction of industrial estates. A variety of price and tax supports were

---

[49] Dholakia (2000), p. 3121.
[50] For a historical study of the origins of such relations, see Patel (1987).
[51] Hirway (2000), p. 301.
[52] Mehta (1989), p. 221.

also provided for private industrialists, especially to the textile industry. The pro-business environment attracted private investment. Given an industrial base to tax, public revenue and public investment were also relatively buoyant. In the words of one analyst, "all put together, per capita investable resources of Gujarat may be perhaps highest in the country."[53] And finally, as already mentioned, labor in Gujarat was relatively productive.

Overall, the rate of economic growth in Gujarat during the 1960s was high but not much higher than the Indian average. What was distinctive about Gujarat was its rapid industrial growth. Agriculture growth was supported by public investment in irrigation, but was mainly extensive.[54] Industry took the lead and was further helped by the discovery of oil during the late 1960s. State government again helped support the diversification of industry during the 1970s. In addition to textiles, a variety of petrochemical industries now developed, along with the engineering goods and cement industries. The overall economic growth rate of Gujarat during the 1970s was a full point above the Indian average, fueled mainly by state-supported industrial development. Between 1960 and 1980, the share of the primary sector in the state's gross product declined from some 42 percent to 21 percent.[55] Unfortunately, industrial growth remained highly concentrated in the Bombay-Ahmadabad corridor, accelerating intrastate inequality. This pattern of development also reflected governmental priorities, focused more on growth than on distributional issues. During the 1960s the poverty rate actually increased in the state, though it started coming down slowly during the 1970s.[56]

It is important to underline that the communal situation in Gujarat was already troubled during the 1960s. Hindu refugees from Pakistan settled in Gujarat, providing support to the Jan Sangh, the predecessor of the BJP. Occupying a state bordering Pakistan, the Muslims in the state were often viewed with suspicion. Wars with Pakistan provided occasions for violence against Muslims. While communal passions were a lot less heated than they have been in recent decades, one analyst records some 3,000 incidents of communal strife during the 1960s.[57] And well before Godhra, there was a major communal riot in 1969 that killed some 1,500 Muslims.

---

[53] Ibid., p. 220.
[54] Hirway (2000), p. 3107.
[55] Mehta (1989), p. 220.
[56] Hirway (1995), p. 2607.
[57] Shah (2007), p. 154.

The 1969 split in the national Congress Party was especially consequential for politics in Gujarat. The split pitched the supporters of Morarji Desai – generally the upper castes – against an emerging coalition of middle and lower strata that coalesced around Indira Gandhi.[58] The Nav Nirman movement of 1974 was a manifestation of this challenge to Indira Gandhi's power by elements of the old Congress; this movement in turn contributed to the national Emergency proclaimed in 1975. Unlike the case of U.P., discussed earlier, Indira Gandhi's Congress Party in Gujarat increasingly became a party of the middle and lower castes and Muslims. Known as the KHAM alliance – an alliance of Kshatriyas, Harijans (scheduled castes), Adivasis (tribals), and Muslims – the Congress Party in Gujarat excluded and alienated members of the hitherto ruling upper castes, especially Patidars. Since the upper castes controlled economic resources, high status and skills, the political struggle in Gujarat during the 1980s become a struggle of elites versus masses, with representatives of middle and lower groups controlling state offices and socioeconomic elites repeatedly challenging this control.

Madhavsinh Solanki was Indira Gandhi's handpicked choice to lead the KHAM coalition in Gujarat. As Solanki tried to consolidate this alliance by offering reserved access to state-controlled positions to alliance members, the Patidars reacted with vengeance, initiating major riots in 1981 and again in 1985. Several characteristics and implications of this growing political conflict are worth underlining. First, Solanki was no radical. While offering access to government-controlled positions to his supporters, he very much sought to appease the regional economic elite by offering them systematic support for production and growth.[59] If the upper castes were not satisfied, it was because they were not used to sharing state power. Second, the riots, often instigated by Patidar youth, targeted vulnerable sections of the population – first the scheduled castes, and later, Muslims – so as to delegitimize Solanki's hold on power. And third, alienated members of the upper castes increasingly looked for a political alternative to Indira's Congress. This search began with support for Morarji Desai's faction of the Congress Party, moved to the Janata Party, and ended during the 1990s with the Patidars embracing the BJP.

Gujarat's economy grew handsomely during the 1970s, far surpassing the sluggish rate of growth of the Indian economy. Large-scale industry

---

[58] For this discussion of political change in Gujarat during the 1970s and 1980s, I am drawing on my own earlier work. For more details, see Kohli (1989), Chapter 9.
[59] Ibid., p. 259.

was the leading sector, facilitated in part by the discovery of oil – hence the growth of the fertilizer and other petrochemical industries – and also by the continuing pro-business tilt of the state government discussed earlier.[60] In spite of growing challenges to the power of the upper castes, the state apparatus still remained under their control. The green revolution in agriculture also helped the growth process. The impact of new agrarian technologies was somewhat limited, however, because nearly half of the cropped area in Gujarat was already under commercial crops, where the discovery of new technologies was uneven. Gujarat also has a very high incidence of landlessness, limiting the income-sharing impact of agriculture growth. Since much of the industrial growth was also capital-intensive, creating minimal employment growth, the impact of growth on poverty alleviation was, unfortunately, minimal.

The rate of economic growth in Gujarat during the 1980s fell behind the national average. Several factors help explain why this might have been so.[61] First and foremost, the growing political turmoil in the state finally began corroding what had become a growth-oriented, pro-business polity. While this shift was not dramatic, public resources were increasingly used to manage coalitional support, detracting from public investment. Political turmoil also hurt private investment. Additional factors contributing to slower growth included a decline in agricultural growth; the green revolution innovations were used up, and the public sector contributed little to new initiatives. Some liberalization of the national economy also hurt Gujarat's textile industry. None of this, however, should be exaggerated. Large-scale industry in Gujarat continued to diversify away from textiles, moving into a variety of new areas. Gujarat's extensive overseas diaspora also increasingly played a positive role in the state's economy, contributing to the growth process.

Developmental Tendencies at the Helm

Since about 1990, politics and economics in Gujarat have undergone important changes. The dominance of the Congress Party started declining in the second half of the 1980s. The upper castes reemerged at the helm, this time in partnership with the BJP, the state's new ruling party. The BJP successfully mobilized Gujarati Hindus as an electoral force by utilizing a variety of strategies, including sharpening the Hindu-Muslim

---

[60] Hirway (1995), p. 2003, also Table 1.
[61] I am drawing here on ibid.

divide. The BJP leaders, in turn, have used state power to actively promote economic growth; they have explicitly sought to emulate the success of the East Asian political economies. A variety of state interventions have been used to attract and support private investors, both domestic and foreign. The results have included rapid economic growth and a decline in poverty. Unfortunately, as in the case of other developmental states, a variety of less desirable trends have also emerged: centralization of power, victimization of Muslims, and growing intrastate inequality.

The upper castes of Gujarat, especially the Patidars, have been in search of a political alternative to the Congress since the 1980s. After various false starts, the BJP and the Gujarati *savarnas*, the upper castes, embraced each other during the 1990s. The BJP has, of course, spearheaded a mobilization of Hindus across India since the late 1980s. This mobilization strategy found special resonance in Gujarat, both because upper-caste Hindus found themselves excluded from the perks of power in this state, and because of the religious attachments and divisions that are part of the Gujarati social fabric. Patidars, Baniyas, and Brahmins, however, hardly constitute a numerical majority. The BJP thus succeeded electorally because it was able to engineer mood swings within the state, especially by employing the militant mobilization of Hindus against Muslims. Since such mood swings do not last, the BJP in power has sought control of the lower-level governing structures and has used public resources as patronage to consolidate the support of the lower strata, especially the tribal population.[62] There is evidence to suggest that such "political normality" tends to hurt the electoral fortunes of the BJP. Scholars have thus reasoned that the killing of some 2,000 Muslims following the Godhra incident in 2002 was part of the BJP's broader strategy to periodically rekindle communal passion, aimed at electoral gain.[63]

Gujarat's chief ministers since 1995 have tended to combine pro-Hindu and pro-industry inclinations. For example, both Dilip Parikh and Suresh Mehta were industrialists and members of the RSS. The most recent, the infamous Narendra Modi, was also a member of the RSS.[64] For now, Modi has come to embody both the anti-Muslim and pro-growth nature of the Gujarati state. Modi has been characterized as a militant Hindu leader who is autocratic, technocratic, and a champion of growth and

---

[62] For a good discussion of the BJP's electoral and ruling strategy, see Shah (2007).

[63] Ibid., p. 152.

[64] "Infamous" because of his role as a bystander as Muslims were killed in Gujarat. Among others, see Yagnik and Sud (2005).

industry.[65] His leadership evokes strong reactions: while a variety of human rights groups would have him prosecuted for a state-sponsored pogrom, India's leading industrialists, such as the Ambanis, have praised him as prime ministerial material.

For the purpose of a political economy analysis, it is important not to focus too exclusively on either specific parties or specific individuals as motors of change. While both the BJP and Modi are important political actors in contemporary Gujarat, the forces moving the regional political economy go much deeper. Since 1990 or so, Gujarat's economy has grown very rapidly, led by growth in manufacturing. In order to understand this outcome, one needs to focus on patterns of collaboration between the political and economic elite, between the state and capital. The Gujarati state has increasingly acted as a developmental state, actively promoting production by supporting private investors. Chances are that, even if the Congress Party displaces the BJP as the ruling party in the near future, the role of Gujarati state as an activist promoter of business interests and economic growth will continue.

As noted, political leaders in Gujarat have prioritized industrialization ever since Gujarat came into being as a state in 1960. This priority reflected mainly the underlying economic interests that the political elite represented but also the values of the leadership, especially the regional influence of Morarji Desai, who led the more conservative wing of the Congress Party. State leaders in turn created a variety of organizations to promote industry and economic growth. These included the Gujarat Industrial Development Corporation (GIPC), the Gujarat Industrial Investment Corporation (GIIC), the Gujarat State Finance Corporation (GSFC), and the Industrial Extension Bureau (Indextb). Between 1960 and 1990, a variety of governments in Gujarat used these organizations, along with more direct policy interventions, to provide financing, power, transportation, and "all the required support to industries, and generally highly positive and supportive attitude [toward] new industries."[66] In other words, the infrastructure of a developmental state already existed in Gujarat prior to the major economic policy shifts of 1991.

Following India's economic decentralization in the 1990s, which devolved policy initiatives to state governments, the ruling elite in Gujarat have aggressively promoted industrial development. The basic pattern has

---

[65] Ibid. Also see Shah (2007) and Mahadevia (2005).
[66] Hirway (2000), p. 3109.

been mainly an intensification of past patterns of collaboration between the rulers and private industrialists. The state government has used a variety of strategies to court and attract private investors. First, an "Agenda for Reform," a policy statement that committed the state government to promoting private sector–led industrial growth, was created by the State Finance Commission in 1992 and was accepted by all the political parties; this political consensus has helped investor confidence in Gujarat.[67] During 1995, the state government again reasserted its pro-business commitment by adopting an industrial policy statement entitled "The Best Now Becomes Even Better."[68] Yet another industrial policy statement in 2000 stressed further diversification of the industrial base, including the promotion of knowledge-based industries, especially by creating Special Economic Zones (SEZs).

Broad policy statements have been taken seriously by private investors because they are backed by real resources. While Gujarat's public finances have been under stress – as have those of most other Indian states – Gujarat's own taxing efforts have been more successful than those of most states, and Gujarat also subsidizes economic activities at a rate higher than most other states. A substantial portion of these subsidies support industrial promotion.[69] The share of public expenditures that is devoted to developmental activities in Gujarat also tends to be higher than that of most other Indian states: during the 1990's, for example, Gujarat devoted 72 percent of its total public expenditure to development, whereas the figure for U.P. was 44 percent, for West Bengal 64 percent, and for Tamil Nadu 70 percent.[70]

Over the last two decades governments in Gujarat have channeled these developmental resources via a variety of specific policy interventions. Most aim to translate broad policy objectives into real outcomes. The first thing to note about these specific policy interventions is that they are highly discretionary. In spite of the rhetoric of "liberalization," government policies have sought to pick and promote winners. The state government divides units it wishes to support into such categories as "thrust industries," "premier units," and "prestigious units."[71] These units tend to be large, often export-oriented, and in industries that the government wishes to promote, such as electronics, biotechnology, and

---

[67] See Awasthi (2000), p. 3183.
[68] See Mahadevia (2005), p. 303.
[69] See Dholakia (2000), pp. 3324–5.
[70] See Sarma (2000), Table 9, p. 3129.
[71] I am drawing here on Hirway (2000) and Dholakia (2000).

engineering products. Industrial diversification – away from the declining textile industry and the well-established petrochemical industries – and toward more knowledge-based industries – has also been the government's explicit goal.

Investors in Gujarat receive a variety of concessions, incentives, and governmental support, especially if investment will promote preferred industries. Concessions are provided in such areas as "turnover tax, sales tax on a whole range of goods such as raw materials, consumable goods, by-products, scrap and waste materials." Incentives include "transport subsidy and capital investment subsidy on a large number of products." On top of all this, preferred industries are eligible for further special incentives.[72] The Gujarat government has also minimized bureaucratic obstacles in the process of "approval and clearance" for private investors, especially for the numerous Gujarati "nonresident investors" wishing to invest in Gujarat.

Significant support for industry in Gujarat also comes in the form of a governmental focus on building the state's infrastructure.[73] Over the last decade or so, the state government has included representatives of the Gujarat Chamber of Commerce and Industries on such boards that are of interest to businessmen as the Electricity Board, the Infrastructure Development Board, and the Environment Management Institute. The political and economic elite have then pushed a variety of public-private partnerships for the development of infrastructure. Power sector reforms in the mid-1990s, for example, have led to the involvement of the private sector in power generation, which in turn has grown rapidly. For construction of roads and ports, the government has pursued a Build-Operate-Transfer policy in which the public sector takes the lead but management ends up in private hands. High-priority industries receive comprehensive infrastructural support. The cozy relationship of state and capital has also led to changes in land policy that enable the transfer of hitherto agricultural or public lands for the purpose of establishing infrastructure and/or new private industries.

The pro-business pattern of state intervention in Gujarat has succeeded in attracting private investors to Gujarat in a big way. After Maharashtra, Gujarat during the post-1991 period has probably received the most private investment in comparison to other Indian states. Much of this investment has been indigenous, though some of it is foreign investment,

---

[72] The quoted material is all from Hirway (2000), p. 3109.
[73] In this paragraph I am drawing on Dholakia (2000), p. 3123.

especially from the Gujarati diaspora. Most of this investment is going into large and medium-sized manufacturing industries, giving Gujarat the flavor of India's workshop. As already noted, both manufacturing growth and overall economic growth in Gujarat have been very rapid during the post-1991 period.

Some concluding observations about Gujarat's high-growth model of the development are in order. First, there is very little in Gujarat's political economy that can be rightly characterized as "liberal" or "free market." Gujarat's model of development is instead pushed forward very much by deliberate state interventions that resemble the interventions of the developmental states of East Asia.[74] Second, high rates of growth in Gujarat have facilitated poverty reduction; income poverty has come down significantly, though considerably less than what might have been expected given such high rates of growth (see Figures 3.4 and 3.5 and Table 3.1). The state's Human Development Index also lags well behind its growth performance.[75] These distributional outcomes also underline some of the less-than-positive attributes of Gujarat's pattern of development: employment generation lags far behind the growth in production because of the capital-intensive nature of manufacturing; and agriculture growth has suffered because public resources are channeled to support private industry.[76] And finally, of course, there is the issue of the exclusionary politics that supports the operation of the narrow ruling alliance. While it would be too strong, and probably analytically untenable, to claim that the politics of *Hindutva* and the political economy of state-led, pro-business economic growth are necessary to sustain each other, the association of the two in Gujarat is more than a mere coincidence. A narrow ruling coalition presents the challenge of how to mobilize electoral majorities; mobilizing the religious majority population is clearly one viable option, at least over the short to medium term.

IV. SOCIAL-DEMOCRATIC POLITICS IN COMMAND:
WEST BENGAL

India does not have any real social-democratic states. It is important to reiterate that the typology of political tendencies I have suggested is meant

---

[74] My discussion of South Korea as a developmental state can be found in Kohli (2004), Chapter 2.
[75] See Hirway (2000).
[76] See Bagchi et al. (2005) and Dholakia (2007).

mainly to underline and accentuate political tendencies in respective states that have persisted for a period; given democracy, politics across Indian states is bound to be evolving. A fairly obvious point is also worth keeping in mind: all Indian states share some core Indian characteristics; they are all part of a poor federal democracy in which the majority of citizens live off agriculture in caste-dominated villages, but in which a capitalist urban economy has also begun to make great strides. If the concept of neo-patrimonial evokes states in sub-Saharan Africa, India does not have any real neo-patrimonial states either. The political economies of U.P. and Bihar have only some tendencies that make them resemble, say, a Nigeria. Similarly, if the term "developmental state" brings to mind a Japan or a South Korea, a state like Gujarat in India is only trying to emulate some of their patterns. Social democracy is similarly associated with Scandinavian countries, known for sharing wealth and power. Some of India's left-leaning states, especially Kerala and West Bengal, have also attempted deliberate redistribution. Since Kerala has already been thoroughly studied,[77] and I have prior knowledge of West Bengal,[78] I use the example of West Bengal here to highlight the social-democratic impulse in some Indian states.

The case of West Bengal evokes controversy. This is in part because the balance sheet of achievements and shortcomings in West Bengal's developmental record over the last three decades is decidedly mixed, but also because, over this period, West Bengal has been governed by a single party, the CPM; the CPM was voted out of power just as this book went to press. The analysis of West Bengal's political economy poses a challenge, then, because any implicit assessment readily becomes an assessment of the "left" in power, evoking as much passion as an assessment of the "right" in power in, say, Gujarat. Some facts of the case, however, are clear and should be noted at the outset. (Table 3.4) In terms of per capita income, poverty, and human development, West Bengal is an average Indian state. After three decades of left-leaning-rule, the high levels of poverty and low levels of human development in the state are a real blight on the left's record. This record even raises the scholarly issue for my analysis of what characterizes the case of the CPM in West Bengal as a "social-democratic" experiment?

---

[77] See, for example, Ramachandran (1997), Kannan (2005), Heller (1999), Nossiter (1982), and Singh (2010).
[78] See the chapters on West Bengal in Kohli (1987) and Kohli (2009).

TABLE 3.4. *Some Developmental Indicators of West Bengal in a Comparative Perspective*

	West Bengal	Hindi-heartland[a] States	South India[b]	All India
Per capita income, 2006–7 (in rupees)	21,753	10,794	26,038	22,580
Economic growth, 1980–2008 (average annual %)	6.5	5.1	6.3	6.2
Economic growth, 1990–2008 (average annual %)	7.2	4.9	6.8	6.1
Poverty head count, 2004–5 (official poverty line) (%)	25.7	37.3	21.2	28.3
Decline in Poverty,[c] 1983–2005 (%)	1.3	0.7	0.9	0.8
Illiteracy,[d] 2005–6	29.1	40.9	23.9	31.7
Human Development Index, 2000	0.59	0.49	0.63	0.58

[a] The three Hindi-heartland states averaged here are Bihar, Uttar Pradesh, and Madhya Pradesh.

[b] The four South Indian states are Andhra Pradesh, Karnataka, Kerala, and Tamil Nadu.

[c] Average per annum percentage decline in head count ratio between 1983 and 2005 from Dev and Ravi (2007), Tables 8, 18, and 19.

[d] Illiteracy is defined as the percentage of the population above the age of six with no schooling.

Sources: Same as in Table 3.1.

The real achievements of the left in power in West Bengal have been the changes over-time in the regional political economy. First, the CPM-led coalition came to power in West Bengal in the late 1970s, when the political situation in the state was highly turbulent, with short-lived governments and considerable political violence; over the last three decades, by contrast, the left has provided relatively stable, public-spirited government. Second, the CPM in power spearheaded significant land reforms and established effective local governments that broke the back of landed power in rural society, contributing to a more even distribution of power. Third, West Bengal's economy has grown handsomely since about 1980 (Table 3.4), propelled initially by robust agricultural growth during the 1980s and then by industry in more recent years. Finally, and most important from the standpoint of a "social-democratic" case, poverty has declined rapidly in West Bengal over the last three decades (Table 3.4). As was clear in Figure 3.5 (also see Figure 3.4), starting from a very high point, poverty came down at a rate of 1.3 percent per annum in

West Bengal; as a matter of fact; the rate of decline has been the most rapid among Indian states. I will suggest later that this decline in poverty is a result of deliberate redistribution and robust economic growth in the context of good governance, tell-tale signs of social-democratic politics at the helm.

Of course, all is not well in West Bengal; there is no Indian state where all is well. The continuing high level of poverty in the state is in part a result of inheritance but also reflects limitations of the CPM's rule. One can view with some sympathy the recent political tensions in West Bengal that have arisen as an elected left-leaning government attempted to attract private investors in order to facilitate industrial growth. The more glaring failures of CPM rule – which are difficult to explain and for which it is hard to muster any sympathy – are evident in limited gains in primary education and health and, most recently, in a failure to pursue with any vigor the pro-poor national program, NREGA. This mixed record probably contributed to the electoral loss of the CPM and its allies. The long era of a democratically elected communist party in power in an Indian region thus came to an end in 2011; new problems require new solutions, and the CPM may have become too rigid and complacent to adapt.[79]

Background

The present state of West Bengal is about one-seventh the size of what used to be the Bengal Presidency during the colonial period. The rest of the old Presidency was carved into the other Indian states of Orissa and Bihar and into the neighboring sovereign state of Bangladesh. The core of the old Presidency, however – including Calcutta, the first capital city of British India, as well as some of the British-controlled jute and tea industries – remained part of West Bengal. It is important to recall that Bengal came under British control rather early. Needing revenues, the British created private property in land by transforming the de facto control over land of indigenous *zamindars* into de jure rights

---

[79] The deeper reasons for the recent electoral loss of the CPM await serious analysis. It is worth noting, however, that the CPM and its left-wing allies received 42 percent of the popular vote to Trinamool Congress's 48 percent in the 2011 elections. The lopsided victory of the latter, then, has as much to do with India's first-past-the-post electoral system and with the unity of the opposition forces as it does with any serious decline in the political base of the left.

and, in return, demanded a share of land wealth. This *zamindari* settlement was deeply consequential for the nature of the regional political economy.[80]

The land settlement transformed upper-caste revenue collectors into mega-landowners. Absent any real roots in the land, these *zamindars* often became absentee landlords – living in Calcutta or in other smaller cities – who cultivated the arts, culture, and lives of leisure. The real control over the land rested in the hands of village-level landlords, the *jotedars*, who often belonged to intermediate castes. Some of the *jotedars* used hired or bonded lower-caste labor to cultivate the land, but many leased the land to a variety of tenants and sharecroppers. The fertile land of the region created enough wealth to support a growing population of poor peasants and layers of land interests above the peasants, culminating in the *zamindars*, who in turn shared this wealth with the colonial state.

Some of the important characteristics of the regional political economy can be traced back to this agrarian system. First, *zamindars* were not always able to meet their revenue obligations to the British and sometimes lost their land. These *zamindaris* were, in turn, sold to new indigenous owners, attracting and absorbing local savings that might, under different circumstances, have promoted indigenous commerce and industry. Second, the layers of interest in land reduced the incentives to improve agrarian productivity. Those investing in *zamindaris* helped to recover their investment mainly by squeezing those below them. Third, the British introduced modern education to the region rather early. Many an offspring of the upper-caste Bengalis, often with roots in land wealth, took advantage of these new opportunities. This led to the emergence of a class of educated Bengali elite, the *bhadralok* (gentlemen elite).[81] Members of this intelligentsia shied away from economic enterprise; they instead took to white-collar jobs, especially the colonial civil service, and eventually to nationalist politics, including radical politics. And finally, absentee landlordism and exploitative production conditions created a restive peasantry, with peasant rebellions relatively common in this part of India.

Certain social structural traits of the region further reinforced the regional tendency toward limited economic dynamism among the indigenous elite and restive politics. A large segment of the Muslim population

---

[80] A good study of the "permanent settlement" that led to the creation of *zamindaris* is Ray (1979).
[81] A good study of the Bengali *bhadhralok* is Broomfield (1968).

of the region eventually ended up in Bangladesh. Some 25 percent of the current population of West Bengal is Muslim. Another quarter belongs to the scheduled castes, and some 5 percent are categorized as scheduled tribes. Muslims, SCs, and STs thus constitute more than half of West Bengal's population; they are also the lower strata of the region, generally poor and illiterate. Caste Hindus of the region – less than half of West Bengal's population – were divided into a small Brahmin and Kayastha elite at the top and a variety of "clean" and "unclean" Shudras below them. It is worth underlining that Kshatriyas (the traditional warrior castes) and Vaishyas (the traditional merchant and trading castes) were generally missing in Hindu Bengal, inclining the Bengali elite to matters cerebral. Over centuries, many members of lower castes in the region embraced Islam, weakening Brahmanic hegemony. A variety of religious reform movements also contributed to the erosion of a strict caste society of the type to be found in the Hindu heartland of India. As many Brahmins and other upper castes became absentee landlords during the colonial period, they left the village society for others to mobilize, an opening exploited by various peasant movements. The indigenous elite thus avoided commerce and enterprise, embracing arts and politics instead, while the lower strata did not readily accept their subordinate status and became available for alternate political commitments.[82]

As a fertile region that was also the seat of the colonial state, Bengal offered important economic opportunities. However, Bengali upper classes often did not take advantage of these opportunities. The British state favored their own, leading to a growing British role in the jute and tea industries, the key export-oriented industries of the region.[83] Commerce and industry attracted Indians from other regions, especially Marwaris from western India, who filled the spaces that Bengalis failed to occupy. Economic development in the region also attracted migrant workers from other Indian regions, giving cities like Calcutta a cosmopolitan flavor. At the time of independence, then, West Bengal was one of India's most highly industrialized states. Nevertheless, the regional economy was relatively vulnerable.[84] First, industry and commerce were controlled by non-Bengalis and heavily integrated with eastern Bengal for imports and markets; both decolonization and partition thus wreaked havoc on West Bengal. Second, much of the industry was concentrated in and around

---

[82] I have developed this argument in some detail in Kohli (2009), Chapter 12.
[83] See Bagchi (1972).
[84] See Bagchi (1998).

Calcutta; the rest of West Bengal was as poor and illiterate as the neighboring state of Bihar and Orissa. And finally, the agricultural economy of the region was hampered by a variety of institutional constraints, especially the pattern of land ownership.

Prior to independence, notable political developments in the region included early nationalist political mobilization, the failure of the Congress to put down any deep roots, and the emergence of radical politics. From the late nineteenth century onward, the educated Bengali elite spearheaded demands for political and social change. Some of these were simply aimed at broader access to the colonial state. Others were focused on reforming the Hindu caste society. And yet others began to question the legitimacy of British presence in India. The classic "divide and rule" colonial strategy led to an attempted partition of Bengal into western and eastern portions – majority Hindu versus majority Muslim populations – further mobilizing the Bengali political class in the early twentieth century.[85] Political leaders were also divided over the appropriate tactics to be used against the British, reformist or militant. Many who preferred the latter were eventually attracted to communism, leading to early support for a communist party in West Bengal.

The Indian national Congress never put down deep roots in Bengal. Of course, following independence, the Congress came to power all over India, including in West Bengal. However, its support base in the region was shallow. The political elite felt that they were more advanced politically than Gandhi and his followers, lending them, at best, lukewarm support. The lower strata were already relatively mobilized; they offered their support to a left-of-center Muslim party that promised land reform. Unlike the situation in many other parts of India, but like that in southern regions such as Madras (eventually the state of Tamil Nadu), the upper castes of West Bengal never established a hegemonic alliance with the lowest strata, an alliance that formed the backbone of Congress support in the Hindi heartland. Moreover, the Congress never established a provincial government in West Bengal prior to independence.

With relatively early industrialization and urbanization, labor emerged as a political factor. Indigenous communist leaders often succeeded in spearheading such efforts. With industry controlled by the British and the Marwaris, communist-led unions combined class appeals with nationalist and ethnic themes: Bengalis versus the rest. Peasant mobilization, by contrast, was seldom led by communists during this early phase. Under

[85] See Sarkar (1973).

the influence of Moscow, Indian communists focused their energies on mobilization of the "proletariat," or industrial workers. Peasants were instead mobilized by a variety of peasant organizations; some were affiliated with political parties (especially the Krishak Praja Party that formed the regional government in the late 1930s), others more autonomous. Eventually, many of these peasant organizations joined the communists during the post-independence period.

In sum, West Bengal experienced early industrialization, but much of it was led by non-Bengalis: the British and Indian entrepreneurs from western India. The indigenous elite had its roots in land wealth. Many of them embraced British-provided higher education and joined the civil service, the professions, and politics, even radical politics. The working classes of the region joined communist-led unions, and peasant organizations succeeded in mobilizing peasants, especially tenants. In such a context the Congress party never put down deep roots.

The Era of Congress Rule

After independence, the Congress Party was India's single most popular party. Its nationalist legitimacy helped it maintain power over most of India, including in West Bengal, but only up until the 1960s. A single Bengali leader with close ties to Nehru, B. C. Roy, ruled West Bengal from 1948 to 1962. After the 1967 elections, a variety of left-leaning parties challenged Congress rule, initiating a decade of political instability that ended only with the emergence of the CPM as the ruling party in 1977. The economy of West Bengal during this period fell behind those of other faster-growing regions of India. While public sector investment helped the regional economy during the 1950s, the private sector in industry remained sluggish. Agricultural growth was also dismal, constrained by both the land system and poor irrigation facilities.

While Congress rule in West Bengal resembled Congress rule elsewhere in India, the similarities were superficial. Unlike the situation in Maharashtra or Gujarat, politics in West Bengal never became pro-business. Also, unlike the case of U.P. and other Hindi-heartland states, the Brahmin-led chains of patronage never quite took root in West Bengal. Moreover, statewide caste movements, such as the backward-class movement, did not materialize in West Bengal. All this requires comment. Early industrialization and the significant presence of industrial capital in Calcutta, as in Bombay and Ahmadabad, could have pushed the state's politics in a pro-business direction during the 1950s and 1960s, but did not. This was mainly a function of the fact that industry in West Bengal was controlled by non-Bengalis. While some Congress leaders were happy to pursue pro-business policies, the significant presence of Marwaris in business played into the hands of the left-leaning intelligentsia of Bengal, who combined appeals of regional nationalism with class politics to mobilize against non-Bengali capitalists.[86] The fact that regional capitalists were far from unified did not help their political case; for example, during the early 1960s, there were six different chambers of commerce, one for Marwaris, one for Muslims, another for businessmen with lineage in former British-owned tea estates and industry, and so on.[87] Unlike the case of Gujarat discussed earlier, then, a cozy ruling alliance adjoining the political and economic elite was never established in West Bengal.

The caste and land-ownership structure in West Bengal also precluded the emergence of a politics akin to that of U.P. or Bihar. Compared to U.P. or Bihar, there were very few Brahmins in West Bengal. Those who were there often became absentee landlords. The hold of Brahmins over the rural society was thus, at best, tenuous. Village-level control was instead exercised by *jotedars* who hailed from a variety of intermediate castes: Mahishyas in the district of Midnapore, the Ugra-Kshatriyas in Burdwan, Mahatos in Purulia, and the Rajbanshis in Cooch Behar.[88] Since Brahmanical hegemony was weak, there was little incentive for these intermediate castes to unite into an anti-Brahmin, backward-caste movement. Caste politics of the kind that prevails in the Hindi-heartland, then – Brahmanical domination, followed by challenges from intermediate and lower castes – has no real parallel in West Bengal.

In spite of a superficial power base, Congress rule in West Bengal during the 1950s provided administrative efficiency. Partition created numerous problems, including an influx of some four million refugees from East Pakistan. These problems absorbed the state leaders. B. C. Roy's close links with Nehru helped West Bengal during this early phase. The dominant political trend in the state, however, was slow but steady mobilization of the lower classes.[89] The early focus of the communists was factory labor. Following the split in international communism between the Soviet Union and China, significant sections of Bengali communists started focusing on the countryside. Several districts of West Bengal already had a

---

[86] Chaudhry (1976), p. 374.
[87] Ibid., p. 381.
[88] Ibid., p. 376.
[89] See, for example, Franda (1972).

tradition of peasant mobilization; urban communist leaders found ready support in these areas. In addition, tribal areas, especially those in the isolated north of the state, proved amenable to radical appeals. From these beginnings emerged the well-known Naxalite movement, whose offshoot, the new Naxalites (or Maoists), continues to flourish in various parts of India today (discussed in Chapter 2). Communist-led labor unions could and did bring industry to a halt, and radical peasant movements forcefully implemented land redistribution legislation. During the 1960s and the 1970s then, West Bengal became one of India's most highly mobilized and unstable states.

As Congress's nationalist hold declined all across India during the 1960s, the communists emerged as a significant alternative political force in West Bengal. The communists were well organized and posed a significant electoral challenge to Congress rule. For roughly a decade, 1967 to 1977, it became difficult for any party to form a stable majority government. Between 1967 and 1972, for example, there were four elections, five different chief ministers, and three spells of president's rule. During these years, West Bengal became nearly ungovernable. A war on the borders over the formation of Bangladesh, more refugees, a land grab sponsored by the Naxalites, industrial strikes led by the communists, state-sponsored repression initiated by Indira Gandhi, and plain hooliganism on the streets of Calcutta contributed to this crisis of governability.[90] This situation changed only after the CPM's electoral victory in 1977.

Between 1948 and 1977 the economy of West Bengal grew at a sluggish pace, and nearly two-thirds of the state's population lived below the poverty line.[91] While West Bengal was one of India's most highly industrialized states at the time of independence, much of the industry was concentrated in and around Calcutta. The significant jute industry also went into decline following the Second World War. Global demand for jute products declined at the end of the war (guinea bags were used in the trenches), and the partition severed the smooth flow of such key inputs as raw jute, which was produced mainly in East Bengal. As many Britis abandoned India, Marwaris moved into the jute industry. Many of thes Marwaris, however, were traders and speculators, not industrialists. Poc management then contributed to the decline of regional industry, as di the tendency of Marwaris to move investment out of the state at the firs sign of political trouble.

---

[90] See Kohli (1990), Chapter 10.
[91] For an overview, see Bhattacharya (1989).

As already noted, unlike the case of Gujarat, the state government in West Bengal did not prioritize private sector–led industrialization. The results were not obvious during the 1950s because of some major public sector investments in the state: for example, Durgapur steel, large irrigation projects, and Nehru's support for Tata steel. All this contributed to modest growth, especially industrial growth. Below the surface, however, the West Bengali government ignored the development of infrastructure, and private sector investment began to move out of the state. The latter trend hastened as labor militancy and political instability grew. Between mid-1960 and mid-1970, then, there was virtually no industrial growth in West Bengal. The state's agriculture also remained sluggish. Lack of investment in irrigation was one constraint, and poor incentives generated by the patterns of land ownership and use was another. The green revolution in paddy also came late to India, benefiting West Bengal mainly during the 1980s.

CPM Rule

The CPM came to power in West Bengal in 1977 and ruled the state until 2011, an unparalleled thirty-five-year electoral reign by a communist party. When the CPM came to power, the political and economic conditions in West Bengal were grave. The economy was stagnant; government and politics were unstable; and nearly two-thirds of the state's population lived below the poverty line. West Bengal remains a state with significant problems: nearly a quarter of the population lives below the poverty line; infrastructure is poor; education and health conditions are near the low Indian average; and, as befits a democracy, the Bengali electorate has been keen to give parties other than the CPM a chance to rule. And yet the CPM in power did facilitate important positive changes: political stability was restored; land reforms were implemented; economic growth resumed; and poverty declined rapidly.

When Congress's electoral fortunes declined during the second half of the 1960s, the CPM and its left-wing allies formed a couple of short-lived coalition governments in the state. The CPM used these short stints in power strategically and pursued some highly visible pro-poor policies in the countryside. While a populist and popular Indira Gandhi could still pose a formidable challenge – especially following the popular Bangladesh war – the CPM used its organizational superiority to consolidate growing support. As a communist party with disciplined cadres, the CPM slowly but surely expanded its base of support, eventually winning the state elections in 1977. While in a position to form a government on its own, the CPM led a coalition of left-wing parties, creating a powerful state government.

It is important to understand the type of communism to which the CPM adhered.[92] The more the CPM accepted the need to contest elections as the legitimate road to power, as well as the need to operate within the constraints of a private enterprise economy, the more the CPM's commitment to fomenting a revolution that would establish a dictatorship of the proletariat was diluted. Once in power in the late 1970s, the CPM essentially became a social-democratic party that sought to facilitate mild redistribution within the constraints of democracy and capitalism. What gave the CPM some advantage over many other Indian political parties with similar commitments was its organizational superiority. One aspect of communism to which the CPM continued to adhere was the democratic-centralist nature of the party. In a highly fragmented political context, organizational coherence gave the CPM a political advantage that it used successfully, not only to win elections repeatedly, but also to implement some pro-poor policies.

Soon after coming to power, the CPM decided to focus its political energy and state resources on the countryside. The CPM leadership reasoned that Calcutta was the responsibility of big business, which was concentrated in, and made profits in, the city. An agrarian focus, by contrast, was both in accordance with the CPM's pro-poor ideology and a smart electoral strategy. Prioritizing implementation of land reforms was also consistent with the interests of those who supported the party, mainly the middle and lower strata in the villages. The CPM's policy priorities thus became securing the land rights of tenant farmers and redistributing land that was above the maximum limit on land ownership allowed by law. It is important to note that these or similar policies were already on the books in most Indian states; they were also consistent with national guidelines. The CPM thus could not readily be blamed by New Delhi for violating the rights of private property or other constitutionally protected rights. The CPM's focus was on implementation; on this front, a well organized party was a significant political asset.

The CPM used the party machinery to penetrate village society. As a ruling party, it also introduced elected local governments at the level of villages. Local government elections brought CPM cadres and others

---

[92] For a more detailed version of the analysis in this paragraph, see Kohli (1987), Chapter 3.

sympathetic to the CPM to power. Downward penetration of the CPM via party and local governments, in turn, enabled the party leadership to isolate the hitherto powerful landlords, the *jotedars*. This significant power shift in the rural society enabled the CPM regime to implement mild but significant land reforms. Over the next two decades, some fifteen million tenants were registered, securing their rights on the land and reducing the share of crops they owed to landlords. The land affected by these tenancy reforms covered some 15 percent of the total cropped area. In addition, some two million households received about half an acre each of above-ceiling surplus lands, totaling some one million acres, or 6.5 percent of the total cropped area of West Bengal. Taken together, then, tenancy reforms and land acquisition benefitted nearly half of all rural households and covered nearly a fifth of all the cropped area of West Bengal.[93]

Except for Kerala, no other Indian state has implemented such extensive land reform. No doubt the magnitude of benefits to poor rural households in West Bengal was very small. However, the margin between destitution and survival in the Indian countryside itself tends to be very small. So, what have been some of the main consequences of the type of agrarian social democracy pursued by the CPM? On the economic front, tenancy reforms and land redistribution led not only to one-time gains, but also to a sharing of long-term agricultural growth.[94] There is evidence to suggest that tenancy reforms helped improve agricultural production.[95] There is also evidence to suggest that the majority who gained from land reforms were members of scheduled castes and tribes.[96] It is thus hard to resist the proposition that the land reforms implemented by the CPM regime have helped the poor in the countryside and that the rapid decline in poverty in West Bengal that is evident in the data is at least in part a result of these redistributive policies.

Land reforms are deeply political. The CPM's motivation in pursuing them was mainly to build and consolidate political support. The fact that the CPM regularly won elections between 1977 and 2011, then, especially with the help of the rural vote, is the most obvious political benefit reaped by the CPM. These political gains, however, have not been unambiguous. The isolation of landlords created an authority vacuum of sorts in the countryside. That vacuum has been filled by party cadres

[93] All of these figures on tenancy reform and land acquisition are from Sengupta and Gazdar (1997), pp. 144 and 168.
[94] Ibid.
[95] Banerjee et al. (2002).
[96] See Bardhan et al. (2009).

and the party-controlled local governments.[97] While this has led to such positive outcomes as the channeling of public resources to the poor – more on this later – rural society in West Bengal has as a result become polarized, with those who support the CPM on one side and those who do not on the other. Over time, party cadres in positions of power have also become complacent, comfortable, and even corrupt.[98] The results include the CPM's declining popularity in West Bengal.

One of the more unexpected developments in West Bengal during the 1980s was an acceleration of agricultural growth.[99] Food grain output in the state grew at nearly 5 percent per annum, compared to the Indian average agricultural growth rate of less than 3 percent during this period. The CPM regime has sought to take credit for this acceleration, but the case that it has resulted from such public policies as land reforms is not very persuasive. Some of the acceleration was simply a recovery from poor performance during an earlier period. Scholars have also pointed out that the land area covered by land reform – less than a quarter of the whole – was too small to account for the accelerated growth.[100] The acceleration, then, resulted mainly from the embrace of the green revolution – higher-yielding paddy – by private producers. Much of the increase in irrigation that facilitated higher cropping intensity was also a product, not of public investment, but of numerous small-scale private investments, such as investments in tube wells. CPM-controlled local governments may have played a positive role in supplying information, but it is not the case that land reforms were mainly responsible for the acceleration in agricultural growth. What is persuasive is a more modest case, namely, that deliberate redistribution in the countryside was certainly not negative for growth, as well as a stronger case, namely, that land reforms facilitated a broad sharing of the fruits of economic growth.[101]

Agricultural growth decelerated in West Bengal during the 1990s but picked up again after 2005.[102] The causes of deceleration include

---

[97] See Chaterjee (2009) and Bhattacharya (2009).

[98] See various essays in the special issue on West Bengal in the *Economic and Political Weekly*, February 28, 2009.

[99] For a good overview, see Guruswamy et al. (2005).

[100] Sengupta and Gazdar (1997), pp. 165–7.

[101] Ibid., p. 169.

[102] Overall agricultural growth between 1980 and 2010 was about 3.5 percent per annum. During the 1980s the growth was focused on cereals and averaged nearly 5 percent per annum. Over the next fifteen years the growth averaged less than 3 percent. Since 2005, the growth rate has again accelerated to some 4.3 percent, now focused not so much on cereals as on vegetables. For data, see Government of West Bengal (2010), Table 5.0, p. 44.

limited public investment in irrigation – a nationwide phenomenon – and the related saturation of gains from the green revolution in paddy. By contrast, the recent acceleration seems to be a result of a growing shift to cash crops, such as vegetables. As incomes in the state rise, this shift seems to be following market logic. The state government in West Bengal, in any case, seems to have concluded that its "rural tilt" had reached a saturation point; toward the end of its tenure, the CPM leadership was concentrating more and more of its energy, not on the countryside, but on the promotion of industry.

As is well known, over time West Bengal has steadily lost its industrial edge in India. A variety of causes have already been noted: the impact of partition; national policies that hurt industry in West Bengal during the 1950s and the 1960s, including the anti-export bias of ISI policies and, related to that, pricing policies, especially freight policies; the failure of the regional government and the region's economic elite to work together, well before the emergence of the CPM; a highly mobilized labor force that discouraged private investors; and the CPM's conscious decision during the 1980s and the 1990s to prioritize the countryside. By the beginning of the new millennium, there was a growing consensus among specialists that the CPM regime needed to prioritize industrial development and that the key constraint on industrial growth was not so much labor activism as it was low rates of profitability in industry.[103] The cumulative impact of decades of neglect has resulted in poor-quality infrastructure and a low level of skills in the state; these factors, along with labor activism, have caused private industry to shy away from the state, calculating that higher rates of profit are to be made elsewhere in India.

Over the last decade, the CPM regime has sought to promote private sector–led industrial growth in West Bengal. A variety of strategies have been pursued. According to government's own documents, they are trying to create "an investor-friendly climate."[104] The government boasts that industrial strikes and man-days lost due to labor strife are declining

---

[103] See, for example, Banerjee et al. (2002). This document was written by nine prominent Bengali economists, clearly hoping to influence public policy in West Bengal. Among the recommendations proposed was the need to prioritize industrial development, not so much by pursuing industrial policy as by creating favorable conditions that will attract private investors, especially small-scale industry. The document did not explain very well the case against industrial policy in West Bengal. In any case, as noted below, the CPM government has by now accepted the need to promote industry in West Bengal, but has also moved toward an activist state pursuing an industrial policy of sorts.

[104] Government of West Bengal (2010), p. 119.

and that the "state government has continued to take measures to boost investors' confidence." Such specific industries as biotechnology information technology, and mines and minerals have been singled out for public support. The government has helped set up "industry specific clusters," "industrial parks," and special economic zones that will be "relaxed and business friendly."[105] As in the case of China, a regional communist government in India has concluded that, if growth is the goal, there are few alternatives but to woo the private sector. We know by now, however, this dramatic policy shift has also created serious problems for the CPM. For example, the effort to acquire land from poor peasants in order to establish private industry has led to numerous confrontations between party cadres and potential supporters, probably causing the CPM electoral support.[106]

While the CPM's efforts to attract private enterprise have led to some well-publicized conflicts, the efforts are not without results. As agriculture growth has slowed, growth in both industry and services has accelerated. West Bengal continues to be one of India's more rapidly growing states. After declining steadily for nearly two decades, West Bengal's share of industrial output in national output stabilized at some 4.4 percent during the 2000s, suggesting that industrial growth in West Bengal is now keeping pace with India's overall industrial growth.[107] Considering the recent past, this is a significant achievement.

No discussion of CPM rule in West Bengal would be complete without noting some glaring weaknesses in the state's developmental record. Educational and health conditions in the state have not improved significantly over the last three decades. Scholars analyzing this outcome have noted that there has been "a near total absence of initiative in public policy" in the areas of health, gender, and illiteracy in West Bengal.[108] During the 1990s, the CPM regime did initiate a campaign to improve literacy. As the data in Table 3.1 shows, however, the results have not been dramatic: as a middle-income state, the human development indicators of West Bengal continue to be middling by Indian standards. Some of this failure of public initiative reflects the dire fiscal situation in the state, which, in turn, is a product of a number of underlying conditions:

[105] Ibid., p. 119.
[106] See, for example, the editorial "Nandigram: Taking People for Granted," in the *Economic and Political Weekly*, January 13, 2007, p. 80.
[107] Government of West Bengal (2010), Table 6.2, p. 106.
[108] Sengupta and Gazdar (1997), p. 194.

failure to tax the rapidly growing service economy; a large public sector wage bill; and less-than-favorable treatment by New Delhi.[109] One suspects, however, that the problem of limited public initiative also runs deeper. The CPM's redistributive interventions, such as land reforms, were deeply political in motivation: altering land relations undercut the power of Congress-supporting landlords and helped the CPM consolidate its power base with the middle and lower strata in the countryside. It may well be that CPM leaders believed that efforts to promote education and health – slow and generalized gains – would not lead to clear electoral dividends.

Another pro-poor program in which West Bengal's record is relatively lackluster is NREGA. As discussed in earlier chapters, this is an important employment-generating program that has the potential to create some 100 days of gainful employment for poor individuals in the countryside. During 2008–9, West Bengal created only twenty-five days of extra employment for every individual participating in this program. Compared to some other Indian states – where the average tends to be closer to fifty days – this is a disappointing performance. Given the CPM's capacity to reach the rural poor via party cadres and party-controlled local governments, one wonders why the program has not been pursued more vigorously. While the issue needs further research, the answer in West Bengal may be the same as in the case of U.P. discussed earlier. NREGA is a centrally sponsored program through which the Congress Party hopes to broaden its base of support among India's poor. Opposition parties like Mayawati's Bahujan Samaj Party and the CPM understand this. Fearing gains for the Congress, non-Congress ruling parties have chosen not to implement NREGA with any vigor; growing electoral competition in this case is hurting rather than helping the rural poor.

To sum up the discussion on West Bengal, and especially on the CPM's role in West Bengal, the record is decidedly mixed. Significant pockets of poverty remain, and health and education conditions have not improved dramatically in the state. And yet there have been significant politically driven achievements. These come to light especially if one adopts a long-term perspective. The CPM regime in 1977 inherited a deeply troubled political economy: unstable politics, a stagnant economy, and massive poverty. Over the last three decades, West Bengal has been moderately well governed, economic growth has returned, and poverty has declined

---

[109] On the need to tax the service economy, see Banerjee et al. (2002). For an analysis of the "discriminatory" treatment of West Bengal by New Delhi, see Guruswamy et al. (2005).

rapidly. At the heart of these positive achievements lies the role of the CPM – a party communist in name but social-democratic in practice – that has successfully implemented modest land reforms, contributing to a more egalitarian polity and economy.

V. CONCLUSION

Some Indian states are growing rapidly. Other Indian states have demonstrated a superior capacity to reduce poverty, even without rapid growth. And in yet other states, neither growth nor poverty reduction has been impressive. In this chapter I have sought to explain such developmental diversity across Indian regions, focusing on how state-level political trends might contribute to such diverse outcomes. For a fuller explanation of regional diversity, a focus on state-level political determinants needs to be complemented by an understanding of the changing national context, a set of changes analyzed in earlier chapters. Moreover, other factors such as geography (coastal or inland) and initial resource endowments are also clearly consequential; my primary focus on "man-made" factors that are influencing patterns of development across Indian states emerges from the political economy concerns of the present study.

I have argued in this chapter that a variety of political tendencies have come to the fore in Indian states and that these tendencies, in turn, especially when they are dominant and persist, have influenced patterns of economic development in these states. In order to support this argument I have discussed some of India's important states. In Uttar Pradesh, for example, I have suggested that neo-patrimonial politicians have been at the helm during the recent period. With a weak sense of public purpose, a state run by such leaders has not been good either at revenue collection or at using public expenditure to promote development. The results have included relatively sluggish economic growth and persistent poverty. By contrast, a narrow developmental coalition of political and economic elite has steered the levers of power in a state like Gujarat. The regional state in such a case has intervened systematically in the markets to promote growth, with considerable success. A different pattern of development has emerged in a state like West Bengal, where a parliamentary communist party, more social-democratic than communist, was in power for nearly three decades. As a well-organized party with a lower-class base, its rulers were able to implement modest land reforms. When agricultural growth picked up, the fruits of economic growth came to be shared widely, bringing down poverty rapidly. Such examples help buttress the claim that how power is organized in Indian states helps explain some of the developmental diversity across these states.

The roots of political diversity across Indian states are harder to explain because they are often located deep in the past, especially the colonial past. In Gujarat, for example, which was earlier part of the undivided state of Maharashtra, and even earlier part of the colonially governed Bombay Presidency, indigenous commercial and industrial elite emerged rather early. Agriculture in the area was also more smallholder in nature, and regional administration was more direct, less dependent on such intermediaries as the *zamindars*. With a social stratum that might stand in the way of commercial and industrial development simply missing, capitalism faced fewer obstacles in the region and took root early. Commercial elite in turn worked closely with regional political elite, even during the nationalist period. Politics in Gujarat since its formation has thus tended to be pro-business. This is not to suggest that some sort of path-dependence was inevitable. On a number of occasions over the last few decades, especially during the Indira Gandhi period, a broad-based political coalition that might have steered politics in Gujarat away from a high-growth path came close to dominating state power. Powerful social groups within the state ensured, however, that such a coalition did not stay in power for long, and that it came to be replaced by a much narrower coalition of political and economic elite. Following the national-level policy changes of 1991, then, a state such as Gujarat, with a developmental coalition at the helm, was much better positioned to take advantage of the new political economy.

Bengal Presidency also experienced early industrialization, but much of this was in the hands of the British, and the Marwaris from western India played an important role in the related commercial developments. The *zamindari* settlement encouraged indigenous Bengali elite to stay away from commerce; they instead took advantage of British-established educational institutions, giving rise to an intelligentsia of sorts, the Bengali *bhadralok*. Absentee landlordism also encouraged a restive peasantry. As the Bengali intelligentsia entered politics, first nationalist and later more radical, they mobilized elements of the lower strata into regional politics. From these beginnings emerged a popular communist party in the region that prioritized modest agrarian redistribution as a strategy for political consolidation. Over the last few decades, as agricultural growth has picked up, an improved tenancy and land situation has enabled poverty in West Bengal to come down rapidly. However, a redistributive thrust can go only so far in a poor economy, a conundrum that a regional communist party has struggled to solve.

Finally, the commercial impulse was simply quite weak in what used to be the old United Provinces, now the state of Uttar Pradesh. *Zamindars* and *taluqadars* dominated the rural economy – which was much of the overall regional economy – and seldom took to commerce. Unlike the case of Bengal, an intelligentsia did not develop in U.P. Without commercial or intellectual dynamism, "pre-modern" upper-caste elites dominated regional politics. A set of political elite, who were socialized in the nationalist movement, might have pulled U.P. out of its "backwardness," but the "best" simply became part of national politics. Politics in U.P. came to be dominated by landowning upper castes who, with their limited political horizons, bickered along factional lines and monopolized the fruits of power. Politics in the state became an end in itself, without any strong conception of the state as serving a public purpose. Over time, the hold of the upper castes was challenged, but caste politics only beget more caste politics, lower-caste leaders arguing that it was now their turn to milk the state. Such neo-patrimonial politics at the helm has hurt any type of development, whether growth-oriented or redistributive.

To conclude, the quality of governance across Indian states is a major issue when trying to explain why development patterns vary so much across India. The type of politics that has come to the fore in these states molds patterns of governmental intervention that, in turn, influence economic outcomes. The roots of political diversity often lie deep in the past, especially in the nature of the regional ruling classes that emerged during the colonial period: a commercially inclined ruling elite gave Gujarat a long-term advantage on the growth front; a radicalized intelligentsia has helped bring down poverty in West Bengal in recent decades; and the absence of both commercial and intellectual development has left U.P. with a ruling elite who treat state power as personal patrimony, hurting both growth and redistribution. Of course, my suggestion that the roots of state-level politics lie deep in the past ought not to be interpreted as a suggestion that these trends were somehow inevitable, or that they can't be altered in the future; just as the future is uncertain today, so it was in the past. The tendencies inherited from the past run deep, but they can be altered, either by slow but steady change that accumulates into qualitative change – for example, slow but steady commercial development – or by major shocks, such as a significant political change produced by democratic politics and new leadership.

Conclusion

India's economy is growing briskly, but many Indians are being left behind. The democratic promise of inclusive growth is not being met. This study has sought both to focus attention on this fact and to explain why it might be so. The facts of the situation are relatively clear. India's economy has grown handsomely since about 1980, and the growth rate is now approaching that of the world's fastest-growing economy, China. Compared both to its own past and to other countries, growth acceleration in India is a major achievement. This impressive growth performance, however, has been accompanied by widening economic inequality along a variety of cleavages: rural versus urban; across Indian regions; and along class lines, especially in the cities. As the rich have gotten richer, the life chances of the poor have not improved proportionately. Poverty has declined at only a modest pace, forcing some 450 million Indians to survive on less than $1.25 per day. Literacy is also improving, but again at a fairly slow pace. Health conditions are especially abysmal: nearly half the children in the country remain underweight and anemic, and some third of Indian women suffer from low body mass index.

If the facts of want amid plenty are relatively clear, why this may be so and what can be done about it are controversial issues. One somewhat sanguine view of India's current developmental trajectory takes comfort in the fact that the Indian economy finally opened up to the world in the early 1990s and grew rapidly as a result. Since poverty and destitution in India are age-old problems, this view might continue, the new growth finally offers the possibility of incorporating the poor into a productive economy. Economic growth also generates public resources that might be used to help those at the bottom. Sooner rather than later, democratic pressures will push the rulers to use these resources constructively to provide improved education, health, and income to the majority of Indians. This is a respectable perspective on contemporary Indian development; at times I too am attracted to it, especially because of the sense of hopefulness it creates. And yet such a view is too sanguine. It is also misleading insofar as it does not take account of how deeply economic changes are embedded in political and social realities. Economic growth in India accelerated only when the ruling elite prioritized growth and slowly but surely created a narrow ruling coalition with the growth producers, commercial and business groups. More important, new economic growth is creating not only new wealth but also new power realities. New private wealth is further empowering India's business classes. These powerful groups, in turn, have begun to mold Indian politics in ways that they hope will make the Indian state even more pro-business. It is not at all obvious why such a state would prioritize distributive goals that favor the underprivileged. Electoral pressures and an occasional farsighted leader can clearly make some difference. However, systematic inclusive growth will require well-organized representation of the underprivileged in the political sphere so as to facilitate a shift, not toward populism, but toward real social-democratic politics. It will also require significant improvement in the capacity of the Indian state to deliver resources and services to the poor, a capacity woefully lacking at present.

In this book, approaching the subject of India's development from a standpoint that views economy, society, and politics as deeply intertwined and focuses on distributive issues, I have explored both national and regional trends in India. The argument that runs through the study is that a narrow ruling alliance of political and business elite increasingly steers national economic policy in India, and that these policies influence economic outcomes. A focus on the narrowness of the ruling coalition helps explain both the forces that have accelerated economic growth in India and the disproportionate distribution of the fruits of that growth. Since the central argument has already been previewed in the Introduction and developed in the following chapters, I will recapitulate it here only briefly. Following the brief recapitulation, I will juxtapose the recent Indian developmental experience against that of some other developing countries, concluding with some reflections on broader themes that go beyond India.

SUMMARY

In this book I have analyzed political change, political economy, and regional diversity in India between 1980 and the present. The focus has been the mutual interaction of states and markets as they mold India's development. I have been especially keen to highlight the winners and losers in the new Indian political economy. Only the briefest summary of the argument is now needed.

India is a complex democracy in which much happens every day, not to mention over the three decades that are the focus of this study. Among a range of political changes, big and small, some that make headlines and others that do not, I have underlined the steadily growing power of business groups in India's national politics as singularly important. I argued in Chapter 1 that this process was actually initiated by Indian politicians during the 1980s as they desperately sought rapid economic growth and embraced business groups as partners in this project. Over time, as the government has created a favorable environment for business to flourish, the power of business groups has grown in India and is now exercised in a wide variety of political arenas: anywhere from molding social values via control of the media, to financing political parties, to influencing public policy (including via corrupt practices), to running for office and winning elections directly. The resulting narrow ruling alliance of state and business elite, in turn, helps explain some important political trends in India. The fact that electoral fragmentation in India has not led to policy incoherence makes sense only against this background; diverse political parties and actors now seem to agree on the basics of policy, especially economic policy. A narrow ruling alliance, however, also creates serious problems for the political elite in terms of how to manage those who are excluded. A variety of legitimacy formulas – at times no more than gimmicks – are thus being tried out to see if they might succeed in mobilizing electoral majorities without disturbing the core ruling alliance; electoral politics and policy making thus increasingly operate on separate tracks, often insulated from each other. Decentralization of sorts also frees the national elite to take credit for "India shining" while lower-level elites are held responsible for failures and shortcomings. Of course, rulers do not fully succeed in managing the excluded; the latter have their own voice and their own initiatives. Indian politics is thus dotted with a variety of movements and actions on the part of the excluded, including some of the most visible manifestations of destitution, such as a growing Naxalite movement involving India's tribal population and farmer suicides.

A state-business alliance has helped propel both India's economic growth and its inequality; this argument was developed in Chapter 2. Following an era of slow growth during the 1970s, India's leaders prioritized economic growth and sought Indian business groups as partners in this endeavor. Slowly but surely business groups responded, especially as they became confident that the era of radical rhetoric and antibusiness policies was over. During the 1980s the Indian state provided indigenous capitalists a variety of favorable policies that helped their profitability and growth. The economy moved to a higher-growth path that has been maintained during the subsequent period. Since the new pro-business policy measures included tax concessions that reduced public revenue, and since the state chose to maintain high levels of public investment, a fiscal and balance-of-payment crisis ensued in the early 1990s. This crisis provided the occasion for a more far reaching "liberalization" of the Indian economy. India's liberalization, however, has been characterized by its own distinctive features that depart significantly from those prescribed by the "Washington consensus." The Indian state maintained a pro-growth expansionary stance and provided various supports to indigenous business groups, including a calibration of external liberalization to ensure that domestic capitalists continued to flourish. India's economy during the post-1991 period has continued to grow handsomely. However, the rate of growth, especially in the industrial sector that liberalization policies have targeted, has not altered dramatically over the last two decades. The real upward shift in India's growth pattern occurred in the early 1980s, when the Indian state embraced Indian capitalists as core allies, and has been maintained ever since.

What has changed significantly following the policy shifts of 1991 are redistributive trends; over the last two decades these trends have become more regressive. The primary motor of these new distributive trends are governmental policies that enable the rich to get richer rapidly, on the one hand, and a pattern of public expenditure that does not compensate all those who are excluded from the new growth, on the other. The fact that India's growth, especially service sector growth, has absorbed those with skills, and that the manufacturing economy has not created enough new jobs to absorb the rapidly growing low-skilled labor force, further contributes to a worsening distributive picture. The reduction in public investment in agriculture has hurt agricultural growth, leaving behind the majority of Indians who continue to live in the countryside. Similarly, the unwillingness of the national state to facilitate industrial growth via public investment is leaving behind India's poorer states, especially the poorly governed poorer states, which are not attracting sufficient private investment to compensate for these policy changes. Since a majority of India's poor live in the countryside and in India's poorer states, the shifting patterns of public investment have been a major culprit in the evolving winner-take-all economy. Of course, given democratic pressures, some of these policies may alter in the near future. Also, major public works programs aimed at creating employment for the rural poor and loan forgiveness for farmers are already in place; it should be added that these programs are possible only because of the buoyant state revenues that the high rates of economic growth have generated. The Indian government's expenditures on public education and health have also gone up in recent years. All this is for the good. However, the quality of implementation of many of these new programs remains uneven. Inequality across a variety of cleavages in India continues to widen; the number of poor remains staggeringly high; and the quality of human development remains abysmally low in spite of three decades of steady economic growth.

Finally, the focus in Chapter 3 shifted from the national level to the level of Indian states. It is well known that Indian states exhibit considerable social and political diversity, often a product of their diverse pasts. Until recently, however, the economic implications of such diversity were not systematic. Of course, even in the past – say, during the colonial period – industry took root in a few Indian states, but not in most. During more recent periods – say, during the period following the onset of the green revolution – a few states with assured irrigation and wheat as the main crop flourished, while many others lagged. Following policy changes in 1991, a fair amount of economic initiative shifted to the level of states. Since then, conditions within states, especially the quality of governance, have become quite consequential for influencing economic outcomes. Some Indian states are growing rapidly, while others are not; poverty has come down rapidly in a few states, but not in most; and in some of India's largest states in the heartland, neither growth nor distributive performance has been impressive.

I sought to explain some of this diversity in Chapter 3 by focusing on diverse political tendencies that have come to the fore in select Indian states. With reference to Gujarat, I suggested that a narrow ruling coalition of political and economic elite is now at the helm and that those in power are trying to emulate the developmental states of East Asia, intervening systematically to facilitate economic growth; Gujarat is also one of India's most rapidly industrializing states. By contrast, personalistic and clientelistic leadership now rules a state like U.P., with unfortunate consequences for both growth and distribution. And finally, with social-democratic politics of a sort in command for nearly three decades, poverty in West Bengal has come down rapidly, even though other human development indicators in the state remain unimpressive. Politics and governance in most Indian states reflect mixed patterns, and their impact on matters economic are not as obvious as they are in some of the states that I have discussed. Still, a focus on the quality and type of governance at the level of states helps explain some of the growing economic diversity across contemporary India. With regard to the roots of this social and political diversity, I have suggested that such roots lie deep in the past, especially in how indigenous caste structures interacted with patterns of land tenure imposed by the colonial state, which, in turn gave rise to diverse regional ruling classes.

initial conditions

To sum up, over the last three decades an India that was committed to a socialist pattern of development has slowly but surely come to be replaced by a pro-business India committed to rapid, private sector–led growth. India's political leaders initiated this change during the 1980s, and over time this trend was reinforced both by the growing power of Indian business groups and by the very global changes that gave rise to the "Washington consensus" on development. The Indian state is now succeeding in attracting private investors, especially indigenous but also foreign, to invest in India, facilitating rapid growth. The growth is spread unevenly, however, as are the fruits of growth. By now a pro-business India seems to be firmly in place, though how such an India will deal with staggering levels of poverty and destitution within the framework of democracy remains, to put it mildly, a major challenge.

INDIA IN A COMPARATIVE PERSPECTIVE

When trying to understand the developmental experiment of any single country, it helps to compare it to others. This enables one to assess not only how well is India doing, but also, equally important, what India can learn from other countries and what other countries might learn from India, both positive and negative. India's democratic capitalist model of development has in recent years facilitated rapid growth but only modest improvement for India's bottom half of the population. This pattern raises several themes of broader significance. In this concluding discussion, I have chosen to focus on three such themes: democracy and growth, democracy and inclusion, and democracy and governance.

Democracy and Growth

Three decades of rapid economic growth in the framework of a democratic polity makes India a somewhat exceptional case in comparison to other developing countries. There are hardly any democratic countries, now or in the past, where a growth rate of nearly 6 percent per annum has been sustained for three decades. What does the Indian case teach us, then, about the more general and ill-understood relationship between democracy and economic growth? In the end, a close understanding of the Indian case does not offer any conclusive evidence on related debates, though the case does raise some deeply important issues.

Of course, scholarly debates on whether democratic or authoritarian regimes are better for growth have remained largely inconclusive (Przeworski et al. 2000). Many observers, however, have not been fully persuaded by such statistical inconclusiveness, especially because of a variety of conceptual and data problems, particularly the problem that authoritarianism is really not a meaningful political category because it lumps together such diverse regimes as, say, the monarchy of Saudi Arabia, the Mobutu regime of Uganda, the former military rulers of Brazil, and the communist party rulers of China. Moreover, the fact that rapid industrialization during the post-World War II period in such Asian countries as South Korea, Taiwan, Malaysia, Vietnam, and China and such Latin American countries as Mexico and Brazil (during some periods) has often been steered by regimes that were less than democratic has left a nagging suspicion among many that all good things may not go together, that certain nondemocratic regimes may actually be well suited to growth promotion. As to why this may be so, a variety of propositions have been put forward in the literature on developmental states that catalogue the potential advantages of nondemocratic regimes:[1] growth-promoting regimes need to be led by technocrats who are insulated from popular pressure; growth requires high rates of saving and lowered consumption, an arrangement that may be harder to implement in democracies; controlling labor, especially holding wages well behind productivity gains and thereby facilitating labor-intensive, export-led growth, is not easy in democracies; and the state and business groups often need to cooperate closely in order to promote growth, an alliance that becomes problematic in democracies.

Three decades of rapid economic growth in democratic India are beginning to challenge such thinking that suggests an elective affinity between certain type of nondemocratic regimes and growth. The recent Indian experience might instead support the argument that there is no inherent tension between democracy and rapid growth (Sen, 1999), or an

---

[1] For a fuller discussion of this literature, see Kohli (2004), especially the concluding chapter.

argument based on the Anglo-American historical experience that goes even further, proposing that democracy is necessary for growth because it helps protect private property rights and opens up space for market leaders to continually modify laws and norms that support sustained economic growth (North, 1990). Does a close understanding of the Indian political economy support such a "liberal" world view? Only on the face of it, I am afraid, and only in part. There is no doubt that a variety of political freedoms and rapid economic growth coexist in India, opening up the possibility of a democratic developmental state. And yet important political changes in India, which have both facilitated rapid growth and are now emerging as a result of that growth, are moving in the direction of a concentration of power in the hands of a political and economic elite, on the one hand, and a simultaneous effort to exclude the majority from meaningful participation in economic decision making, on the other. As noted in the body of the discussion in earlier chapters, economic decision making in India is increasingly in the hands of technocrats who remain relatively insulated from popular pressure. Except when elections approach, close cooperation between the state and business groups has become the norm; high rates of saving and low levels of consumption coexist; and the pressure to transform unionized labor into a more "flexible" labor force is building in the political economy. So, yes, political freedom and economic growth coexist in India, but it is also the case that India is increasingly a two-track polity, with competitiveness on the electoral track and a substantial concentration of power on the track that is truly consequential for the well-being of the majority.

The coexistence of political freedom and rapid growth nevertheless makes India normatively a more attractive model of development than many developmental states of yore that have facilitated rapid industrialization under the tutelage of brutal regimes. Moreover, as many developing countries democratize and hope to grow rapidly in a globalized world, the prospect of replicating a South Korean or Chinese pathway to rapid growth seems relatively remote. In this context, the Indian case gains interest: what sort of developmental state is India? Does India represent a case of a democratic developmental state? If so, how does it differ from the East Asian developmental states? What lessons can others draw from the Indian case? A full answer to these questions would require another study. A few related observations, however, can be made here.

Countries such as Japan, South Korea, and Taiwan have industrialized rapidly under the leadership of developmental states. The core shared features of these developmental states are well known: authoritarian regimes committed to economic growth; heavy state intervention in markets via industrial policy and picking winners; creation of a disciplined and pro-ductive labor force; close collaboration between the state and business elites; and the use of economic nationalism as a glue to hold the politi-cal economy together (Johnson, 1987). The emerging model of develop-ment in India shares some of these features but also differs in important respects. Shared features include a state commitment to growth; close collaboration between political and economic elites to achieve this goal; considerable state intervention in the economy; and elements of economic nationalism, including limited use of foreign investment for growth pro-motion. Given democracy and today's more globalized world, however, even on some of these dimensions India differs from the East Asian cases in terms of degree: the commitment to growth in India on occasion needs to be more plural so as to accommodate electoral pressure; the alliance of state and business elites needs to be more covert; and economic nation-alism has to be tempered so as to accommodate membership in WTO and the other pressures and opportunities of a globalized economy. On other dimensions, however, the Indian model is quite different from those pursued earlier in some East Asian countries; three such distinctions are especially worth underlining.

First, by the time the Indian state committed itself to rapid economic growth during the 1980s, a robust private sector already existed in India. Unlike many East Asian cases, therefore, the role of the Indian state in growth promotion was not so much creating capitalism from scratch as it was working with and supporting existing capitalists. State intervention in the economy in India has thus been more facilitative than transfor-mative. While India too has an active industrial policy, and on occasion Indian leaders have picked winners (for example, Rajiv Gandhi's active support of the computer industry or, at the state level, as discussed earlier, in a state like Gujarat), there are very few examples in India of the scale of government intervention that, say, the South Korean state adopted in order to build a ship industry from scratch (Amsden, 1989). Second, India's growth is not so much export-driven as it is based on produc-tion for a substantial domestic market. Only part of this is a matter of size; notice China's export proclivity. For the rest, this Indian proclivity reflects continuity with a prolonged import-substitution past; the inabil-ity of Indian industry to be as globally competitive as, say, that of China; and continuing governmental preference for such a model of develop-ment. And third, the labor situation in India is quite different than it was in the heyday of the developmental states of East Asia. The neglect of primary education and a focus instead on higher education in India has given an advantage to service and manufacturing industries that employ skilled labor at the expense of an export-oriented manufacturing industry that might have employed low-skilled workers who were nevertheless literate and productive. Democracy and a long tradition of an activist and unionized labor force also distinguish the Indian labor situation sharply from that of East Asia.

To sum up this brief discussion on democracy and growth, the Indian example does strengthen the case that high rates of economic growth can be achieved within the framework of a democracy. However, champions of all-good-things-go-together views should not be triumphant; the concentration of power at the apex and exclusion of the majority from meaningful participation remain troubling trends in India. For those wanting to learn from the Indian version of a democratic developmental state, it will also be important to bear in mind some of the preconditions on which India's growth rests: democracy in India was already quite well established when the high-growth era began; a robust indigenous capitalist sector was already in place, waiting and pushing for the Indian state to become pro-business; and success in service sector exports required significant prior public investment in the development of a skilled labor force.

Democracy and Inclusion

If on the growth dimension India's recent experience may appear to offer lessons to others, India's poor record on the inclusion front is bound to make others wonder how much of a model of development India really is; on this dimension, at least, India needs to look for lessons elsewhere. As one thinks of India's record on inclusion in a comparative perspective, it helps to distinguish economic from political inclusion, each of which can now be discussed in brief.

On the dimension of economic inequality, it is clear that such inequality in India has been getting more and more skewed over the last two decades. Some observers do not find such developments disconcerting. This is because, first, in spite of growing inequality, India in a comparative perspective remains a country of modest inequality: India's Gini coefficient in 2005 was 37, while that of China in the same year was 42, and that of Brazil, one of the world's most unequal countries, was 54 (in 2009).[2] While such cross-national comparisons are fraught with

---

[2] This data as well as the data in the following discussion is taken from the World Bank's online data source, World Development Indicators.

data problems (for example, inequality in India is assessed from data on consumption and not directly from income), they do provide broad indicators. India's modest inequality is also part of a larger Asian pattern, say, in comparison to Latin America, in which access to land has historically been less unequal. Some may then take comfort in this comparative assessment, concluding that India can afford to become even more unequal before the matter becomes politically consequential. Such a conclusion, however, is not warranted. Not only is sharp income inequality not desirable normatively – an issue on which observers can differ – but political tolerance for inequality varies across societies. New inequality is always more irksome than old, established inequality. Class inequality may be less politically damaging in India – in part because grievances do not readily accumulate across diverse regions and in part because India has long lived with a rigid caste hierarchy – but both regional inequality and inequality across the rural-urban divide can easily be politicized within the framework of a democracy. And second, some other observers may be more accepting of growing inequality in India because they consider such trends inevitable in the process of rapid growth: after all, inequality is growing even in China! Such a view, in turn, might be informed by a belief that growing inequality results from high rates of return on scarce capital and skills needed in the process of rapid industrialization. Systematic studies, however, do not support these conclusions.[3] Rather, it is increasingly accepted that the relationship of growth to inequality is mediated by policies. It is thus clear from the earlier discussion that among the important determinants of growing inequality in India is the decline of public investment in agriculture and in India's poor regions. There is nothing inevitable about such policy choices.

High rates of poverty and low levels of human development underline the failure of inclusive development in India. Global comparisons only make the issue starker. Whereas 16 percent of China's population lives below the World Bank standard of poverty – below $1.25 per day, adjusted for purchasing power parity – and only 4 percent in middle-income Brazil, the figure for India is a staggering 42 percent. India's literacy rate is well below that of China and Brazil, as is life expectancy. Of 1,000 live births, some 50 Indian children die as infants, compared to only 17 in China and Brazil. The most heartbreaking data to come out

---

[3] For a discussion of the evidence on the "Kuznets curve," which proposed that one should expect inequality to increase as countries move through the middle stages of development, see Fields (2001), Chapter 5.

of India concerns the weight-for-age malnourishment of children: while 5 percent of children below the age of five are malnourished in China (and only 2 percent in Brazil), some 44 percent of Indian children remain malnourished; this compares to sub-Saharan Africa's average of some 25 percent. No decent society should claim it is "shining" when nearly half its children remain undernourished.

A number of factors that have contributed to these outcomes in India have been discussed throughout this study. A comparative perspective helps to further underline some of these, while pointing to a few others. The relative success of inclusive growth in East Asia, for example, owed much to early land redistribution and then to systematic pursuit of labor-intensive manufactured exports. Significant investment in primary education also helped raise the bottom in East Asia, especially via the well-known benefits to children that flow from improving female literacy. By contrast, land redistribution in India seldom reached the tiller. India's neglect of primary education is also well known. And the recent pattern of rapid economic growth has failed to create enough new jobs to make a serious dent in poverty. Growing inequality has also retarded the trickle-down impact of rapid growth. To be fair, with buoyant public revenue, the Indian state in recent years has renewed efforts to improve primary education and to create jobs for the poor via public works programs. An effort is also under way to rethink how to improve the effectiveness of various other government programs that are aimed to help the poor but seldom do. Unfortunately, much of the new thinking in India on how to benefit the poor is defeatist in the sense that, after years of public sector failure, the pro-business ruling groups in India seem to have no confidence in the state's constructive role. Instead of any serious effort to reform the state's capacity, the new solutions all tilt toward strategies with minimum involvement of the state: cash transfers, private schools, and private health provision. While the tendency to make a virtue of defeat is pervasive in India, it is hugely unlikely that the well-being of poor Indians can be improved rapidly without effective public provision of services and jobs, and equally unlikely that this effectiveness, in turn, can be improved without improving the downward reach of the state.

Finally, a brief comment on the issue of political inclusion is in order. Given a well-established democracy in India, one might expect that, sooner rather than later, the poor majority of India would express its electoral will in the political sphere, successfully tilting the Indian state in a pro-poor direction. This is, in fact, not all that likely – or, if it comes to pass, it will do so only after considerable organization and struggle on the part of the poor. That the power of numbers has never readily equaled the power of wealth in well-established democracies is a view that has long been shared by thoughtful Marxist and liberal scholars.[4] This is because the rich and the powerful in successful democracies devise various institutional mechanisms to insulate substantive decision making from popular pressure. While the rich are far from omnipotent, and their efforts at insulation do not always succeed – social democracy remains a possibility – business and other elite groups do tend to enjoy power disproportionate to their numbers in all democracies. In light of this comparative observation, it is not surprising that a major political development in contemporary India is the effort under way by Indian business groups – in partnership, of course, with segments of India's political class – to create institutional mechanisms that will help insulate substantive economic decisions from mass pressure. A variety of such efforts were discussed in Chapter 1, though I suggested that these efforts are also being challenged; whether India can create a truly pro-business state remains an open question. What is clear at present is that while the poor and the downtrodden in India participate actively in the electoral sphere – in that sense, Indian democracy remains quite inclusive – their impact on economic policies that mold life chances remains quite limited.

Democracy and Governance

India's democracy is relatively well institutionalized, but the quality of government offered by India's democratic state is, at best, uneven. The quality of governance also declines as one travels down the political hierarchy. When put in a comparative perspective, the gap between a well-instituted democracy and poor governance in India appears both large and exceptional. Many well-established democracies in the world, especially in advanced industrial countries, provide moderately good government in the sense that they "make the trains run on time"; they collect taxes, provide social services, build infrastructure, and implement a variety of governmental policies and programs. By contrast, where states do not provide effective governance – say, in large parts of Africa – even democracy often tends to become neo-patrimonial and fractured. In parts

---

[4] For a good Marxist account of the underlying dynamics, see Miliband (1969). For liberal accounts that tend to agree that business groups develop veto power in democracies, see Dahl (1978) and Lindblom (1982). With reference to India, I developed some related ideas in my very first book, Kohli (1987).

of India, too, poorly functioning democracy and a low quality of governance coexist. On the whole, however, what is remarkable is that India is a well-functioning electoral democracy that delivers a poor quality of government. At the heart of this gap lie poorly functioning public institutions, both political and bureaucratic.

Much has been written about India's democratic exceptionalism: origins, consolidation, and, over time, deinstitutionalization.[5] The decline of political parties and growing political competitiveness threatened India's democracy during the 1970s and 1980s. As already discussed, over the last two decades the growing role of business in India's national-level politics and the related convergence of views on economic policy across India's political class have set the boundaries of Indian politics, limiting the worst consequences of deinstitutionalization. However, as also discussed earlier, maintaining a narrow ruling coalition of political and economic elite is generating a new problem for Indian democracy, the problem of how to win elections while pursuing pro-business, pro-growth policies. Without strong parties, a variety of legitimacy formulas are being tried out that might do the trick of winning elections without providing for any substantial redistribution. Populist pressures are always lurking, at times just below the surface and at other times, especially at the state level, expressed in full daylight. While none of these new pressures threaten Indian democracy as such, they do implicate the quality of government offered by the Indian state.

If good governance involves diagnosing and pursuing solutions to pressing social problems, much of India's democratic state does not govern well. Of course, there are significant exceptions to this rule. Macroeconomic and foreign policy at the national center often reflect a keen understanding of the relevant issues. The same, unfortunately, does not hold true for a variety of other issue areas, including education, health, infrastructure, agriculture, and the pursuit of antipoverty programs. Growing corruption at the apex also erodes the capacity to govern effectively. Some state governments govern well, but again, only in select issue areas. For example, as discussed earlier, the state in Gujarat is proving to be very good at growth promotion but often at the expense of excluding religious minorities, and the left-leaning leadership in West Bengal has rapidly brought down poverty but failed to create a more flexible ruling

[5] My own understanding of these issues is developed in Kohli (1989) and Kohli (2004). The bibliographies in these works also provide references to numerous other relevant studies.

coalition that would also support growth promotion. Most state governments, by contrast, offer an even more mixed picture on governance, with neo-patrimonial political tendencies dominant in several major Indian states. The roots of poor-quality governance in India are clearly complex; some of these have been analyzed earlier. An important proximate cause is the weakness of the Indian political parties. Well-functioning parties socialize leaders, establish bonds between leaders and followers, help create durable coalitions of potentially conflicting interests, and generate longer-term political horizons. Without strong parties, popular but poor-quality leaders often come to the fore in India, especially at the state level, but also, with the growing role of state leaders at the national level, at the apex. The focus of these leaders, if not on channeling private resources for public use, is, at best, on how to win the next set of elections. Diagnosing and solving pressing public policy problems is typically not the focus of this political class. Neglect of the public domain then contributes to an accumulation of pressing problems.

If the quality and concerns of the political leadership is one important component of the poor quality of governance in India, the other component is the quality of the bureaucracy. Once again, the apex of the Indian bureaucracy, including the civil and foreign services, is staffed by professional, competent, publicly oriented officials. While not quite the "steel frame" that served the British in India, India's top-level bureaucracy remains critical to governing India. However, the quality of the bureaucracy declines as one moves down the political hierarchy, especially at the level of states, districts, and village and town governments. At times, good-quality bureaucrats find it difficult to perform their jobs due to the conflicting priorities of political leaders, but just as often, or even more often, the professionalism and competence of the lower-level bureaucracy is severely wanting. Even well-conceived policies flounder in the hands of these bureaucrats.

Of course, the declining quality of the bureaucracy as one travels down the political hierarchy broadly mirrors the shape of Indian society, flourishing at the apex but a mass of poverty, illiteracy, and poor health at the bottom. If one accepts this parallel coexistence as an analysis, however, one would be led to conclude that the quality of lower-level bureaucracy in India will improve only when the entire society modernizes. It will be a long time before that comes to pass, if it comes to pass at all. A comparative perspective suggests instead that if the state is to take a lead in solving some pressing social and economic problems, state organizations should not simply mirror the society; they should instead stand some distance apart from society, more responsive to orders from above and less easily captured by the powerful in society. Well-functioning lower-level bureaucracies in countries like Japan and South Korea have been created by emphasizing professionalism, discipline, and a finely tuned systems of rewards and punishment. While India may never fully emulate such East Asian cases, some improvement in the quality of lower-level bureaucracy will remain important for implementing the policies that matter most for poor Indians.

To conclude, the creation of inclusive political and effective bureaucratic institutions remains India's foremost developmental challenge. Rapid economic growth is clearly India's major achievement; it should be celebrated. However, this growth is leaving many behind. If the growth is to be inclusive, it is not likely to be achieved mainly via civil society activism or via market-oriented solutions. A variety of public interventions will be needed, including creating incentives to make the growth process itself more employment-generating, providing public investment in agriculture and in India's poor states, implementing antipoverty programs effectively, and providing such public services as health and education. To succeed, all such interventions will require both appropriate political leadership – leadership that represents enduring, inclusive coalitions in power – and effective bureaucratic institutions. If the idea that India can move toward such a state appears quixotic, consider this: the task of generating inclusive growth in India is sizable, and there is no historical evidence to suggest that unguided markets on their own can create a more inclusive society; either the Indian state will become more social-democratic and more effective, or the challenge of inclusive reform will be unmet. Political reform in India thus remains an important precondition for constructive state intervention to create inclusive economic growth.

References

Note: Not all the materials I consulted are listed here. Only those materials that are cited in the book are listed. For a fuller listing, please consult the bibliographies in my earlier writings listed herein.

Agarwala, Rina (2008). "From Work to Welfare: A New Class Movement in India." In Rina Agarwala and Ronald Herring, eds., *Whatever Happened to Class? Reflections From South Asia.* New York: Routledge, 91–108.

Ahluwalia, Isher Judge (1985). *Industrial Growth in India: Stagnation since the Mid-Sixties.* Delhi: Oxford University Press.

Ahluwalia, Montek S. (2000). "Economic Performance of States in Post-Reform Period." *Economic and Political Weekly,* May 6, pp. 1637–48.

Ahluwalia, Montek S. (2002). "Economic Reforms in India since 1991: Has Gradualism Worked?" *Journal of Economic Perspectives,* v. 16, no. 3 (Summer), pp. 67–88.

Alfaro, Laura, and Anusha Chari (2009). "India Transformed? Insights from the Firm Level, 1988–2007." Paper presented at the NCAER-Brookings India Policy Forum 2009, New Delhi, July 14–15.

Amsden, Alice (1989). *Asia's Next Giant: South Korea and Late Industrialization.* New York: Oxford University Press.

Anand, Bharat, Dmitri Byzalov, and Devesh Kapur (2006). "The Dimensions and Implications of Media Inequality in India." Paper prepared for the annual meeting of the American Political Science Association, Philadelphia, Pennsylvania, August 30–September 3.

Appu, P. A. (1996). *Land Reforms in India.* New Delhi: Vikas Publishing.

Awasthi, Dinesh (2000). "Recent Changes in Gujarat Industry: Issues and Evidence." *Economic and Political Weekly,* v. 35, no. 35/36 (August 26), pp. 3183–7.

Bagchi, Amiya Kumar (1972). *Private Investments in India.* Cambridge: Cambridge University Press.

Bagchi, Amiya Kumar (1998). "Studies on the Economy of West Bengal since Independence." *Economic and Political Weekly*, Nov. 21–Dec. 4, pp. 2973–8.

Bagchi, Amiya Kumar, Panchan Das, and Sadhan Kumar Chattopadhyay (2005). "Growth and Structural Change in the Economy of Gujarat, 1970–2000." *Economic and Political Weekly*, July 9, pp. 3039–47.

Balakrishnan, Pulapre et al. (2008). "Agricultural Growth in India since 1991." Development Research Group, Department of Economic Analysis and Policy, Reserve Bank of India, Study No. 27.

Banerjee, Abhijit (2002). "Empowerment and Efficiency: Tenancy Reform in West Bengal." *Journal of Political Economy*, v. 110, no. 2, pp. 239–79.

Banerjee, Abhijit, and Thomas Piketty (2005). "Top Indian Incomes, 1956–2000." *World Bank Economic Review*, v. 19, no. 1, pp. 1–20.

Banerjee, Abhijit, Pranab Bardhan, Kaushik Basu, Mrinal Datta Chaudriri, Maitreesh Ghatar, Ashok Sanjay Guha, Mukul Majumdar, Dilip Mookherjee, and Debraj Ray (2002). "Strategy for Economic Reform in West Bengal." *Economic and Political Weekly*, October 12, pp. 4203–18.

Banga, Rashmi (2008). "Critical Issues in India's Service-Led Growth." In Asian Development Bank, *Industrial Performance and Private Sector Development in India*. New Delhi: Oxford University Press, Chapter 1.

Bardhan, Pranab (1998). *The Political Economy of Development in India*. Delhi: Oxford University Press.

Bardhan, Pranab, Sandip Mitra, Dilip Mookerjee, and Abhirup Sarkar (2009). "Local Democracy and Clientelism: Implications for Political Stability in Rural West Bengal." *Economic and Political Weekly*, Feb. 28, pp. 46–58.

Basant, Rakesh (2000). "Corporate Response to Economic Reforms." *Economic and Political Weekly*, March 4, pp. 813–22.

Basu, Amrita (2001). "The Dialectics of Hindu Nationalism." In Atul Kohli, ed., *The Success of India's Democracy*. New York: Cambridge University Press, pp. 163–89.

Basu, Amrita (2010). "Gender and Politics in India." In Pratap Mehta and Niraja Gopal Dayal, eds., *Oxford Handbook of Indian Politics*. New Delhi: Oxford University Press.

Besley, Timothy, Robin Burgess, and Berta Esteve-Volart (2007). "The Policy Origins of Poverty and Growth in India." In Timothy Besley and Louise J. Cord, eds., *Delivering on the Promise of Pro-poor Growth*. Washington, DC: Palgrave Macmillan and the World Bank, 49–78.

Bhagwati, Jagdish N., and Padma Desai (1970). *India: Planning for Industrialization*. London: Oxford University Press.

Bhagwati, Jagdish N., and T. N. Srinivasan (1975). *India*. New York: National Bureau of Economic Research, distributed by Columbia University Press.

Bhattacharya, B. B. (1989). "West Bengal Economy: Stagnation and Growth." In Malcolm S. Adiseshiah, ed., *The Economies of the States of the Indian Union*, New Delhi: Lancer International, 131–42.

Bhattacharya, B. B., and S. Sakthivel (2004). "Regional Growth and Disparity in India." *Economic and Political Weekly*, March 6, pp. 1071–7.

Bhattacharya, Dwaipayan (2009). "Of Control and Factions: The Changing 'Party-Society' in Rural West Bengal." *Economic and Political Weekly*, Feb. 28, pp. 59–69.

Brass, Paul (1965). *Factional Politics in an Indian State: The Congress Party in Uttar Pradesh*. Berkeley: University of California Press.

Brass, Paul (1981). "Congress, the Lok Dal and the Middle Castes: An Analysis of the 1977 and 1984 Parliamentary Elections in Uttar Pradesh." *Pacific Affairs*, v. 54, no. 1 (Spring), pp. 5–41.

Brass, Paul (1988). "The Punjab Crisis and the Unity of India." In Atul Kohli, ed., *India's Democracy: An Analysis of Changing State-Society Relations*. Princeton, NJ: Princeton University Press.

Broomfield, John (1968). *Elite Conflict in a Plural Society*. Berkeley: University of California Press.

Candland, Christopher (2007). *Labor, Democratization and Development in India and Pakistan*. London: Routledge.

Carras, Mary (1979). *Indira Gandhi: A Political Biography*. Boston: Beacon Press.

Chakravarty, Sukhamoy (1988). *Development Planning: The Indian Experience*. Delhi: Oxford University Press.

Chandra, Bipan, et al. (1998). *India's Struggle for Independence, 1857–1947*. New Delhi: Penguin.

Chandra, Bipan, et al. (1999). *India after Independence*. New Delhi: Viking, Penguin Books.

Chandra, Kanchan (2004). *Why Ethnic Parties Succeed: Patronage and Ethnic Head Counts in India*. Cambridge: Cambridge University Press.

Chaterjee, Partha (2009). "The Coming Crisis in West Bengal." *Economic and Political Weekly*, v. 44, no. 9 (Feb. 28), pp. 42–3.

Chaudhry, Nirmal Chandra Basu Ray (1976). "West Bengal: Vortex of Ideological Politics." In Narain (1976), pp. 360–403.

Chaudhuri, Sudip (2002). "Economic Reforms and Industrial Structure in India." *Economic and Political Weekly*, January 12, pp. 155–62.

Chen, Shaohua, and Martin Ravallion (2008). "The Developing World Is Poorer than We Thought but No Less Successful in the Fight against Poverty." World Bank, Poverty Research Working Paper 470, August.

Corbridge, Stuart, and John Harriss (2000). *Reinventing India: Liberalization, Hindu Nationalism and Popular Democracy*. Cambridge, UK: Polity.

Dahl, Robert (1978). "Pluralism Revisited." *Comparative Politics*, v. 10, no. 2, pp. 191–203.

Damodaran, Harish (2008). *India's New Capitalists: Caste, Business and Industry in a Modern Nation*. New Delhi: Permanent Black.

Dasgupta, Jyoitindra (1970). *Language Conflict and National Development: Group Policy and National Language Policy in India*. Berkeley: University of California Press.

Dasgupta, Sukti, and Ajit Singh (2005). "Will Services Be the New Engine of Growth in India?" Centre for Business Research, University of Cambridge, Working Paper No. 310.

Datt, Gaurav, and Martin Ravallion (1998). "Why Have Some Indian States Done Better than Others at Reducing Rural Poverty?" *Economica*, no. 257, pp. 17–38.

D'Costa, Anthony (2005). *The Long March to Capitalism*. Houndsmill, Basingstoke: Palgrave Macmillan.

D'Costa, Anthony (2009). "Economic Nationalism in Motion: Steel, Auto and Software Industries in India." Unpublished manuscript.

Deaton, Angus, and Jean Dreze (2002). "Poverty and Inequality in India." *Economic and Political Weekly*, September 7, pp. 3729–48.

Deaton, Angus, and Jean Dreze (2009). "Food and Nutrition in India: Facts and Interpretations." *Economic and Political Weekly*, Feb. 14, pp. 42–63.

Deaton, Angus, and Valerie Kozel (2005). *The Great Indian Poverty Debate*. Delhi: MacMillan India Limited.

De Long, Bradford (2003). "India since Independence: An Analytic Growth Narrative." In Dani Rodrik, ed., *In Search of Prosperity: Analytic Narratives on Economic Growth*. Princeton, NJ: Princeton University Press.

Dev, Mahendra S. (2009). "Challenges for Revival of Indian Agriculture." *Agricultural Economics Research Review*, v. 22 (Jan.–June), pp. 21–45.

Dev, Mahendra S., and C. Ravi (2007). "Poverty and Inequality in India." *Economic and Political Weekly*, v. 42, no. 6, pp. 509–21.

Dholakia, Archana (2000a). "Fiscal Imbalance in Gujarat." *Economic and Political Weekly*, August 26, pp. 3217–27.

Dholakia, Ravindra M. (2000). "Liberalisation in Gujarat: Review of Recent Experience." *Economic and Political Weekly*, v. 35, no. 35/36 (August 26), pp. 3121–4.

Dholakia, Ravindra M. (2007). "Sources of Economic Growth and Acceleration in Gujarat." *Economic and Political Weekly*, March 3, pp. 770–8.

Diamond, Larry Jay (1988). *Class, Ethnicity and Democracy in Nigeria*. Basingstoke: MacMillan.

Dreze, Jean, and Haris Gazdar (1997). "Uttar Pradesh: The Burden of India." In Jean Dreze and Amartya Sen, eds., *Indian Development: Selected Regional Perspectives*. Delhi: Oxford University Press, pp. 33–127.

Dreze, Jean, and Reetika Khera (2009). "Battle for Work." *Frontline*, v. 26, No. 1, Jan. 3–16.

Dreze, Jean, and Amartya Sen (2005). *India: Development and Participation*. New York: Oxford University Press.

Engineer, Asghar Ali (2003). *The Gujarat Carnage*. Hyderabrad: Orient Longman.

Evans, Peter (1995). *Embedded Autonomy: State and Industrial Transformation*. Princeton, NJ: Princeton University Press.

Fields, Gary S. (2001). *Distribution and Development: A New Look at the Developing World*. Cambridge, MA: MIT Press.

Franda, Marcus (1972). *Radical Politics in West Bengal*. Cambridge, MA: MIT Press.

Frankel, Francine (1978). *India's Political Economy, 1947–77: The Gradual Revolution*. Princeton, NJ: Princeton University Press.

Frankel, Francine (2005). *India's Political Economy, 1947–2004: The Gradual Revolution*. New Delhi: Oxford University Press.

Frankel, Francine, and M. S. A. Rao, eds. (1990). *Dominance and State Power in Modern India: Decline of a Social Order* (2 volumes). New Delhi: Oxford University Press.

Ghate, Prabhu (2009). "A Quick Study of NREGA: Implementation Issues in Selected States." Unpublished manuscript.

Ghosh, Buddhadeb, and Girish Kumar (2003). *State Politics and Panchayats in India*. New Delhi: Manohar Books.

Gopal, S. (1984). *Jawaharlal Nehru: A Biography* (3 volumes). New Delhi: Oxford University Press.

Gordon, James, and Poonam Gupta (2004). "Understanding India's Services Revolution." International Monetary Fund, Working Paper 04/171.

Government of Gujarat (2008). *Socio-Economic Review: Gujarat State, 2007–2008*. Gandhinagar, Gujarat: Directorate of Economics and Statistics.

Government of India (2007). *National Family Health Survey – 3 (NFHS-3)*. New Delhi: International Institute for Population Sciences.

Government of India (2007a). *Uttar Pradesh Development Report* (2 volumes). New Delhi: Academic Foundation (for the Planning Commission).

Government of India (2009a). *Identification of BPL Households in Rural India* (Saxena Report). Ministry of Rural Development.

Government of India (2009b). *Planning Commission Report of the Expert Group to Review the Methodology for Estimation of Poverty* (Tendulkar Report).

Government of West Bengal (2010). *Economic Review 2009–10*. Kolkata: Saraswaty Press Limited.

Guha, Ramachandra (2007). "Adivasis, Naxalites and Indian Democracy." *Economic and Political Weekly*, August 11, pp. 3305–12.

Guha, Ramachandra (2007). *India after Gandhi: The History of the World's Largest Democracy*. New York: Harper Collins.

Guruswamy, Mohan, Kamal Sharma, and Jeevan Prakash Mohanty (2005). "Economic Growth and Development in West Bengal: Reality versus Perception." *Economic and Political Weekly*, May 21, pp. 2151–7.

Hansen, Thomas Blom (1999). *The Saffron Wave: Democracy and Hindu Nationalism in Modern India*. Princeton, NJ: Princeton University Press.

Hansen, Thomas Blom, and Christopher Jaffrelot, eds. (1998). *The BJP and the Compulsions of Politics in India*. Delhi: Oxford University Press.

Hanson, A. H. (1966). *The Process of Planning*. London: Oxford University Press.

Harriss, John (1999). "What Is Happening in Rural West Bengal?" *Economic and Political Weekly*, June 12, 1237–47.

Harriss, John (2003). "Do Political Regimes Matter? Poverty Reduction and Regime Difference Across India." In Peter P. Houtzager and Mick Moore, eds., *Changing Paths: International Development and the New Politics of Inclusion*. Ann Arbor: University of Michigan Press, pp. 204–31.

Hasan, Zoya (1990). "Power and Mobilization: Patterns of Resilience and Change in Uttar Pradesh Politics." In Frankel and Rao (1990), pp. 133–203.

Heller, Patrick (1999). *The Labor of Development: Workers and the Transformation of Capitalism in Kerala, India*. Ithaca, NY: Cornell University Press.

Herring, Ronald (1983). *Land to the Tiller: The Political Economy of Agrarian Reform in South Asia*. New Haven, CT: Yale University Press.

Himanshu (2007). "Recent Trends in Poverty and Inequality. Some Preliminary Results." *Economic and Political Weekly*, Feb. 10, pp. 497–508.

Hirway, Indira (1995). "Selective Development and Widening Disparities in Gujarat." *Economic and Political Weekly*, v. 30, no. 41/43 (October 14–21), pp. 2003–18.

Hirway, Indira (2000). "Dynamics of Development in Gujarat: Some Issues." *Economic and Political Weekly*, v. 35, no. 35/36 (August 26), pp. 3106–20.

Jaffrelot, Christophe (1996). *The Hindu Nationalist Movement and Indian Politics*. New York: Columbia University Press.

Jaffrelot, Christophe (2003). *India's Silent Revolution: The Rise of the Lower Castes in North India*. New York: Columbia University Press.

Jayadev, Arjun, Sripad Motiram, and Vamsi Vakulabharanam (2007). "Patterns of Wealth Disparities in India during the Liberalization Era." *Economic and Political Weekly*, September 22, pp. 3853–63.

Jayakar, Pupul (1992). *Indira Gandhi: An Intimate Biography*. New York: Pantheon.

Jenkins, Rob (1999). *Democratic Politics and Economic Reform in India*. Cambridge: Cambridge University Press.

Jha, Praveen, and Subrat Das (2007). "Fiscal Strains in the Era of Neo-liberal Reforms: A Study of Uttar Pradesh." In Pai (2007), pp. 308–44.

Johnson, Chalmers (1962). *Peasant Nationalism and Communist Power: The Emergence of Revolutionary China*. Stanford, CA: Stanford University Press.

Johnson, Chalmers (1987). "Political Institutions and Economic Performance." In Fredric Deyo, ed., *The Political Economy of New Asian Industrialism*. Ithaca, NY: Cornell University Press, pp. 136–64.

Kannan, K. P. (2005). "Kerala's Turnaround in Growth: Role of Social Development, Remittances and Reform." *Economic and Political Weekly*, February 5, 548–54.

Kapur, Devesh (2010). *Diaspora, Development and Democracy: The Domestic Impact of International Migration from India*. Princeton, NJ: Princeton University Press.

Kapur, Devesh, and Milan Vaishnav (2011). "Quid Pro Quo: Uncovering Black Money in Indian Elections." Unpublished manuscript, University of Pennsylvania.

Katzenstein, Mary, Smitu Kothari, and Uday Mehta (2001). "Social Movement Politics in India." In Atul Kohli, ed., *The Success of India's Democracy*. New York: Cambridge University Press.

Kochanek, Stanley (1987). "Briefcase Politics in India: The Congress Party and the Business Elite." *Asian Survey*, v. 27, no. 12 (Dec. 1987), pp. 1278–1301.

Kochanek, Stanley (1996a). "Liberalisation and Business Lobbying in India." *Journal of Commonwealth and Comparative Politics*, v. 34, no. 3 (Nov. 1996), pp. 155–73.

Kochanek, Stanley (1996b). "The Transformation of Interest Politics in India." *Pacific Affairs*, v. 68, no. 4, pp. 529–50.

Kochhar, Kalpana, et al. (2006). "India's Pattern of Development: What Happened, What Follows?" *Journal of Monetary Economics*, v. 53, no. 5 (July), pp. 981–1019.

Kohli, Atul (1987). *The State and Poverty in India: The Politics of Reform*. Cambridge: Cambridge University Press.

Kohli, Atul, ed. (1988). *India's Democracy: An Analysis of Changing State-Society Relations*. Princeton, NJ: Princeton Unviersity Press.

Kohli, Atul (1989). "Politics of Economic Liberalisation in India." *World Development*, v. 17, no. 3, pp. 305–28.

Kohli, Atul (1990). *Democracy and Discontent: India's Growing Crisis of Governability.* New York: Cambridge University Press.

Kohli, Atul (1997). "Can Democracies Accommodate Ethnic Nationalism? Rise and Decline of Self-Determination Movements in India." *Journal of Asian Studies*, v. 56, no. 2 (May), pp. 325–44.

Kohli, Atul, ed. (2001). *The Success of India's Democracy.* New York: Cambridge University Press.

Kohli, Atul (2004). *State-Directed Development: Political Power and Industrialization in the Global Periphery.* New York: Cambridge University Press.

Kohli, Atul (2006a). "Politics of Economic Growth in India, 1980–2005, Part I: The 1980s." *Economic and Political Weekly*, April 1, pp. 1251–9.

Kohli, Atul (2006b). "Politics of Economic Growth in India, 1980–2005, Part II: The 1990s, and Beyond." *Economic and Political Weekly*, April 8, pp. 1361–70.

Kohli, Atul (2009). "Nationalist versus Dependent Capitalist Development: Alternate Pathways of Asia and Latin America in a Globalized World." *Studies in Comparative International Development*, December.

Kothari, Rajni (1970). *Politics in India.* Delhi: Orient Longman.

Kudaisya, Gyanesh (2007). "Constructing the 'Heartland': Uttar Pradesh in India's Body-Politic." In Pai (2007), pp. 1–31.

Kumar, Chattopadhyay (2005). "Growth and Structural Change in the Economy of Gujarat, 1970–2000." *Economic and Political Weekly*, July 9, pp. 3039–47.

Kumar, Girish (2006). *Local Democracy in India: Interpreting Democracy.* New Delhi: Sage Publication.

Kumar, Nagesh (2000). "Economic Reforms and Their Macro-Economic Impact." *Economic and Political Weekly*, March 4, pp. 803–12.

Kumar, Vivek (2007). "Bahujan Samaj Party: Some Issues of Democracy and Governance." In Pai (2007), pp. 241–70.

Lewis, Arthur W. (1977). *The Evolution of the International Economic Order.* Princeton, NJ: Princeton University Press.

Lewis, John P. (1995). *India's Political Economy: Governance and Reform.* Delhi: Oxford University Press.

Lindblom, Charles (1982). "Another State of Mind." *American Political Science Review*, v. 76, no. 1 (March 9–21).

Mahadevia, Darshini (2005). "From Stealth to Aggression: Economic Reforms and Communal Politics in Gujarat." In Jos. Mooij, ed., *The Politics of Economic Reforms in India.* New Delhi: Sage Publications.

Mallick, Ross (1994). *Development Policy of a Communist Government since 1977.* Cambridge: Cambridge University Press.

Manor, James (2011). "Congress Party and the 'Great Transformation.' In Sanjay Ruparelia et al., eds., *Understanding India's New Political Economy: A Great Transformation?* New York: Taylor and Francis Ltd.

Mazumdar, Surajit (2008). "Crony Capitalism and India, Before and After Liberalization: II." Working Paper 4, Institute for Studies in Industrial Development, New Delhi.

Mehta, Sanat (1989). "Gujarat Development: Opportunities and Constraints." In Malcolm S. Adiseshiah, ed., *The Economies of the States of the Indian Union.* New Delhi: Lancer International.

Miliband, Ralph (1969). *The State in Capitalist Society.* New York: Basic Books.

Mohan, Rakesh (2002). "Fiscal Correction for Economic Growth: Data Analysis and Suggestions." *Economic and Political Weekly,* June 10, pp. 20–27.

Mookherjee, Dilip (1992). "Indian Economy at the Crossroads." *Economic and Political Weekly,* April 11–18, pp. 791–801.

Moore, Barrington, Jr. (1966). *Social Origins of Dictatorship and Democracy.* Boston: Beacon Press.

Mukherjee, Pranab (1984). *Beyond Survival: Emerging Dimensions of India Economy.* Delhi: Vikas Publishing House.

Myrdal, Gunnar (1968). *Asian Drama* (3 volumes). New York: Pantheon.

Nagaraj, R. (2000). "Indian Economy since 1980: Virtuous Growth or Polarisation." *Economic and Political Weekly,* August 5, pp. 2831–9.

Nagaraj, R. (2003). "Industrial Policy and Performance since 1980: Which Way Now?" *Economic and Political Weekly,* v. 38, no. 35 (August 30), pp. 3707–15.

Nagaraj, R. (2009). "Is Services Sector Output Overestimated? An Inquiry." *Economic and Political Weekly,* January, pp. 40–5.

Narain, Iqbal, ed. (1976). *State Politics in India.* Meerut: Meenakski Prakashan.

Nayar, Baldev Raj (1989). *India's Mixed Economy: The Role of Ideology and Interest in Its Development:* Delhi: Popular Prakashan.

Nayar, Baldev Raj (2001). "Opening Up and Openness of Indian Economy." *Economic and Political Weekly,* September 15, pp. 3529–37.

Nayyar, Gaurav (2005). "Growth and Poverty in Rural India: An Analysis of Inter-State Differences." *Economic and Political Weekly,* April 6, pp. 1031–9.

Nayyar, Gaurav (2008). "Economic Growth and Regional Inequality in India." *Economic and Political Weekly,* February 9, pp. 58–65.

North, Douglas C. (1990). *Institutions, Institutional Change, and Economic Performance.* New York: Cambridge University Press.

Nossiter, T. J. (1982). *Communism in Kerala: A Study in Political Adaptation.* Berkeley: University of California Press.

Pai, Sudha, ed. (2007). *Political Process in Uttar Pradesh: Identity, Economic Reforms and Governance.* Delhi: Pearson Longman.

Panagariya, Arvind (2008). *India: The Emerging Giant.* New York: Oxford University Press.

Pandey, Gyan (1978). *Ascendancy of the Congress in U.P., 1926–34: A Study in Imperfect Mobilization.* Delhi: Oxford University Press.

Paranjape, H. K. (1980). "New Statement on Industrial Policy." *Economic and Political Weekly,* September 20, pp. 1592–1597.

Patel, I. G. (1992). "New Economic Policies: A Historical Perspective." *Economic and Political Weekly,* January 4–11, pp. 41–46.

Patel, Sujata (1987). *The Making of Industrial Relations: The Ahmedabad Textile Industry.* Delhi: Oxford University Press.

Patnaik, Prabbat (1999). "The Performance of the Indian Economy in the 1990s." *Social Scientist,* v. 27, nos. 5–6 (May–June), pp. 3–16.

Pedersen, Jorgen Dige (2000). "Explaining Economic Liberalisation in India: State and Society Perspectives." *World Development*, v. 28, no. 2, pp. 265–82.

Pocock, David F. (1972). *Kanbi and Patidar: A Study of the Patidar Community of Gujarat.* Oxford: Clarendon Press.

Przeworski, Adam, et al. (2000). *Democracy and Development: Political Institutions and Material Well-being in the World, 1950–1990.* New York: Cambridge University Press.

Raj, K. N. (1966). *Indian Economic Growth: Performance and Prospects.* New Delhi: Allied Publishers.

Ramachandran, V. K. (1997). "On Kerala's Development Achievements." In Jean Dreze and Amartya Sen, eds., *Indian Development: Selected Regional Perspectives.* Delhi: Oxford University Press, pp. 205–56.

Ramaswamy, K. V. (2007). "Regional Dimension of Growth and Employment." *Economic and Political Weekly*, December 8, pp. 47–56.

Ray, Ratnalekha (1979). *Change in Bengal Agrarian Society, 1760–1850.* New Delhi: People's Publishing House.

Rodrik, Dani, and Arvind Subramanium (2004). "From 'Hindu Growth' to Produtivity Surge: The Mystery of the Indian Growth Transition." KSG working paper no. RWP04–13.

Rudolph, Lloyd, and Susanne Rudolph (1987). *In Pursuit of Lakshmi.* Chicago: University of Chicago Press.

Ruparelia, Sanjay (2005). "Managing the United Progressive Alliance: The Challenges Ahead." *Economic and Political Weekly*, v. 40, no. 24 (June 11), pp. 2407–2412.

Ruparelia, Sanjay (2011). "Expanding Indian Democracy: The Paradox of the Third Force." In Sanjay Ruparelia et al., eds., *Understanding India's New Political Economy: A Great Transformation?* New York: Taylor and Francis Ltd.

Sandbrook, Richard, et al. (2007). *Social Democracy in the Global Periphery.* New York: Cambridge University Press.

Sarkar, Sumit (1973). *The Swadeshi Movement in Bengal, 1760–1908.* New Delhi: People's Publishing House.

Sarkar, Sumit (1989). *Modern India, 1885–1947.* London: Macmillan.

Sarma, Atul (2000). "Gujarat Finances." *Economic and Political Weekly*, v. 35, no. 35/36 (August 26), pp. 3125–31.

Sen, A. K. (1999). *Development as Freedom.* Oxford: Oxford University Press.

Sengupta, Arjun (2001). *Reforms, Equity and the IMF.* Delhi: Har Anand Publication.

Sengupta, Mitu (2004). *"The Politics of Market Reform in India: The Fragile Basis of Paradigm Shift."* Unpublished Ph.D. thesis, Department of Political Science, University of Toronto.

Sengupta, Sunil, and Haris Gazdar (1997). "Agrarian Politics and Rural Development in West Bengal." In Jean Dreze and Amartya Sen, eds., *Indian Development: Selected Regional Perspectives.* Delhi: Oxford University Press, pp. 129–204.

Serra, N., and Joseph E. Stiglitz, eds. (2008). *Washington Consensus Reconsidered: Toward New Global Governance.* New York: Oxford University Press.

Shah, Ghanshyam (1975). *Caste Association and Political Process in Gujarat: A Study of the Kshatriya Sabha*. Bombay: Popular Prakashan.

Shah, Ghanshyam (2007). "Gujarat After Godhra." In Ramashray Roy and Paul Wallace, eds., *India's 2004 Elections: Grass-roots and National Perspectives*. New Delhi: Sage Publications, pp. 151–79.

Sheth, Pravin N. (1976). "Gujarat: The Case of Small Majority Politics." In Narain (1976), pp. 68–87.

Shetty, S. L. (2003). "Growth of SDP and Structural Changes in State Economies: Interstate Comparisons." *Economic and Political Weekly*, December 6, pp. 5189–5200.

Singh, Ajit Kumar (2007). "The Economy of Uttar Pradesh since the 1990s: Economic Stagnation and Fiscal Crisis." In Pai (2007), pp. 273–94.

Singh, Prerna (2010). "*Worlds Apart: A Comparative Analysis of Social Development in India*." Unpublished Ph.D. dissertation, Department of Politics, Princeton University.

Sridharan, E. (2006). "Parties, the Party System and Collective Action for State Funding of Elections." In Peter Ronald de Souza and E. Sridharan, eds., *India's Political Parties*. New Delhi: Sage Publications.

Srinivasan, T. N., and S. Tendulkar (2003). *Reintegrating India with the World Economy*. Washington, DC: Institute for International Economics.

Srivastava, Saraswati (1976). "Uttar Pradesh: Politics of Neglected Development." In Narain (1976), pp. 323–69.

Stone, Brewers (1988). "Institutional Decay and the Traditionalization of Politics: The Uttar Pradesh Congress Party." *Asian Survey*, v. 28, no. 10 (October), pp. 1018–30.

Teitelbaum, Emmanuel (2008). "Was the Indian Labor Movement Ever Co-opted." In Rina Agarwala and Ronald Herring, eds., *Whatever Happened to Class? Reflections from South Asia*. New York: Routledge, 50–72.

Uppal, Yogesh (2007). "The Disadvantaged Incumbents: Estimating Incumbency Effects in Indian State Legislatures," unpublished manuscript, available at http://mpra.ub.uni.muenchen.de/8515/.

Vaidyanathan, A. (2006). "Farmers' Suicides and the Agrarian Crisis." *Economic and Political Weekly*, September 23, pp. 4009–13.

Vaidyanathan, A. (2010). *Agricultural Growth in India*. New Delhi: Oxford University Press.

Varshney, Ashutosh (1991). "India, Pakistan and Kashmir: Antinomies of Nationalism." *Asian Survey*, v. 31, no. 11, pp. 997–1019.

Varshney, Ashutosh (1995). *Democracy, Development and the Countryside: Urban-Rural Struggles in India*. New York: Cambridge University Press.

Varshney, Ashutosh (2003). *Ethnic Conflict and Civic Life: Hindus and Muslims in India*. New Haven, CT: Yale University Press.

Verma, Anil K. (2007). "Backward-Caste Politics in Uttar Pradesh: An Analysis of the Samajwadi Party." In Pai (2007), pp. 157–90.

Virmani, Arvind (2004a). "India's Economic Growth: From Socialist Rate of Growth to Bharatiya Rate of Growth." Working Paper No. 122, *Indian Council for Research on International Economic Relations*, New Delhi, India.

Virmani, Arvind (2004b). "Sources of India's Economic Growth: Trends in Total Factor Productivity." Working Paper No. 131, *Indian Council for Research on International Economic Relations*, New Delhi, India.

Wallack, Jessica Seddon (2003). "Structural Breaks in Indian Macroeconomic Data." *Economic and Political Weekly*, October 11, pp. 4312–15.

Weiner, Myron (1967). *Party Building in a New Nation: The Indian National Congress*. Chicago: University of Chicago Press.

Weiner, Myron (1991). *The Child and the State in India*. Princeton, NJ: Princeton University Press.

Weiner, Myron (2001). "The Struggle for Equality: Caste in Indian Politics." In Atul Kohli, ed., *The Success of India's Democracy*. New York: Cambridge University Press.

Widmalm, Sten (2006). *Kashmir in Comparative Perspective: Democracy and Violent Separatism in India*. New Delhi: Oxford University Press.

Wilkinson, Steven (2004). *Votes and Violence: Electoral Competition and Ethnic Riots in India*. New York: Cambridge University Press.

Williamson, John (1990). "What Washington Means by Policy Reform." In John Williamson, ed., *Latin American Adjustment: How Much Has Happened*. Washington, DC: Institute for International Economics, 7–38.

World Bank (2004). India: Investment Climate and Manufacturing Industry. Washington, DC: World Bank.

Yagnik, Achyut, and Nikita Sud (2005). "Hindutva and Beyond: The Political Topography of Gujarat." Unpublished manuscript.

Ye, Min (2007). "Embedded States: The Economic Transitions of China and India." Unpublished Ph.D. dissertation, Department of Politics, Princeton University.

Index

Note: Footnotes are not indexed.

BJP, 8, 30, 35, 41, 61, 66, 71, 179,
  183, 185
  and electoral finances, 54
  and the Godhra incident, 73–74
  economic approach of, 41
  economic nationalism of, 40
  electoral strategy of, 62–64
  in U.P., 174
  role in Gujarat, 187–189
Bofors scandal, 53
Bombay, 30, 156, 163, 179, 184, 185,
  199, 210
Bombay Club, 40, 58
Bombay Presidency, 180
BPL, 131
Brahmanical domination, 15, 16, 69,
  136, 158, 159, 200
Brahmins, 15, 16, 69, 70, 136, 159,
  161, 162, 164, 165, 166, 188,
  197, 200
Brazil, 47, 86, 218, 221, 222
briefcase politics, 55
Britain, 179
British colonialism, 52, 57, 73, 156,
  161, 163, 182, 195, 197, 198,
  201, 210, 225–226
  economic impact, 80–81
  legacy, 19–20
Bundelkhand, 175
Burdwan, 200
Business and Economy, 50
Business Digest, 50
business groups. *See also* pro-business
  policies
  and electoral finances, 51–55
  and lobbying for government favors,
  55–56
  overview of political role, 6–7
  political attitudes toward, 49–50
  rising power of, 41–59
Business Today, 50

Calcutta, 163, 195, 196, 197, 199,
  201, 203
capitalists. *See* business groups
caste politics
  as protest politics, 69–70

caste politics, as protest politics. *See
  also* backward castes; *dalits*;
  middle castes
chambers of commerce, 57–58
Chhattisgarh, 75
Chidambaram, P., 47
China, 20, 23, 46, 74, 79, 94, 121,
  129, 133, 138, 200, 207, 212,
  218, 219, 220, 221, 222
CII. *See* Confederation of Indian
  Industry
class inequality, post-reforms,
  128–129
class politics. *See* business groups;
  lower-class politics; revolutionary
  politics
colonialism. *See* British colonialism
communal conflict, in Guarat, 185
Communist Party of India (Maoists).
  See CPIMaoists
Communist Party of India (Marxist).
  See CPM
Confederation of Indian Industry, 7,
  38, 53, 58
  political influence of, 57–58
Congo, 154
Congress (O), 168
Congress Party, 2, 8, 15, 20, 27, 29,
  35, 41, 52, 62, 63, 65, 69, 71, 72,
  73, 81, 153, 198, 202
  and electoral finances, 52–54
  changes under Indira Gandhi,
  24–26
  economic approach, 41
  electoral strategies of, 60–61
  rule in Gujarat, 183–186
  rule in U.P., 165–171
  rule in West Bengal, 199–202
  under Nehru, 22–23
Cooch Behar, 200
corruption. *See also* G-2 scandal;
  neo-patrimonial politics
  and state-business relations, 55–56
CPI-Maoists, 75. *See also*
  revolutionary politics
CPM, 50, 199
  electoral finances, 54

neglect of education and health,
207–208
neglect of NREGA, 208
social democratic politics in,
overview, 16–17
WIPRO, 108
World Bank, 125, 131, 132, 221, 222
World Economic Forum, 7
World Values Survey, 49, 50
World War II, 201
WTO, 12, 37, 114, 220

Yadav, Laloo Prasad, 69
Yadav, Mulayam Singh, 69
role in U.P., 173
Yadavs, 173

zamindari abolition, 85, 164,
167
zamindari settlement, 210
zamindars, 162, 164, 181, 195, 196,
210, 211
Zimbabwe, 154